Xi Zhongxun: Father of a Great Nation's Leader

Xia Meng, Wang Xiaoqiang

Published by
ACA Publishing Ltd.
University House
11-13 Lower Grosvenor Place,
London SW1W 0EX, UK
Tel: +44 (0)20 7834 7676
Fax: +44 (0)20 7973 0076
E-mail: info@alaincharlesasia.com
Web:www.alaincharlesasia.com
Beijing Office
Tel: +86(0)10 8472 1250
Fax: +86(0)10 5885 0639

Authors: Xia Meng and Wang Xiaoqiang
Editors: David Lammie and Martin Savery
Translator: Shanghai SBY Translation Co., Ltd.
Cover art: Daniel Li

Published by ACA Publishing Ltd in association
with the People's Publishing House

© 2014, by People's Publishing House, Beijing, China
ALL RIGHTS RESERVED. NO PART OF THIS
PUBLICATION MAY BE REPRODUCED IN MATERIAL FORM,
BY ANY MEANS, WHETHER GRAPHIC,
ELECTRONIC, MECHANICAL OR OTHER, INCLUDING
PHOTOCOPYING OR INFORMATION STORAGE, IN WHOLE OR IN PART, AND
MAY NOT BE USED TO PREPARE
OTHER PUBLICATIONS WITHOUT WRITTEN
PERMISSION FROM THE PUBLISHER.

The greatest care has been taken to ensure accuracy but the
publisher can accept no responsibility for errors or omissions, or
for any liability occasioned by relying on its content.

ISBN 978-1-910760-02-4

A catalogue record for *Xi Zhongxun: Father of a Great Nation's Leader*
is available from the National Bibliographic Service of the British Library.

Glossary of Terms

CMC	Central Military Commission
CPC	Communist Party of China
CPG	central people's government
CPPCC	Chinese people's political consultative conference
KMT	Kuomintang (Nationalist Party)
NGO	non-government organisation
NPC	national people's congress
PLA	People's Liberation Army
PRC	People's Republic of China
SEZ	special economic zone
SOE	state-owned enterprise
SDPC	state development planning commission
SPC	state planning commission
TCM	traditional Chinese medicine

Democratic figures/personages refer to people of note who are 'members of non-CPC political parties'

Preface

The reform and opening up of China ushered in the socialist road with Chinese characteristics and sparked the dawn of a new era. The immortal and meritorious services of Deng Xiaoping, the initiator, chief designer and commander-in-chief of that road, will be eternally engraved on the minds of the Chinese people. He accomplished these outstanding feats with his selfless comrades-in-arms and senior army generals blazing a trail, and going through fire and water with him. The founding fathers and commanders-in-chief of the reform and opening up prompted hundreds of millions of Chinese people to embark together on the new journey that we are still following today. Their eminent contributions deserve to be documented and their deeds should be remembered and admired. They are the role models and examples for the broad masses of party members and cadres to follow on the new journey of reform and opening up.

To cherish the memory of these founding fathers of reform and opening up and to enable readers, especially party members and cadres, to know them better and to learn from them as role models, we decided to publish the *Pictorial Biographies of the Founding Fathers of China's Reform and Opening Up* series. To present these books to readers at the earliest opportunity, we will publish this series volume by volume as each book is completed.

China has entered a new era of reform and opening up. The party central committee with comrade Xi Jinping as general secretary has declared the epoch-making new manifesto of reform and opening up. The implementation of the manifesto requires the devotion and joint efforts of brave generals keeping pace with the times, losing no time moving ahead, fearing no upheavals, abolishing outdated laws and regulations, and defying the negative statements of others; it requires innumerable cadres hurling themselves into the reform and opening-up process; and it requires the collective efforts of hundreds of millions of people. Only in this way can our great cause keep on advancing!

People's Publishing House, August 2014

Alain Charles Asia (ACA) Publishing Ltd is delighted to be associated with the People's Publishing House to bring this book to an English-speaking readership.

ACA, formerly known as ACP (Alain Charles Publishing) Ltd Beijing, was founded in October 1989 and was the first foreign-owned publishing company to be allowed to open an office in China.

In 2007, ACP Beijing was renamed ACA Publishing Ltd to better reflect its focus on China and the Asia-Pacific region. The company specialises in publishing books about China for international readers and has offices in Beijing and London.

ACA Publishing Ltd, October 2016

Contents

Chapter 1   A Peasant Boy from the Dancun Plateau............1

Chapter 2   Becoming a Party Member in Prison............11

Chapter 3   Gunfire from the Liangdang Mutiny............15

Chapter 4   Meeting Liu Zhidan and Xie Zichang............23

Chapter 5   Establishing the Zhaojin Revolutionary Base............28

Chapter 6   Striving to Overcome the Dangerous Situation at the Chenjiapo Conference............36

Chapter 7   'Baby-faced' Chairman of the Border Region Government....42

Chapter 8   Wrongfully Purged............51

Chapter 9   Northwest Soviet Zone Becomes Foothold for Red Army Long March............57

Chapter 10   Guarding the Southern Entrance to Yan'an............61

Chapter 11   'Putting the Party's Interests First'............70

Chapter 12   Guarding the Northern Entrance to Yan'an............80

Chapter 13   Revolutionary 'Correspondence'............88

Chapter 14   Yetai Mountain Counterattacks............93

Chapter 15   Nine Letters from Mao Zedong............99

Chapter 16   Instigating the Hengshan Uprising............107

Chapter 17   All Border Region Forces 'Under the Unified Command of Peng Dehuai and Xi Zhongxun'............113

Chapter 18   Rectifying 'Leftism' in Land Reform with the 'Total Approval' of Mao Zedong............123

Chapter 19   "All for the Front and All for the Development of the New Zone"...131

Chapter 20   Managing and Developing the Great Northwest............140

Chapter 21 Plenipotentiary Appointed by the Central People's Government....152

Chapter 22 Mao Zedong Says: "You are More Formidable than Zhuge Liang"...159

Chapter 23 'An Accomplished Head of the Central Publicity Department'..166

Chapter 24 'Majordomo' of the State Council..173

Chapter 25 Premier Zhou Enlai's 'Minister of Internal Affairs'................179

Chapter 26 Declaration of Endowed Military Commands........................194

Chapter 27 Establishing the State Council Petition System.....................198

Chapter 28 Keeping a Clear Head Amid the Frenzy of the Great Leap Forward..202

Chapter 29 Protecting the Ancient City Walls of Xi'an on Three Occasions...216

Chapter 30 Appreciation of Shaanxi Opera in Beijing................................221

Chapter 31 The Liu Zhidan Novel Incident..230

Chapter 32 Being Wronged for 16 Years and Twice Sent Down to Luoyang.....237

Chapter 33 Sent South at Age 65 to Govern Guangdong..........................245

Chapter 34 Decisive Action to Redress Miscarriages of Justice...............253

Chapter 35 Tackling the Root Causes of the 'Illegal Emigration' Frenzy..260

Chapter 36 'Lobbying' the Central Government to Let Guangdong 'Take the First Step'..267

Chapter 37 'Blazing a New Trail' to Advocate the Establishment of SEZs..277

Chapter 38 Return to Zhongnanhai..291

Chapter 39 All Rivers Flow to the Sea: Emotional Ties to China............306

Epilogue...322

Chronology of Xi Zhongxun's Life..326

Notes..342

Chapter 1

A Peasant Boy from the Dancun Plateau

The Guanzhong plain in the central Chinese province of Shaanxi has witnessed considerable glory and hardship throughout the country's long history. Thirteen dynasties, including the Qin, Han, Sui and Tang, founded their capital here. This is a place that has staged so many historic events that the great Tang poet, Du Fu, was moved to describe it "a towering imperial state since ancient times". One of its most famous counties is Fuping, which borders Qiaoshan mountain to the north and the Wei river to the south. It combines the boldness of the loess plateau and the vastness of the Guanzhong plain, having a commanding view over the whole region. Fuping boasts a history of more than 2,400 years since it became a county in 456BC during the reign of Emperor Ligong in the Qin dynasty.

Zhonghe village, Dancun town

Xi Zhongxun: Father of a Great Nation's Leader

Fuping (富平) in Chinese means 'prosperity and peace', which the early inhabitants hoped would be propitious. According to the words of a well-known local ballad, the county has prospered thanks to a number of talented locals, including: "Yang Jue, the upright official; Wang Jian, the courageous general; Lian Yue, the model of filial piety; Zhang Dan, the loyal official; Sun Piyang, the prince's teacher; and Wei Zheng, an emperor's minister, who killed the Dragon King in his dream". The ballad tells the stories of those who dedicated their lives to bettering the nation and its people, bequeathing a legacy of enduring myths. A number of heroes have also emerged in more modern times, including Zhang Qingyun, Jiao Zijing, Zhang Yi'an and Hu Jingyi, who have done much to save the nation and its people.[1]

On 15 October 1913 (16 September according to China's lunar calendar), Xi Zhongxun was born to an ordinary peasant family on the Dancun plateau in the west of Fuping (now under the administration of Zhonghe village, Dancun town). The Xi family connection to Fuping dates back to the late 19th century. In early 1885, in the 11th year of the reign of Emperor Guangxu, Xi Zhongxun's grandparents, Xi Yongsheng and his wife whose maiden name was Zhang, together with their son and daughter, were travelling after having been displaced from their original home. Their three-year journey westward from Dengzhou, Henan province, finally ended near the Ducun river to the east of Dancun. Here, they decided to settle, serving as hired hands and tenant peasants, living on a small plot of land.

The Dancun plateau covers a relatively small area but the loess soil is highly fertile. A local saying goes: "Fertilise in Dancun, harvest in Ducun." However, Fuping went through a disastrous three-year drought during the first years of Emperor Guangxu. Vast areas of land were abandoned and the population slumped as the famished fled to nearby provinces such as Henan, Hubei, Shandong and Sichuan. As a result of this migration, the people of Dancun are said to be spread across "18 counties in nine provinces".

Now working as an itinerant peddler, Xi Yongsheng died from an illness, leaving his wife and children to live a hand-to-mouth existence. The eldest son, who was known affectionately as Tiger, enlisted in the army. The second son, Xi Zongde, took charge of the household, while the daughter, who was known as Danǔ (big sister), and the third son, Xi Zongren, helped with the farm work.

Xi Zongde was partially literate and enjoyed great prestige in the village. His wife, Chai Caihua, came from a poor, peasant family in a neighbouring village. Indeed, the family was so poor that she had to borrow a pair of embroidered shoes for her wedding ceremony.

One autumn around 1900, Tiger, who had served in the army for a number of years, came back home unexpectedly. He said he was escorting Empress Dowager Cixi and Emperor Guangxu to the city of Xi'an, the national capital of 12 former dynasties. Tiger had been deafened by cannon in a battle with invading troops, known as the Eight-Power Allied Forces.[2] He departed home abruptly, without even having a family meal, but he did leave the family a large quantity of silver. Thanks to their newfound wealth, the Xis were able to buy land, and even opened premises for curing tobacco leaves. After that, the fortunes of the family improved.[3]

Xi Zhongxun was the eldest son of the family. According to genealogical tradition in China, which has established names for the different generations – Guo, Yu, Yong, Zong, Zhong, Zheng, Ming and Tong – this generation should feature the name 'Zhong' (meaning 'awarded'). After consulting with some educated people, Xi Zongde named his son Zhongxun (中勋), in the hope that the boy would go on to lead a good life. This name was slightly modified to Zhongxun (仲勋), and was later changed again by Yan Musan, his head teacher at Licheng middle school. Yan regarded the

The former site of Ducun primary school

character 中 (meaning 'middle') to be loaded with too much meaning, so an extra component was added to indicate 'impartiality' and 'integrity'. Xi Zhongxun also went by the childhood name Xiangjin (literally meaning 'similar'). Reflecting on his name, Xi Zhongxun said: "The nickname given by my father and my family name Xi form the name Xi Xiangjin." This is the opposite of the line '*xing xiang jin, xi xiang yuan*' found in the *Three Character Classic*, a 13th century text widely studied in Chinese schools, which means 'humans are similar in nature, while their habits differentiate them'. "As a result, some of my classmates asked me how I had got such a strange name," said Xi Zhongxun.[4]

In the spring of 1922, the eight-year-old Xi Zhongxun attended Ducun primary school in the east of the village. Chai Guodong, his cousin and classmate, recalled Xi with considerable admiration. "The work was rather difficult. We had to read and recite texts, but after our studies, Zhongxun would come to my home and play all the time. However, the next morning, he was always the first one out of about 100 students to recite the texts. He was a really smart boy."

On 7 September 1958, Xi Zhongxun returned to Ducun primary school to visit teachers and students

The motto of Licheng middle school: "Elucidating the latest knowledge, cultivating the ideal personality, creating a healthy society"

Lakeview tower, located in the southern part of Fuping's First Higher primary school

Between March and April 1925, Ducun primary school organised two visits to Licheng middle school in Zhuangli town, about 6km to the north. They went to attend memorial services for Sun Yat-sen[5] and Hu Jingyi.[6] This experience of life outside the Dancun plateau enthralled the teenage Xi.

In the spring of 1926, Xi Zhongxun was admitted with distinction to the higher primary section of Licheng middle school. He was one of only a few publicly funded children, and was an excellent student in both conduct and study, according to his classmate Liu Maokun, who was responsible for compiling class rankings. "Zhongxun always topped the list," Liu later recalled.

Licheng middle school was established by Hu Jingyi in 1920. The name 'Licheng' was taken from a famous passage in the *Great Learning*, one of the four Confucian classics: "thoughts purified; hearts rectified; personalities cultivated; families regulated; the state well governed; and the whole world will then be tranquil and in peace". Hu inscribed the school motto of 21 Chinese characters, translated as "elucidating the latest

Xi Zhongxun's classroom at Licheng middle school

knowledge, cultivating the ideal personality, creating a healthy society". The motto was designed to encourage students to put the country and the people first, to forge ahead and take on responsibilities in a pioneering spirit. The school song also cautioned students "against being pedantic and not to neglect social duties at the expense of their studies".

This school was one of the first in northern Shaanxi to spread the word of Marxism. Under the guidance of Yan Musan, Xi actively participated in various activities, and gained access to progressive publications such as *China Youth* (中国青年 *Zhongguo Qingnian*) and *Advancing Together* (共进 *Gongjin*). In March 1926, just one month after his enrolment at the school, Xi joined Licheng youth association. Issue 123 of *China Youth* (June 1926) reported: "The Licheng youth association, established in Licheng middle school, Fuping county, has more than 30 active members." At the age of 13, and having been introduced by Song Wenmei[7] and Wu Zhizhen, Xi joined the Communist Youth League of China.

Also in May, the Licheng Party Group, the earliest Communist Party organisation in Fuping, was established under the chairmanship of Yan.

Hu Jingyi (1892-1925), who styled himself as 'Liseng' (the monk with the bamboo rain hat), was born in Zhuangli, Fuping, Shaanxi. He was a renowned military general in Shaanxi. In October 1924, he launched a coup with Feng Yuxiang and Sun Yue, two other patriotic generals. Later, he supervised the administration of Henan province. Hu was praised by Li Dazhao, one of the founders of the CPC, as "a reliable person with whom our party can cooperate in future"

In June 2000, Qi Xin paid a visit to Licheng middle school, the alma mater of Xi Zhongxun. She was accompanied by Li Zhanshu (fifth from left), a member of the standing committee of Shaanxi provincial party committee

In July, a mass rally against local bullies was held in Zhuangli town. Xi marched at the front of the demonstration with other progressive students. In addition, directed by the party, he went to nearby villages, including Shike, Dongjiazhuang, Jingjiayou and Santiaogou, to hand out leaflets, put up placards and hold mass rallies. Since Xi Zhongxun, Song Wenmei and Cheng Jianwen[8] all attended Ducun primary school, their revolutionary activities initiated in Licheng middle school led them to become known as the "three heroes of Ducun village".

Xi stayed at Licheng middle school for only one year, but he had clear memories of this period in his life. "At that time I knew the Communist Party was doing good things for the people, and I was determined to fight under its direction to the very end."

In the spring of 1927, Xi transferred to the First Higher primary school of Fuping county. Yan, who had previously been dismissed by the Licheng middle school board, had by then taken over as the headmaster of the First Higher primary school.

The library of Licheng middle school

The school was located in the southeast corner of the old walled town of Fuping. Lakeview tower in the campus was then the highest building in the county. The balcony at the top of the tower afforded a panoramic view of the beautiful surrounding scenery: "to the south, rice fields, lotus plants and lakes; to the north, a river running incessantly under a bridge; to the west, a holy Buddhist pagoda glitters radiantly; to the east, the many households that make up Dou village." At that time, Xi had become a self-supporting student, without government funds, but this required sacrifices. For example, he had to make a weekly walk of about 15km from school to home to bring steamed buns and pickles back to school.

Apart from studying hard, Xi also took an active part in revolutionary activities, such as the May Day celebrations, and demonstrations against the counter-revolutionary warlords, Zhang Zuolin and He Jingwei. *Shaanxi National Daily* reported on 20 May 1927: "The 9 May national humiliation commemoration meeting[9] held in Fuping turned out to be a major event with an unprecedentedly high participation rate."

In the second half of the year, collaboration between the Chinese Communists and the Nationalist army to rid the country of warlords came

Fuping county today

to an end. The Nationalists turned on the Communists, in what became known as the White Terror. In this climate, all revolutionary activities had to be carried out underground. The Fuping special branch of the Communist Party of China (CPC) secretly held a meeting to discuss whether to enrol Xi Zhongxun as a party member. As Xi was still under 14, and his transfer from Licheng middle school had only occurred a few months before, his application was declined. In his later years, Yan looked upon this event with regret. "Based on his revolutionary performance, Zhongxun was in fact a highly qualified party member at that time," he said.

Chapter 2

Becoming a Party Member in Prison

In the spring of 1928, Xi Zhongxun was enrolled at the No.3 Normal University of Shaanxi province. Situated in Sanyuan county, the university was the alma mater of Yan Musan and an important front for revolutionary activity in Weibei.[1]

Shortly after his enrolment, a student revolt influenced by 'leftist adventurism' led to Xi Zhongxun being thrown into prison for more than four months. The authorities arrested several progressive students including Xi Zhongxun and Wu Tingjun, a cadre of the student movement of Sanyuan CPC committee. They were sent to Xi'an military tribunal two months later. One day in April, Wu Tingjun confided to Xi Zhongxun that he had been officially admitted to the CPC but he remained a member of the Communist Youth League to facilitate activities with cross-party elements. Xi Zhongxun was not yet 15 at that time.

Under the leadership of Wu Tingjun, Xi Zhongxun turned his prison cell into a classroom and devoted his time to incessant struggle. They gave up their allowance of four strings of cash[2] per head in order to improve the diet of their fellow inmates, who were deserters from the army of the prominent warlord Ma Hongbin.[3] The students were forced to wear heavy shackles, so the deserters tore pieces of cloth from their own trousers to bandage the sore limbs of their fellow inmates. Throughout his time in prison, Xi Zhongxun followed the lead of his older fellow student. "All my actions there were conducted according to the strict directions of Wu Tingjun," he later recalled.

When Song Zheyuan, governor of Shaanxi province, personally interrogated the students in August 1928 and concluded that they were just fresh-faced children, he decided to release them on bail. The bail

The site of the former No.3 Normal University of Shaanxi, which today houses a kindergarten

conditions were met thanks to the connections of one of Xi Zhongxun's uncles, Xi Zongren. According to Xi Zhongyao, a younger male cousin of Xi Zhongxun: "My father [Xi Zongren] approached a compatriot from Dancun village," he said. "He ran a store in Xi'an, which was put up as security, and we then brought him back."

Xi Zhongxun's return home was a great relief to his father Xi Zongde, who had a breakdown due to constant overwork. Xi Zongde did not complain about his son's decision to devote himself to the revolutionary cause, but he gave him some pragmatic advice. "You are too young now," he said. "You can work as a CPC representative when you are grown up. For the time being, it is best if you can help the poor."

Unfortunately, Xi Zongde did not live to see his son carry out his wishes. He died of an illness in November 1928, leaving the young Xi Zhongxun distraught.

While in prison, Xi Zhongxun was affected by serious eczema and was unable to move about comfortably. His friend Song Wenmei paid him a visit and found out that Xi Zhongxun had been admitted to the CPC while in prison. Song decided to relay the news to the party organisation in Fuping as soon as he could.

Although Xi Zhongxun still yearned to return to school and "enrich his knowledge", that path was blocked by his time in prison on suspicion of membership of the CPC.

Xi Zhongxun and his younger brother Xi Zhongkai

At that time, the Guanzhong plain was suffering from a succession of natural disasters and severe famine. The 15-year-old Xi Zhongxun joined the famine refugees who resorted to bartering salt for grain. They would collect salt produced by panning in the salt flats east of Fuping and exchange it for basic foods such as maize and black-eyed peas from the mountains in the north. This miserable existence and the terrible famine haunted Xi Zhongxun, who also had to endure the loss of his mother, who died suddenly of disease in June 1929. The young Xi Zhongxun was too poor to afford a proper burial. He had no other choice but to place her meagre coffin in the concierge's lodge pending a hasty burial two years later.

The harsh conditions experienced by working people and the tragic sufferings in his own life had a profound impact on the young Xi Zhongxun. He was particularly struck by *The Young Wanderer*, a novel written by the contemporary author Jiang Guangci. There were striking similarities between Xi Zhongxun's own struggles and those of the protagonist.

At this time, a fund-raising and relief committee was established in Wuzi region in Sanyuan county, adjacent to Dancun. Xi Zhongxun contacted Huang Ziwen,[4] director of the committee, enthusiastically joined in the fund-raising activities and secretly recruited his sworn brother, Comrade Zhou Dongzhi[5] and his young compatriots Hu Zhenqing, Yao Wanzhong and Liu Mingshi as party members.

In the winter of 1929, Xi Zhongxun joined the peasant association of Dancun in its fight against Zhang Changqing's militia. The peasant association members acquired more than a score of handguns, tied Zhang Changqing to the gate tower of Shijia village, held a mass rally and read out a list of 20 crimes committed by Zhang. However, Zhang was able to escape and this led to the authorities launching a ruthless attack on the village in retaliation. Dang Zhengxue, an association member and an uncle-in-law of Xi Zhongxun, tried to reason with the attackers, but he was detained in the gate tower. Carrying only a length of hemp rope, Xi Zhongxun went to try to free Dang Zhengxue but he was unsuccessful, and Dang was killed. Xi was greatly troubled about this episode, as he explained years later in conversation with his younger brother Xi Zhongkai.

That was Xi Zhongxun's first experience of participating in mass work and armed struggle as a party member, during which time he recruited other party members and laid foundations for the future. "I led only a few armed insurrections," he later said, "and mobilised the masses to participate in grain distribution and guerrilla raids in my hometown in the west of Fuping in the winter of 1932, relying on the foothold I established there as a result of my activities in 1929."

Chapter 3

Gunfire from the Liangdang Mutiny

In the small hours of 2 April 1932, heavy gunfire broke the silence of the night sky over the mountainous county of Liangdang, in Longnan. The Liangdang mutiny, as it became known, was commanded by Xi Zhongxun and Liu Linpu and had started on schedule. Three reactionary company commanders were shot dead and, on hearing gunfire, the battalion commander fled to Xishan mountain. At the break of dawn, a 300-strong revolutionary troop gathered beside the Yaogou canal outside the north gate of the county and marched alongside the chilly waters of the Guangxiang river in the direction of the Sun temple to the north.

Just over two years earlier, on 6 February 1930 (8 January in the traditional Chinese calendar), Xi Zhongxun headed west towards Changwu as instructed by the party for troop manoeuvres with Wang Dexiu's detachment affiliated to the local armed forces of Bi Meixuan.

During March and April 1930, Xi Zhongxun, Li Bingrong and Li Tesheng held two confidential meetings in Yaowang cave outside the west gate to Changwu county and decided to set up a party group, work with the Second Detachment as the centre and separately go to the companies to rally the troops. Later, Xi Zhongxun was promoted from troop clerk to officer cadet of the second company. In the course of mobilising the soldiers for daily combat, the party group set up a Red Army friendship association.

In June, 1930, Zhen Shoushan reorganised the troop to be the second detachment of the first division of the Northwest army. One month later, the Second Company in which Xi Zhongxun served was relocated to the garrison at Tingkou, which in ancient times used to function as an important relay station on the Silk Road. Here, Xi Zhongxun influenced at least three people – mule and horse store owner Wang Zhixuan, gentleman Liu Shirong and primary school headmaster Liu Jingtian – to join the revolution with Wang's store as their clandestine meeting place.

In November 1930, the troop was incorporated by Yang Hucheng[1] into the second battalion, third regiment of the third brigade of Shaanxi Cavalry and moved to Binxian county. Xi Zhongxun's title was again changed, to special service leader of the second company. A battalion committee was established about that time, with Li Bingrong and Li Tesheng as secretaries of battalion branches, each consisting of more than 30 party members.

At the start of spring 1931, troop movements involved considerable risks. Liu Zhidan,[2] tasked with troop movement of the Third Brigade, was put behind bars in Binxian county by Brigade Commander Su Yusheng. One of Liu Zhidan's followers, Wang Shitai,[3] went to consult with Xi Zhongxun about their future. Asked about the prospect of obtaining some weapons and carrying them away, Xi Zhongxun argued that it was very difficult to steal them from warlords and then transport them to a safe location because of the disadvantageous location of Binxian county near the Xi'an-Lanzhou highway. However, in the end, the raid did succeed, although there were casualties. Wang Shitai was instantly impressed by Xi Zhongxun. "My first meeting and conversation with Zhongxun left a deep impression on me," he said. "This young man made a fairly realistic analysis of the situation."

In April, Su Yusheng and his troops betrayed Yang Hucheng. Xi Zhongxun, Li

The former site of Yaowang cave in Changwu county

Bingrong and Li Tesheng convened a meeting of core party members to discuss the matter and proposed the slogan 'Eliminating the First Regiment and Depending on Yang Hucheng'. The second battalion launched violent

Xi Zhongxun in the period of troop movements

attacks against the First Regiment led by Su Yusheng in Binxian county. The battle ended just before Yang Hucheng's troops arrived. Subsequently, the troops were reorganised by Yang to become the first battalion, second regiment of the third brigade of Shaanxi garrison.

In May, the first battalion was moved to Beicang, Fengxiang county, for garrison duty, where Xi Zhongxun took over as secretary of the battalion committee. Party work in the military progressed gradually – all four companies of the battalion had their own party branches, each of which included more than 20 party members. During this period, the Shaanxi provincial party committee twice sent people to foment uprisings.

In the winter of 1931, the First Battalion set out for Longnan to fight against Sichuan servicemen. After the battle, the troops were stationed in Shaanxi and Gansu, the battalion headquarters, the first company and the machine gun company in Fengzhou county, the second company in Shuangshipu (now Fengxian county) and the third company in Liangdang county. Up to this point, the troops had changed their banners (indicating a change of allegiance) three times and their defence sector was very stretched.

The revolutionary activities alerted senior figures. The regimental commander changed three of the four company commanders of the battalion, chiefly targeting the Machine Gun Company. Company Commander Li Bingrong was transferred and the company was dissolved and reorganised. Xi Zhongxun brought military supplies clerical staffer Liu Shulin to work in the reorganised company and actively won over the squad leader and platoon leader. He also trained Liu Xixian, a teacher at Wenchang Palace National Model primary school, to become a revolutionary activist and used his house as a place for underground meetings. As Liu Shulin recollected: "Xi Zhongxun told me that mother [the party organisation] ordered us to admit party members by making friends with them and winning them over gradually." Xi Zhongxun, Liu Shulin, Liu Xixian and others posed for a photograph. This image of the 'sworn brotherhood' is the earliest surviving photo of Xi Zhongxun.

In March 1932, the regimental headquarters abruptly decided to move the garrison, ordering the first battalion to travel more than 50km southwestwards to be stationed in the counties of Huixian and Chengxian

The 'sworn brotherhood', including Xi Zhongxun (far left), Liu Shulin (second from left) and Liu Xixian (far right)

The former site of Wenchang Palace National Model primary school in Fengzhou

Liu Linpu

The former site of the Liangdang mutiny

in Gansu province. The decision backfired and created deep unrest among the soldiers. The situation was extremely urgent. In late March, Xi Zhongxun and Liu Linpu,[4] secretary and special delegate respectively of Shaanxi provincial military committee, held a meeting in the ancient temple on Fenghe mountain in the north of Shuangshipu and decided to take advantage of the garrison change to stage a mutiny in Liangdang, Gansu province, and march north to rendezvous with the guerrillas directed by Liu Zhidan in Shaanxi and Gansu.

On 1 April, the whole battalion was stationed in Liangdang: the first company in the southern end of North Street, the second company in South Street, the battalion headquarters in the residence of a landlord in the west of the county government, the third company in the area around the county government and West Street, and the Machine Gun Company in North Street. At 9pm, Xi Zhongxun hosted a battalion committee meeting in a mule and horse store in North Street, where it was decided that Liu Linpu would direct the mutiny and Xi Zhongxun would organise and lead the entire battalion.

The mutiny went according to plan. At noon on 3 April, in the Sun temple, the troops were reorganised as the fifth detachment of the Shaanxi and Gansu Guerrillas of the Chinese Workers' and Peasants' Red Army. Liu Linpu was appointed political commissar, Xi Zhongxun secretary of the detachment committee and Wu Jincai detachment leader, only to be replaced by Xu Tianjie a few days later. Using an incomplete map for directions, the troops crossed the Wei river and entered Shaanxi, only to be blocked by the KMT army near the Jincai river in Linyou county. Xi Zhongxun convened a battalion committee conference which decided that Xu Tianjie should lead the troops on a detour to Yueyu temple in Yongshou county to regroup and be put on standby. Xi Zhongxun and Zuo Wenhui went to Tingkou to make preparations for crossing the Jing river, and Liu Linpu and Lü Jianren left for Qianxian county to negotiate with Liu Wenbo's troops in order to buy time.

Three days later, news came that the troops had been besieged and attacked by a bandit troop headed by Wang Jiezi while they were taking up position in Yueyu temple. Xi Zhongxun was forced to temporarily take shelter in a cave dwelling of Wang Zhixuan's mule and horse store.

Liu Linpu and Lü Jianren heard of the defeat and were arrested on the way to report it to the Xi'an provincial party committee. Soon afterwards, Liu Linpu was killed, at just 23 years old.

The Liangdang mutiny was a tragic event but it reverberated through Shaanxi and Gansu provinces and went down in the annals of the revolutionary movement in northwest China.

The Sun temple

Chapter 4

Meeting Liu Zhidan and Xie Zichang

In early June 1932, Xi Zhongxun returned secretly to his home town. After meeting with Cheng Jianwen, minister of organisation of the Shaanxi provincial party committee, Xi made up his mind to head north to Zhaojin to see the Shaanxi and Gansu guerrillas, and Liu Zhidan, in particular.

Zhaojin lies at the southern foot of Qiaoshan mountain, with Ziwuling mountain in the north. It overlooks Weibei plateau to the south, and faces the main Xianyu road to the east. Close by is the Sanjia plateau in Zhengning county, Gansu province, with its high mountains, deep valleys and dense woodland. With the help of Zhou Mingde, a village peasant and third uncle

Yangliuping in Zhaojin

Liu Zhidan

Xie Zichang

of Zhou Dongzhi, Xi Zhongxun hastened to Zhaojin under the guise of a salt trader. He stayed in Zhou's house on Laoye mountain.

At the beginning of September, Xi Zhongxun met with Xie Zichang[1] and Liu Zhidan in Yangliuping, to the west of Zhaojin. These two legendary figures of northwest China's revolutionary movement had a high regard for Xi Zhongxun due to his involvement in the Liangdang mutiny, and asked him to establish a revolutionary base and guerrilla force.

His first task was to collect grain and winter clothes and raise funds, before the Shaanxi and Gansu guerrillas could head south to engage in warfare. "In the past we had no base, so we should build one now," Xie Zichang told Xi Zhongxun. "Many refugees fled here due to the famine in Guanzhong plain. You are familiar with the locals, which is ideal for your work here. We have no guns or ammunition left for you. You should mobilise the masses to set up peasant associations, organise guerrilla forces and carry out guerrilla warfare."

Liu Zhidan gave encouragement to Xi but was realistic in his assessment of the situation. "Setbacks are inevitable in a revolution," he said. "We can start afresh." He designated a special team, comprising his own guards, to work in Zhaojin and told Xi Zhongxun: "You come from Zhaojin and you have also planted crops. You can get along quite well with the peasants. You should certainly assume responsibility for setting up the base. After the troops leave, you may encounter enormous hardships. As long as you stick to the correct policies and put your trust in the masses, any difficulties can surely be overcome."

Earlier that summer, the Shaanxi provincial party committee formulated two resolutions. The first, on 1 June, was to establish the 'New Shaanxi-Gansu border region soviet zone and guerrillas' and the second, on 25 August, was the 'fourth suppression of the imperialist KMT and the establishment of a new Shaanxi-Gansu border region soviet zone'. In accordance with the directives of the provincial party committee and the trust placed in him by Liu Zhidan and Xie Zichang, Xi Zhongxun stayed in Zhaojin and assumed the task of establishing the base.

Xi Zhongxun built a shed beside Zhou Dongzhi's house and asked someone to bring his aunt to live with him. He planted crops with the masses every day and called on his younger male cousins, Xi Zhongjie and Chai Guodong, as well as his brother Xi Zhongkai to join the revolution.

The Laoye mountain ridge runs northwest-southeast and is situated more

Laoye mountain

than 6km southeast of Zhaojin Street. Xi Zhongxun and Zhou Dongzhi mobilised the masses to set up peasant labour unions in the surrounding villages of Nantangzi, Jinpenwan, Beiliang, Chenjiapo, Hanjiashan, Yangshan and Hujiaxiang. They also recruited a group of party activists, including Wang Jinzhu from Laoye mountain, Ji Shouxiang (Ji Laoliu) and Hu Jianhai from Hujiaxiang, Yu Dehai from Nantangzi, the brothers Wang Zhizhou and Wang Zhilin from Jinpenwan, Wang Mantang from Beiliang and Wang Wanliang from Fangershang. "Some of these men were sworn brothers", so many of them were "intimately related".[2] This was the first revolutionary backbone force to be trained from among the poor peasants in the Zhaojin area, in preparation for the establishment of cadres for red political power.

The militia often came to track down and arrest them. It was not safe for Xi Zhongxun to stay in the village in the evening; instead, he slept in a cave dwelling half-way up the hill, burning charcoal for warmth. He recalled in later years and with deep emotion that "everything would have been impossible without the kind help of ordinary people".

In late October, Chen Kemin, the commander of the special service squadron, turned traitor and killed the squad leader, Cheng Shuangyin. As Xi Zhongxun recollected: "It was cotton harvest time when I brought the special service unit to Wuzi region."

The Weibei soviet zone, centred on the Wuzi and Xinzi districts of Sanyuan county, was situated at the juncture of the counties of Sanyuan, Fuping, Yaoxian, Jingyang and Chunhua. It was the first revolutionary base established by the CPC in Shaanxi. The special service unit was reorganised as the second detachment of Weibei guerrillas in the rear of the Wuzi district with Xi Zhongxun as the political instructor in command of fighting despotic landlords, establishing peasant unions and distributing grain and land in the west plateau of Yaoxian county and the villages of Huali and Rangniu.

Driven by 'leftist' adventurism, mass rallies and demonstrations were held in Weibei soviet zone for three consecutive days to commemorate the October revolution. On 9 November, the authorities mustered a militia in six counties, including Sanyuan and Fuping, in addition to a garrison battalion to suppress and ransack the soviet zone.

Xi Zhongxun moved to Zhaojin, but many arrests were taking place here so he decided to move the rear Wuzi district guerrillas to Xunyi county. He secretly returned to his home village of Dancun armed with two light machine guns, two handguns and two rifles. At the end of the year, he established a Dancun party branch in the house of Yue Qiangmin, his classmate from Tangjiapu village, with Yao Wanzhong as secretary. He also helped set up a Dancun guerrilla force, led by Yue Qiangming and Liu Mingfeng. The frontline Wuzi district guerrilla force also came to Dancun and Xi Zhongxun became its political commissar.

The local people were desperately short of food as the year came to a close. Xi Zhongxun encouraged the masses to improve grain distribution in west Fuping; within two weeks their numbers had surged to several thousand and the peasant society was consequently established. In January 1933, Jia Tuofu[3] wrote in *Report on the Struggle in Weibei* that: "Mass work to distribute grain and kill despotic landlords was also carried out in Ducun, Dancun and Panlong which, together with Wuzi district, formed a Red Army base independent of rule by the KMT or despotic landlords in Fuping."

In February 1933, Xi Zhongxun took up the position of secretary of the Communist Youth League in Sanyuan county, separately developed a group of party members from among the province's Third middle school and Wang Taiji's troops stationed in Sanyuan, and established the party organisation there under the direction of county Party Secretary Zhao Boping.[4]

A sabre used by Dancun guerrillas

Chapter 5

Establishing the Zhaojin Revolutionary Base

In late February 1933, Xi Zhongxun held two conversations with Meng Jian, secretary of the Shaanxi provincial party committee, in 38 Hotel in Dongguan Street, Xi'an, and learned of the specific responsibilities assigned to him in the 26th Red Army.

The 26th Red Army was created out of the Shaanxi and Gansu guerrilla forces on 24 December 1932. Its political commissar, Du Heng, demanded they "fight against Xia Yushan's militia first, which provoked the local militia to join forces against the Red Army. Then, it burnt the Fragrant hills temple, thereby alienating more than 1,000 monks. The more they fought, the more enemies they made and the more territory they lost".[1] Xi Zhongxun made his first acquaintance with Du Heng, who was returning from Xi'an, in an underground location in Wuzi region. Du Heng's impression and attitude towards Xi Zhongxun's leadership of the Liangdang mutiny was 'ambivalent'. Xi Zhongxun then went south to join the Second Red Regiment in Weibei, temporarily acting as the political instructor of the Young Pioneers and gradually becoming aware of the errors of the 'leftist' opportunist line.

On 8 March, the Shaanxi-Gansu border region special CPC committee was founded on Rabbit ridge, Zhaojin. Jin Like was appointed secretary and Xi Zhongxun was made a member of the special party committee and chairman of the military committee, predominantly in charge of the local armed forces and of preparations for establishing political power. Afterwards, Xi also worked as secretary of the special young pioneers committee.

Months previously, Xi Zhongxun built revolutionary mass organisations in the Laoye mountain region, which sowed the seeds of revolution. In

Rabbit ridge

Zhaojin, he led Zhou Dongzhi, Ji Shouxiang, Wang Mantang and Wang Wanliang to survey and mobilise the villagers, to rapidly organise the Peasant Association, the Poor Peasants Group and the Red Guards[1] and to energetically lead the masses in the task of grain distribution. The guerrilla movement was also expanded and more than 20 guerrilla groups were quickly established in Xunyi, Yaoxian and Chunhua.

On the solid foundation of mass work and armed struggle, on 5 April 1933, tomb-sweeping day, the Shaanxi-Gansu border region special CPC committee held a congress of workers, peasants and soldiers at Rabbit ridge. They established the Shaanxi-Gansu border region revolutionary committee and selected Zhou Dongzhi, who came from a peasant background, as chairman and Xi Zhongxun as vice chairman and secretary of the party. Seen from a distance, the east-west Rabbit ridge looks like an alert rabbit, lying still but poised to move at the first sign of danger. Liangxia was a hamlet comprising just a few households, where the Red Army soldiers, cadres and the masses went about their business.

The revolutionary committee was composed of members in charge of land, grain, the economy and the elimination of counter-revolutionaries. These tasks were headed, respectively, by Wang Mantang, Ji Shouxiang, Yang Zaiquan and Wang Wanliang. Huang Ziwen effectively functioned as secretary-general. The committee also had a political security team with Zhou Dongzhi as the political instructor. Pursuant to *The Chinese Soviet*

Government Organisation Act, grassroots political power was immediately established and the revolutionary committee led the political power system in the districts, villages and towns, including district-level revolutionary committees in Zhaojin, Anziwa and Taoqu plateau, and town-level ones in Fragrant hills, Yuyuan, Chenjiapo, Heitianyu, Jinpenwan, Xiufang valley, Beiliang, Laoye mountain, Qijieshi and Malanchuan. Together, these structures created a fairly complete political power system.

The revolutionary committee vigorously implemented laws and decrees, including *The Land Law of the Chinese Soviet Republic*, adhered to the principle that the crops belonged to the planters, demarcated land boundaries by means of staking and pegging, redistributed only land in valleys rather than in mountainous areas, confiscated surplus land from rich peasants, and explicitly advocated a policy of protecting middle-income peasants who were short of land and supplementing their land holdings. Land distribution started in Xiufang valley. More than 130 hectares of land from Yaoxian county school and Fragrant hills temple was distributed to Yuyuan villagers and more than 300 hectares of land held by the Li and Mei landlords was given to the villagers of Jinpen. In the meantime, it banned landlords from renting out land to tenants and the KMT from levying exorbitant tariffs, also introduced new policies relating to the distribution of grain, cattle and sheep, and barred smoking, gambling and foot binding. All these measures won widespread local support.

The revolutionary committee also encouraged the masses to till more land and produce more grain. It set up charity granaries so that "the starving masses from elsewhere could eat crops that had been gathered and stored to help them". [2]

In the same month, the 26th Red Army party committee decided to reorganise the headquarters of the Shaanxi-Gansu border region guerrilla force and appointed Xi Zhongxun as political commissar and Huang Ziwen as commander-in-chief. The aim was to get rid of troops that were not committed to the cause and avoid any infringement on the benefits due to poor peasants resulting from the 'wrong' policy of simply 'recruiting anyone who wanted to join the revolution'. The reorganised headquarters led an overhaul of the troops, which involved ruthlessly dismissing members with an 'impure' background, rearranging the troops into three guerrilla forces in Yaoxi, Chunhua and Xunyi, and establishing political systems so that they could fully carry out their function of being the main armed forces safeguarding the revolutionary base area.

Xuejia Stockade village

Also in the same month, the leading Shaanxi-Gansu border region party, along with political and military forces, set up base in Xuejia Stockade village, so named because of a traditional Chinese story in which Xue Gang stationed troops there to revolt against the Tang dynasty. Xuejia featured precipices in the east, west and south, linked with other ridges via a suspension bridge in the northwest. The guerrilla headquarters organised the masses to rebuild the village, construct fortifications, repair caves and shore up the castle walls. It made good use of four natural caves to set up an encampment for the guerrillas, a clothing factory, hospital, a machine maintenance facility, a location for the leadership organisation, a military munitions depot and a makeshift prison.

Xuejia Stockade Village Clothing Factory was one of the earliest in the Red Army's history, staffed by 30-40 women who worked in peacetime and served as guerrillas in wartime. The medical care personnel mostly treated the wounded using traditional Chinese medicine (TCM) techniques, for example using dressings soaked in medicinal herbs. There were 60-70 workers in the machine maintenance facility, while skilled workers were brought in from Xi'an by the Shaanxi provincial party committee. The 'braided hemp grenades' that they produced played a significant role in the 'siege' warfare. The holes made in the rock floor to house the moulds that were used to make the grenades can still be seen today.

The Zhaojin revolutionary base, founded under the leadership of Liu Zhidan and Xi Zhongxun, was the first of its kind in northwest China. More than 80 years on, many old revolutionary sites have been kept intact. This photo shows Cave 1, the former site of the guerrilla base camp

Cave 2, the former site of the Red Army hospital and clothing factory

Cave 3, the former site of the machine maintenance facility

The holes housing grenade moulds in the machine maintenance facility

Xi Zhongxun: Father of a Great Nation's Leader

Cave 4, the former home of the special committee and revolutionary committee, along with a warehouse

In an effort to promote the circulation of goods, the revolutionary committee set up a market in Tingzi valley underneath Xuejia Stockade village on the principle that the masses would be given priority in buying and selling grain and vegetables. It also meant that the Red Army could receive their share of grain. The market was extremely popular with the masses. It was initially open five days a week, but soon transactions took place on a daily basis.

The agrarian revolutionary war (1927-1937), as it became known, along with other economic reforms, helped the Shaanxi-Gansu border region soviet zone, centred on Zhaojin, consolidate and expand the area under its control. It now covered an area of more than 50 sq km at the juncture of Yaoxian, Xunyi, Chunhua and Yijun counties. It was the first revolutionary base to be successfully established by the CPC in mountainous northwest China.

Wang Shitai, who was once commander of the second regiment of the Red Army, praised Xi Zhongxun's work during this period. "Zhongxun was secretary of the Shaanxi-Gansu border region special military committee

Establishing the Zhaojin Revolutionary Base

The historic plank pathway built by the Red Army along the face of a cliff

and political commissar of the headquarters," he said. "He led and directed many military actions. He also took charge of making preparations to establish democratic political power in the revolutionary base, tasked with much specific work. Despite holding the position of chairman of the revolutionary committee, Zhou Dongzhi, though honest and uneducated, was selected by senior officers because of his background as a peasant labourer. It was Xi Zhongxun who did most of the work, got involved in all activities, big or small, and directed and managed the troops in person."[3]

In late May 1933, the political guard led by Xi Zhongxun and Huang Ziwen was assaulted by brigands headed by Chen Kemin at Saddle slope. In ensuring the safe evacuation of Huang Ziwen and other soldiers, Xi Zhongxun was wounded and his blood spilled into the earth of the soviet zone.

Chapter 6

Striving to Overcome the Dangerous Situation at the Chenjiapo Conference

On 17 June 1933, the Shaanxi-Gansu border region special CPC committee and the 26th Red Army party committee held a joint conference in Beiliang, Zhaojin in which Du Heng, in his capacity as political commissar, ordered the second regiment of the Red Army to march south to Weihua after repeated setbacks. Xi Zhongxun, who was recuperating in Xuejia Stockade village, failed to attend the conference. As Zhang Xiushan,[1] who took over Xi Zhongxun's post as political commissar of the guerrilla headquarters, recalled: "The secretary of the Border Region Special Party Committee Jin Like disagreed with the proposal of moving south but applauded the suggestions of Liu Zhidan. Xi Zhongxun wasn't there, but he entrusted Jin Like to express his own opinion that they should persist in fighting in Shaanxi, Gansu and Ningxia."

Beiliang

Striving to Overcome the Dangerous Situation at the Chenjiapo Conference

Wang Taiji (1906-1934), from Lintong in Shaanxi province, was admitted to Guangzhou Huangpu military academy in 1924 as one of its first students. He became a party member while in the academy. He led and participated in the Weihua insurgency and died a heroic death in Xi'an in 1934. Once the commander of the 42nd Division of 26th Red Army, he was also one of the founders of the Shaanxi-Gansu border region revolutionary base

Liu Zhidan and Wang Shitai were forced to lead more than 300 soldiers of the second regiment of the Red Army south to Weihua only to meet with various reversals. Yuan Yuedong, who was then secretary of the Shaanxi provincial party committee, and Du Heng were arrested and then betrayed the party. The Shaanxi party and league organisations suffered the most serious damage.

In these desperate hours, Wang Taiji, commander of the cavalry regiment of the 17th KMT army, led his troops in revolt. After enduring tough fighting, his troops marched towards Zhaojin under the new title of the army of volunteers for the war of resistance against Japan in northwest China. At that time, the newly incorporated Yaoxian county guerrilla force led by Zhang Bangying and Chen Xueding and the fourth regiment of the Red Army reorganised from the Weibei guerrillas and headed by Yang Sen and Huang Zixiang, advanced to Zhaojin.

When Wang Taiji's insurgent force arrived in Zhaojin, Xi Zhongxun was still recovering from his wounds, but the news so invigorated him that he personally led the political guards and three guerrilla forces in the west of Yaoxian, Chunhua and Xunyi counties to meet up with them. After various twists and turns, they eventually met each other in Xiufang valley at the foot of Xuejia Stockade village in the evening. Clasping Wang Taiji's hands, Xi Zhongxun spoke out: "Welcome, Comrade Taiji!" Touched with a little embarrassment, Wang Taiji responded: "Look! I brought here only a small number of soldiers." Xi Zhongxun consoled him with a smile. "Those who wanted to run away have fled already, leaving behind only those who are firmly committed to the revolutionary cause," he said. "With these loyal forces, we have a better chance for further expansion!"[2]

Then, lacking any directives from the party organisation or a strategy agreed in advance, and facing the danger that the KMT army might arrive at the mountain at any moment, the revolutionary forces held different opinions about whether they should stick it out in the base. Neither party could convince the other.

On 14 August 1933, the Joint Conference of the Shaanxi-Gansu border region party, administrative and military leadership was convened in Chenjiapo and chaired by Qin Wushan,[3] secretary of the special party committee and Xi Zhongxun, secretary of the special military committee. The conference prioritised rebuilding the main forces of the Red Army and turning around the passive situation. Ten or more high-ranking party cadres attended the conference, including Li Miaozhai, Zhang Xiushan, Gao Gang,[4] Zhang Bangying, Chen Xueding, Yang Sen, Huang Zixiang, Wang Bodong, Huang Luobin and Zhao Baosheng (also known as Bao Sen).

The former site of the Chenjiapo conference

Jinpenwan

Chenjiapo is situated on a northwest-southeast slope, with ridges in the west and ravines in the east. It was located on the only route from Xuejia Stockade village to Beiliang, Jinpenwan, Hujiaxiang, Gaoshanhuai and even Weibei.

The conference lasted from the afternoon until the following day when the sun shone in the sky. The participants discussed three topics, the first of which was whether or not the three troop formations should act under a unified command. Some pessimists thought that it was a huge task to bring together the main forces and guerrillas from all counties. Nonetheless, a majority advocated pooling together these different forces under a centralised command. The second issue focused on the candidate for commander-in-chief. The majority of participants recommended Wang Taiji for the post, but a minority disagreed on the grounds that they regarded this as the army of volunteers leading the Red Army. The last issue concerned the position of Gao Gang as political commissar; a majority gave their assent to the proposition. The conference went along with the opinion of the majority, including Xi Zhongxun, Qin Wushan and Zhang Xiushan, to allow the Shaanxi-Gansu border region red army to take unified command of the army of volunteers, the fourth regiment of the Red Army and the guerrillas. It also recommended Wang Taiji as commander-in-chief and Gao Gang as political commissar. As proposed by Xi Zhongxun, Liu Zhidan was appointed as both deputy commander-in-chief and chief of staff. Given that Liu had not yet returned from the south, his appointment was temporarily deferred.

The Chenjiapo conference took 'Building and Expanding the Shaanxi-Gansu Border Region Soviet Zone' as its central slogan, worked out a strategy to concentrate efforts on small-scale fighting, accumulating small victories, carrying out extensive guerrilla activity and conducting in-depth work among the masses. In order to save a perilous situation, troops were encouraged to clench their fists and gather their strength to fight in this historic revolutionary struggle in the Shaanxi-Gansu border region. It was regarded as a historic conference in enhancing the unified leadership of the party over the Red Army and the guerrillas, in rebuilding the main forces of the Red Army, turning around the military situation, evacuating Zhaojin and opening up the Shaanxi-Gansu border region revolutionary base with Nanliang as the centre.

The newly established main forces in the Shaanxi-Gansu border region eradicated one of Lei Tianyi's militia troops in Rangniu village and Xia Yushan's militia in Miaowan. They also attacked Liu Lin's militia, wiped out a troop of the Dimiao militia and then conquered Zhanghong town in Xunyi county. A string of victories helped advance the reputation of the Red Army forces. When the main Red Army forces launched out-flanking attacks, Xi Zhongxun, together with Li Miaozhai and Zhang Xiushan, led the soldiers and civilians to repeatedly defeat the enemy using 'braided hemp grenades' and registered the first victory in safeguarding Xuejia Stockade village.

As Xi Zhongxun remembered in later years: "After that [the Chenjiapo conference], they marched to the north, taking away good guns, under the leadership of Gao Gang, the political commissar. Later, I organised guerrilla groups in Xunyi, Chunhua and western Yaoxian county. The masses' revolutionary fervour was very high. All you needed to do was to mobilise and lead them. They were like dry brushwood – you just needed a spark to ignite them. You only needed a few people to set up a guerrilla group at that time, even one person alone could do it. Then the guerrilla group would be established, followed by guns and munitions. We implemented unified management of the militias that sometimes sent us guns and munitions. I was happy to work in that way during that period."[5]

After Liu Zhidan returned on the day of the mid-autumn festival, the first thing he did was to visit Xi Zhongxun in recuperation. He said excitedly: "Things went very well! The end result of the Chenjiapo conference was to reject the wrong road and return to the correct path."

Chapter 7

'Baby-faced' Chairman of the Border Region Government

On 12 October 1933, confronted by the massed forces of four regular KMT regiments and a 6,000-strong militia from all counties, Liu Zhidan decided to evacuate the main forces of the Red Army from Zhaojin.

The Zhaojin soviet zone was the first attempt by the party and the Red Army in northwest China to establish a revolutionary base in a mountainous area, which also happened to be the home of the 26th Red Army. In early November 1933, a joint conference of administrative and military directors from the Shaanxi-Gansu border region CPC was held in Baojia Stockade village in Heshui county, Gansu province. Here, it was decided to develop three guerrilla zones centred on Anding (now Zichang county in Shaanxi province), Nanliang and Zhaojin. Meanwhile, Xi Zhongxun remained in Zhaojin because "he had a solid base among the masses there. He hid in the forest during the day and carried on work among the masses at night".[1]

On the eve of the spring festival in 1934, Xi Zhongxun hastened to Nanliang to work as secretary of the headquarters of the second guerrilla group and political instructor of the army of volunteers.

Nanliang village is situated in the east of Huachi county, Gansu province, near the border with Shaanxi. It lies at the southern foot of Daliang mountain, at the juncture of the counties of Huachi, Heshui, Fuxian and Bao'an (now Zhidan). The upper reaches of the Hulu river and several of its tributaries criss-cross the land, creating many gullies and ravines.

Xi Zhongxun's task on arriving in Nanliang was to "set up mass organisations, establish armed revolutionary forces, launch guerrilla warfare, open up a revolutionary base and establish worker-peasant political power". He helped the guerrillas as they eliminated the militia in Yanjia hollow, East Huachi county and Nanliang village, as well as the armed

Nanliang

forces of local landlords in Erjiang valley. He also took the lead in carrying out organisational work and mobilising the masses to distribute grain, cattle and sheep to individual households. A peasant labourers' association, poor peasant society, peasant union and a Red Guards unit were set up in Two-Generals valley, White Horse Temple valley, Nanliang, Liyuan, Leopard valley, Justice valley, Five-Village valley and White Horse valley. Xi Zhongxun dispatched Wu Daifeng and Liu Yuesan to organise the guerrillas in Bao'an county, Wang Ziliang to reorganise the guerrillas in Heshui county, Wu Yaxiong to set up a guerrilla group in Ansai county and Yang Pisheng to organise the expansion of the Army of Volunteers.

"Xi Zhongxun taught us how to fight against local despots, distribute farmland and protect the land," said Jiang Chengying, a Red Guards veteran. "The land was well protected, the landlords were overthrown and the oppression was eliminated. Most of the residents here were poor refugees from northern Shaanxi. Xi had such a good relationship with the masses, old and young, that they rushed to see him whenever he came to their home."[2]

The Red area in the Shaanxi-Gansu border region centred on Nanliang quickly expanded to 14 other counties: Bao'an, Ansai, Ganquan, Fuxian, Qingyang (now Qingcheng county in Gansu province), Heshui, Ningxian, Zhengning, Xunyi, Chunhua, Yaoxian, Tongguan (now Tongchuan city in Shaanxi province), Yijun and Zhongbu (now Huangling county in Shaanxi province). The Party Committee of the 42nd division of the Red Army held a mass meeting in Sihetai village in the Xiaohe valley and voted to establish the Shaanxi-Gansu border region revolutionary committee, with Xi Zhongxun elected as chairman and Huang Ziwen as secretary-general on 25 February 1934. This committee was reconvened in Zhaiziwan on 28 May 1934.

During this period, Xi Zhongxun and Liu Zhidan yearned to make contact with the upper echelons of the party, frequently asking comrades to look for them and giving them shoe-shaped gold or silver ingots as travelling allowances – but to no avail.

In October 1934, the Shaanxi-Gansu border region military and administrative cadre school was founded in Liyuan village, with Liu Zhidan appointed as principal and Xi Zhongxun as political commissar.

Liyuan

One day, Xi entered the school when Liu was organising military drills. Liu immediately saluted and invited his comrade to review the troops, which made Xi embarrassed. Liu Zhidan later told Xi Zhongxun that CPC members should uphold the political power built with their own hands; otherwise, civilians would not respect it.

As the revolutionary base continued to expand, it became increasingly important to develop the soviet government. From 1-6 November 1934, the Shaanxi-Gansu border region conference of workers, peasants and soldiers was held in Laoye temple in Liyuan, where more than 100 representatives from all walks of life joined in heated discussion about all the vital issues concerning the construction of a revolutionary base. As one of the conference moderators, Xi Zhongxun drafted numerous important documents. The conference established the Shaanxi-Gansu border region soviet government and democratically elected Xi Zhongxun as its chairman, Jia Shengxiu and Niu Yongqing as vice chairmen and Cai Ziwei as political secretary-general. It chose candidates for the committees on land, labour, finance, grain, culture, supervision of workers and peasants, purges and

The seals of (from left to right): the Shaanxi-Gansu soviet government; the Union of Worldwide Proletariats and Oppressed Nations; and the Shaanxi-Gansu border region revolutionary committee

The larger hall of Laoye temple in Liyuan

women. It also set up subordinate committees on eradicating the practice of foot-binding and banning smoking and gambling, and passed resolutions on politics, military affairs, land, finance and grain.

The red sun shone brightly on the Shaanxi-Gansu plateau in early winter. On the morning of 7 November 1934, the grand opening ceremony of the Shaanxi-Gansu border region soviet government was held in Liyuan. A platform was set up in the Qingyin building, opposite the temple. Altogether more than 3,000 official representatives, Red Army soldiers and local people from many kilometres around attended the ceremony. The red logo 'Opening Ceremony of the Shaanxi-Gansu Border Region Soviet Government' dazzled in the sunlight, hammer-and-sickle flags fluttered in the breeze and the sound of drumbeats and chanting filled the air.

Xi Zhongxun made a gracious and eloquent speech that called for further expansion of the armed forces, extensive mobilisation of the masses, an intensification of fighting and struggles for greater victories. He and Liu Zhidan jointly reviewed the troops.

The declaration of the establishment of the Shaanxi-Gansu border region soviet government, which formally consolidated the revolutionary base, was a milestone in the revolutionary history of the Shaanxi and Gansu border region and for the whole of northwest China.

In the same month, the official journal of the soviet government, *The Red Northwest*, was published for the first time.

The government at that time was stationed in Zhaiziwan, which was not far south of Nanliang. The masses were accustomed to calling it the 'Nanliang government'. Xi Zhongxun became its chairman at the age of just 21, so the masses affectionately called him the "baby-faced chairman". Whenever they encountered problems, they consulted Xi, who received them without delay. "You did quite a good job," said Liu Zhidan. "We will remain invincible as long as we serve in your style."

Xi Zhongxun did a huge amount of ground-breaking work in the areas of political power construction and economic and social development. He and Liu Zhidan also led the formulation of 10 major policies relating to land, finance, grain, the military, militias, bandits, social development, purges, intellectuals, captives, culture and education.

Red political power flourished. During 1934 and 1935, two district-level revolutionary committees were established, in the south and east of the Shaanxi-Gansu border region. Twenty county-level revolutionary committees were also set up, five of which were in Longdong district of

Qingyin building

Zhaiziwan

Gansu province (Huachi, Heshui, Qingbei, Chi'an and Xinning), two were near the Shaanxi-Gansu border (Xinzheng and Yonghong), and 13 counties were in Shaanxi province, namely, Zhongyi, Fuxi, Ansai, Chi'an, Chichun, Fugan, Hongquan, Fugan, Dingbian, Chichuan, Jingbian, Chunyao and Chishui.

Based on the practice of land distribution in Zhaojin, the border region government carried out its 'agrarian revolutionary war'. It confiscated land leased by landlords and rich peasants, who were only allowed to acquire their own distributed land so long as they worked it. Only land located in valleys and the central area was distributed at first; distribution of mountainous land and land in border regions could be carried out later. When it came to allocating land, priority was given to the family members of Red Army soldiers.

The border region government set up a market in Liyuan. When it opened it was bustling with activity, with people coming to the market from many kilometres around. Business was brisk. A protective policy was adopted for the merchants in the non-revolutionary 'white' area to sell mountain produce and livestock, shipping goods and materials such as cloth and cotton in and out to satisfy the demands of the army and the masses. The measures taken to foster and protect markets meant that everyday necessities were freely available: "The cadres used flashlights and the soldiers used enamel bowls."[3]

To promote economic activity, the border region government also issued a currency for the revolutionary base, known by civilians as the soviet bill. This currency was printed using a woodblock, and painted with tung oil on white flat cloth. A total of Rmb3,000 was issued initially, in denominations of Rmb1, Rmb0.5, Rmb0.2 and Rmb0.1; Rmb1 was equivalent to the value of a silver dollar. The border region government set up exchange offices in Liyuan where the currency could be exchanged at any time.

Culture and education developed rapidly in this part of northwest China. In the past, there hadn't even been a school in Nanliang. The border region government founded the First Lenin primary school in Sihetai, Xiaohe valley in February 1934. The teachers and students erected wooden planks as desks, piled up stones to use as benches, used slate for blackboards and soot as

Former site of the Shaanxi-Gansu border region soviet government in Zhaiziwan

ink. The textbook incorporated rhymes and jingles to convey revolutionary messages. They included simple, clear and easy-to-understand lines such as "Marx and Engels are mentors of world revolution" and "kill the despotic gentry with knives and shoot the White Army with rifles".[4]

Upon its foundation, the border region government issued a decree: any party, administrative or military cadre embezzling Rmb10 or more should be shot. "No cadre committed embezzlement thanks to this decree," recalled Xi Zhongxun.

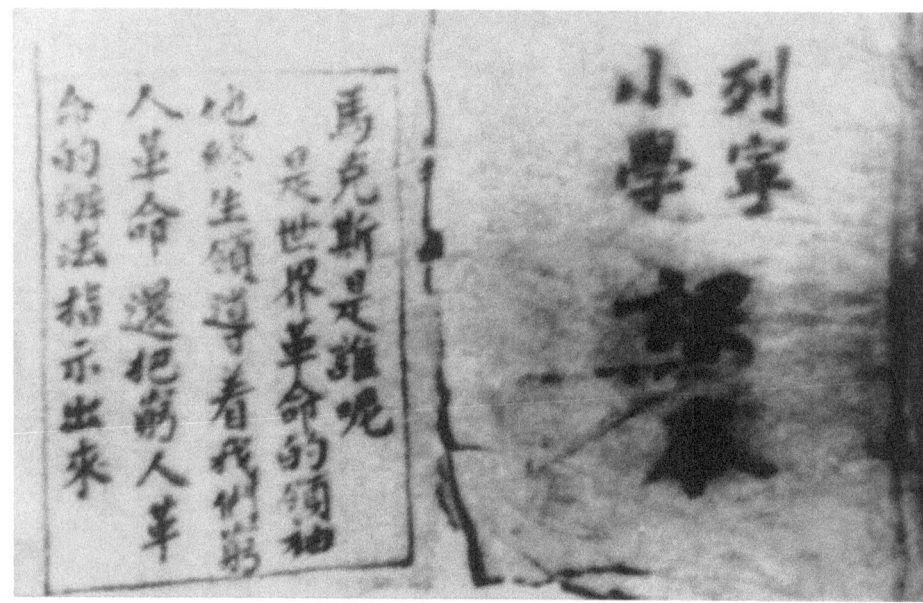

Lenin primary school textbook; the text on the left-hand page reads: "Who is Marx? Karl Marx was a world revolutionary leader, who directed workers' revolutions throughout his lifetime and pointed out the methods for such revolutions"

Chapter 8

Wrongfully Purged

The Communist Party of China northwest working committee in Zhoujiaxian (now in Zichang county) was founded on 5 February 1935, and Xi Zhongxun was elected as a committee member. Its establishment confirmed the unified leadership of the party over the Shaanxi-Gansu border region revolutionary base and the Northern Shaanxi revolutionary base, and the formation of a revolutionary base in northwest China.

In the middle of that month, the KMT authorities launched their second large-scale 'suppression' in the revolutionary base in northwest China. When Liu Zhidan transferred the main forces of the Red Army to fight in

The historic site of the Shaanxi-Gansu border region soviet government in Yizigou village, Xiasiwan

northern Shaanxi, Xi Zhongxun commanded the Second Guerrilla unit and the Red Guards in Nanliang to switch their positions, erect red flags, light bonfires and stealthily deploy their troops in Laoye mountain to pin down Ma Hongbin's forces in the soviet zone for a month or more.

On 13 April 1935, Xi Zhongxun evacuated more than 100 workers, Red Guards and Qingyang guerrillas from Zhaiziwan and moved east to Luohe valley (now in Ganquan county, Shaanxi province). He was besieged twice by enemies on the journey. Not until he was out of danger did Xi Zhongxun happen to notice that his feet were bleeding due to his hard riding of the white horse. Later, Liu Zhidan patted the horse and commented: "What a brave white horse to save its master!"

In May, the Shaanxi-Gansu border region party, administrative and military office transferred to Siwan at the foot of Luohe valley. The border region government, now stationed in Yizigou village, set up a market in Hupitou, issued the soviet currency, established Lenin primary schools in Qiaozhen town, Yanjiagou village and Wangjiaping, and built military

The cave in Yizigou where Xi Zhongxun once lived

schools in Wangjiaping to train soldiers and administrative cadres. Xi Zhongxun also designated Wang Zhongxiu, Wang Dayou and Wang Dianbin to organise guerrilla groups in the counties of Luochuan, Bao'an, Jingbian, Dingbian and Anbian.

The scorching July sun shone over the Shaanxi-Gansu plateau, but political clouds were gathering in the form of Zhu Lizhi, the representative dispatched to northwest China by Kong Yuan, who was the north China representative of the central government, and Nie Hongjun, who was the representative of the Interim Shanghai Central Office.

Zhu Lizhi believed that a one-sided report by Guo Hongtao, who worked as a committee member and departmental director of the northwest workers' committee, made wrong judgments about the situation, and designated Li Jinglin and Hui Bihai to help with the work in the Shaanxi-Gansu border region. After assuming the post of secretary of the special party committee, Li Jinglin fought against the rich peasants when he learned of their identities. Hui Bihai led the working group of the 'agrarian revolutionary war' to carry out 'field inspections' using ultra-leftist methods, driving the rich peasants 'into the mountains to eat grass' after redistributing their belongings. The masses frantically redistributed whatever they saw. Yang Yuting, chairman of the financial committee of the soviet government, once passed by the Luohe river. The masses went so far as to sail from the other side of the bank to expropriate public funds that he was carrying. Xi Zhongxun criticised these actions and rectified the problem before removing Hui Bihai from his post at the next special party committee meeting.

Word came in early September 1935 that the 25th Red Army led by Xu Haidong and Cheng Zihua was moving to fight in the Shaanxi-Gansu border region. Xi Zhongxun and Liu Jingfan assigned individuals to give the officers and men of the 25th Red Army cattle and sheep as a reward for their great deeds.

In mid-September, Xi Zhongxun chaired a conference in Yongning mountain and delivered an ebullient speech to welcome the arrival of the 25th Red Army in northern Shaanxi.

However, the situation in the Shaanxi-Gansu border region was quite perilous. Chiang Kai-shek obstructed and intercepted the Red Army's long march and assembled 100,000 troops to step up military 'suppression' in the Shaanxi-Gansu soviet zone.

After the 25th Red Army joined forces with the 26th and 27th Red Army, the 15th Red army group was set up with Xu Haidong elected as commander, Cheng Zihua as political commissar and Liu Zhidan as deputy commander and chief of staff.

The CPC northwest working committee was dissolved on 17 September 1935, and replaced by the newly created Shaanxi-Gansu-Shanxi provincial party committee, with Zhu Lizhi as secretary and Guo Hongtao as deputy secretary. The northwest military committee was also reorganised with Nie Hongjun as chairman. Upon its foundation, the Shaanxi-Gansu-Shanxi provincial party committee firmly believed that the 'rightist' organisations and their members were mainly in the Shaanxi-Gansu border region party organisation and the 26th Red Army, and began to make arrests in Yongping town on 21 September 1935.

"The list contained more than 30 names, including mine and [Liu] Jingfan's who attended the conference," recalled Xi Zhongxun. "It also included the vice chairman, the correspondent and secretary-general, who

The prison in Huichuantong pawnshop in Wayao where Xi Zhongxun was confined

were all thought to be rightists. I sensed something was wrong and had some dubious men arrested. In the end, only nine were arrested and the rest were freed once I had given a personal guarantee: if they did something wrong, I would be arrested without delay. As time passed, an increasing number of people were arrested across the region. At that time the arrested could not be sent back without the letters signed in my name. Consequently, many people were released in my name and this gave me cause for considerable disquiet."[1]

"As a result, an absurd phenomenon emerged: the Red Army spared no effort in fighting Chiang Kai-shek's troops and scored a series of victories, while the exponents of 'leftist' opportunism took actions to seize power and then arrest a huge number of cadres, including Liu Zhidan and other senior cadres in the 26th Red Army and in the Shaanxi-Gansu border region. The white reactionary army took advantage by launching massive attacks and the border region shrank day by day, which sowed the seeds of misgivings among the masses; landlords and rich peasants took the opportunity to make mischief, by encouraging 'defections' in counties such as Bao'an, Ansai, Dingbian and Jingbian. The revolutionary base had entered a perilous phase."[2]

Someone suggested to Xi Zhongxun that he should escape in order to save himself from useless sacrifice. "Even if they were to kill me, I couldn't leave here," he retorted. "These comrades were given pardons in my name. How can I take flight?"

In no time Xi Zhongxun was arrested, having been wrongly identified as a 'secretary of the rightist front committee'. Nie Hongjun wrote in a letter to Xi Zhongxun: "Comrade Zhongxun, I feel it imperative to have a talk with you because of your ambiguous and non-proletarian attitude in the crackdown on counter-revolutionaries."[3] Xi faced three criminal charges: cursing the masses as 'bandits'; failing to launch the agrarian revolutionary war in mountainous areas by restricting land redistribution to valley areas; and tipping off rich peasants.

Xi Zhongxun and Liu Zhidan were locked up in the cave of Huichuantong pawnshop in Wayao village. The makeshift prison was freezing, and the inmates had to sleep on rice straw laid on the floor, with their hands and feet tied up and lice crawling over their bodies. They were given little food and not allowed to drink water or go to the toilet. They were subjected to arbitrary torture by their jailers and forced to admit they were rightists and counter-revolutionaries.

Liu Zhidan's daughter Liu Lizhen, who was just six years old at the time, went to see her father with her mother. "My mother was told that a pit had been dug to bury my father," she said. "My mother took me to see it. What a deep pit for a man! She burst into tears at the sight of it."[4]

The wrongful crackdown on counter-revolutionaries threw the only soviet zone in northern Shaanxi into turmoil.

Chapter 9

Northwest Soviet Zone Becomes Foothold for Red Army Long March

Just as the dangers posed by the wrongful crackdown on counter-revolutionaries threatened to spiral out of control, events took a favourable turn thanks to the arrival of the Central CPC Red Army on their Long March.

Mao Zedong arriving in northern Shaanxi after the Long March

The CPC Red Army, marching to Hadapu after innumerable trials and hardships, were overjoyed to read in the newspaper that Liu Zhidan's Red Army troop was stationed in northern Shaanxi. Mao Zedong pointed out at a conference for senior military cadres in the temple of Guan Yu in Hadapu on 20 September 1935 that the national crisis was deepening on a daily basis. "We must take further actions and march northwards to resist Japanese aggression, as planned," he said. "First, we should march to northern Shaanxi to meet up with Liu Zhidan's Red Army troops. It is only 350-400km to Liu's revolutionary base in northern Shaanxi. We should press on and continue to advance northwards."[1]

In October 1935, the central CPC Red Army arrived in Wuqi after their successful Long March of 12,500km. On their arrival, Mao Zedong and Zhang Wentian[2] immediately issued the order to: stop arresting, stop interrogating and stop killing people; everything will be resolved by the central authorities.

On 7 November 1935, the central authorities were stationed in Wayao village and they established a five-member party affairs committee directed by Qin Bangxian and composed of Dong Biwu, Wang Shoudao, Zhang Yunyi, Li Weihan and Guo Hongtao. They were tasked with addressing the problems left over by the wrongful crackdown on counter-revolutionaries in northern Shaanxi. After investigation, the groundless accusations made against Liu Zhidan and others were overturned. Altogether 18 prisoners, including Xi Zhongxun, Liu Zhidan and Yang Sen, were set free, and other comrades followed.

"The revolutionary base in northern Shaanxi is safe now!" Both soldiers and civilians were exultant and lost no time in spreading the news.

Former site of the party school of the CPC central committee in Wayao

Northwest Soviet Zone Becomes Foothold for Red Army Long March

Comrades of the Red Army CPC central committee said: "If the 'Leftist' opportunism had destroyed the revolutionary base, there would have been no place for the CPC central committee to recuperate." Until now, the northwest soviet zone, comprising the Shaanxi-Gansu border region revolutionary base and its counterpart in northern Shaanxi, had provided a foothold for the Long Marchers and it became a bridgehead for the central Red Army's war of resistance against Japan.

Whenever he recalled this period, no matter how many years had passed, Xi Zhongxun could never suppress his excitement. "The revolutionary bases would have been destroyed without the arrival of Mao Zedong in northern Shaanxi," he said. "He would not have encountered us if he had arrived four days later; without Mao's order of 'Spare him!' I would have perished in the earth since they had already dug pits to bury us alive."

During his study in the party school of the CPC central committee in Wayao village, Xi Zhongxun acted as leader of the Third Drill Squad. On 27 December 1935, Xi was present at the party activist conference of the CPC central committee convened in the party school, when he met Mao Zedong for the first time. He had long admired Mao, since listening to his report *On Tactics Against Japanese Imperialism*. He was deeply impressed on meeting the man. "I listened to Chairman Mao's report attentively," Xi said. "I felt that what he said was completely true and realistic and the path he advocated was thoroughly correct. I felt the fog lifting and a big boost in confidence. I was overjoyed to hear Chairman Mao speak for the first time."[3]

He also met Zhou Enlai for the first time. "I saw a man in the distance who wore the black cotton uniform of the Red Army, with a long beard and eyes that shone with vigour below thick, dashing eyebrows. The intelligence that radiated in his bright eyes enabled him to have a keen insight into all matters, which engendered a feeling of profound respect."[4]

In his later years, Xi Zhongxun spent much time evaluating the historic experiences of the Shaanxi-Gansu border region revolutionary base. He observed in his article *Review of History* that: "The party organisations, the Red Army soldiers and the masses experienced 10 years of counter-revolutionary 'suppression' and disturbance created by 'leftist' and 'rightist' approaches to the agrarian revolutionary war. Having overcome innumerable trials and tribulations, the red sun finally dispelled the dark clouds; victories reddened the mountains and trees on the Shaanxi-Gansu plateau and disseminated the seeds of the soviet to western China where the revolutionary situation was comparatively backward. It became the only base where revolutionary achievements survived the failure of 'leftist' opportunism advocated by Wang Ming, and contributed considerably to the liberation of the Chinese people under the leadership of the CPC."

Wang Shitai, an old comrade-in-arms of Xi Zhongxun, had intimate knowledge of the revolutionary process adopted by Xi Zhongxun to establish the Shaanxi-Gansu border region revolutionary base. "During the Long March in 1935, the CPC central committee and the CPC Red Army braved extreme difficulties and came to northern Shaanxi," he said. "Chairman Mao stressed the importance of the Shaanxi-Gansu-Ningxia border region functioning as the foothold of the CPC central committee and the CPC Red Army as well as the starting point of the War of Resistance Against Japan. Without this revolutionary base, the CPC central committee would have faced enormous disasters and dangers. Nor could it have established a firm foothold in northwest China. There is no doubt that the achievements of this period should be attributed to everyone. Nonetheless, I believe that it was Comrade Zhongxun who should take most credit for establishing the Zhaojin revolutionary base and the Nanliang revolutionary base amid all the difficulties and hardships."[5]

Zhou Enlai, newly arrived in northern Shaanxi

Chapter 10

Guarding the Southern Entrance to Yan'an

In January 1936, the CPC central committee designated Xi Zhongxun to work in the soviet government, newly established in Guanzhong special zone (based on the former southern Shaanxi-Gansu border region) as vice chairman of the soviet government and secretary of the party and league. In late February 1936, Xi arrived in Nanyi village, Xinzheng county (now Zhengning county, Gansu province), where the Guanzhong

The courtyard in Nanyi village where Xi Zhongxun once lived

special zone party and administrative office was stationed. In April 1936, 11 divisions of the Northeast army launched massive attacks in Guanzhong where the special party committee was disbanded and the cadres scattered and withdrew. Similar to what happened following the withdrawal from Zhaojin, Xi Zhongxun took up the post as secretary of the Guanzhong working committee and stayed behind for the fighting that followed.

In May 1936, Xi Zhongxun was dispatched to withdraw from Guanzhong and join the Red Army's Field Army in the west, commanded by Peng Dehuai on their westward march. After liberating the town of Quzi on 1 June 1936, Xi Zhongxun organised the Quxian-Huanxian county CPC working committee and served as secretary. He mobilised the masses to pool together stone rollers and millstones in Bazhu plateau so that rice and flour milling could continue day and night to ensure adequate supplies for the troops.

On 4 June, Huanxian county was liberated. Xi Zhongxun rushed over to the city of Hongde in the north of Huanxian, organised the Huanxian county party committee and assumed the post of secretary. The county party

The ruins where the Quxian-Huanxian county working committee was stationed

Bazhu plateau

committee office was set up in the Xingerpu district of Hongde. Because of the wartime situation, it needed to be relocated frequently.

After spending about three months in Huanxian, Xi Zhongxun succeeded in completing all the establishment and organisational work. At the same time, he set up the Huanxian county soviet government. The county party committee had its own guard as well as offices for organisation, propaganda, military affairs, labour unions, youth and women. He personally recruited the first group of party members and set up three district-level guerrilla groups in the counties of Huanxian, Hongde and Hujia Dongzi. There were 40 or more guerrillas with access to over 30 rifles and handguns.

In mid-August 1936, Li Fuchun, secretary of the Shaanxi-Gansu border region provincial party committee, talked with Xi Zhongxun in Helianwan and announced that the central government had decided to relocate Xi to Bao'an county (which was then where the CPC central committee was stationed) for new tasks.

An important reason for the move was that nearly all the revolutionary bases in the Guanzhong plain had been lost in the few months since Xi Zhongxun had left, and the central government urgently needed to designate someone who was familiar with the situation there to lead the struggle.

Unfortunately, central government leaders had only just begun to be aware of the unfair treatment of the comrades who had suffered from the wrongful crackdown on counter-revolutionaries. Li Weihan[1] (Luo Mai), then director of the organisation department of the CPC central committee, said later in Yan'an: "I was not familiar with the situation at that time and I followed too many wrong proposals. It was especially unfair for Comrade Zhongxun to be designated to work as secretary of the county party committee there." He also recollected in his later years: "Since the 'leftist' line had not been exposed and criticised, cadres and military cadres in the Shaanxi-Gansu border region soviet zone were still labelled as opportunists. As a result, their assignments, especially those of some senior cadres, were usually unfair."[2]

On 15 September 1936, Xi Zhongxun attended a plenary session of the political bureau of the central committee, along with two other local cadres. It was the first time he had attended a central government meeting. On

The former site where the CPC central committee was stationed in Bao'an county, Shaanxi province

seeing Xi Zhongxun, Mao Zedong clasped his hands and showered him with praise. "So young, still just a baby!" he said.

The party central committee assigned Xi Zhongxun to organise the work in Guanzhong as secretary of the special party committee. Xi once said he had twice been asked to guard the south gate for the party central committee, and that this was the first occasion. Zhang Wentian, responsible for the work of the central government, urged Xi to "try mobilising the militia leaders to join the united front, including the head of the neighbourhood administrative system and the joint defence directors."

Xi Zhongxun felt great responsibility to be working once again in Guanzhong, which was strategically located in the southernmost part of the Shaanxi-Gansu-Ningxia special zone and surrounded by KMT-controlled areas to the south, east and west. It was also just 200km from Xi'an. KMT diehards coveted the capture of this 'capsule-shaped strip'. The five counties under the jurisdiction of the Guanzhong special zone − Chunyao, Chishui, Yonghong, Xinzheng and Xinning − had all been occupied by the KMT army, which had established strongholds in all the central cities. Only Pingdao valley in Xinning county had escaped their control. As a consequence, the guerrillas in Guanzhong had no choice but to disperse and conduct their activities in a clandestine manner.

Along the way, they had to fight against the enemies they encountered on a daily basis in addition to crossing enemy lines, climbing mountains, fording ditches and trekking through forests. All this left them little time to celebrate the mid-autumn festival.

In early October 1936, Xi Zhongxun arrived at Shimen mountain, Xunyi county and exchanged information with Zhang Fengqi, who was guarding Guanzhong at Shimen pass. In mid October, Xi chaired the Guanzhong party activist conference in Qijieshi with more than 30 people present that decided to reorganise and expand the county guerrilla groups, centralise their fighting capabilities, conduct sporadic actions and establish the Guanzhong guerrilla headquarters with Guo Bingkun as commander and Xi Zhongxun as political commissar. The delegates also agreed to carry out united front work to the best of their ability, to win over progressive and non-aligned militias and members of the neighbourhood administrative system, and to combat a handful of extremist

Shimen mountain

reactionaries. It was also decided to reorganise party work in every locality, to invigorate the whole party's organisational life, to restore soviet political power in all counties and to establish new soviet zones. The official in charge of liaison, Zhang Guide, remembered: "When I met him [Xi Zhongxun] for the first time, he told me that the situation was grim. Militarily speaking, the enemy had the advantage; politically speaking, we had the advantage."[3]

Xi Zhongxun quickly applied himself to the work situation in Guanzhong. The Guanzhong guerrillas triumphed in fighting on the Mayuan plateau, in Xinzheng county, Rangniu village, Chunyao county and Guojiazhang, Chishui county and purged a host of bandits in Guanzhong. The number of guerrillas grew by 14 to 500 members in total, and local political power was largely restored. New soviet zones were developed in the three districts along the Jinghe river, including Xiaoqiao in Chunyao county and Yaoxiang mountain in Tongyi county.

In mid-December 1936, the special party committee had not yet received news about the 'Xi'an incident' on 12 December, in which Chiang Kai-shek was arrested by the former Manchurian warlord Zhang Xueliang, which led to a truce between the KMT and the communists. Ignorant of these important developments, the special party committee ordered the Red Army and guerrillas to launch attacks and persuaded the militias and neighbourhoods in the administrative system to turn in their weapons voluntarily. Within 10 days, control had been re-established over the entire Guanzhong soviet zone and soviet governments were set up in the counties of Chunyao, Chishui, Xinzheng and Xinning, where party work was resumed. This expansion of the soviet zones in Guanzhong and the attacks on the KMT army continued until Peng Dehuai[4] conveyed new instructions to the leadership, including Xi Zhongxun, following the Xi'an incident.

Li Weihan, secretary of the CPC Shaanxi-Gansu provincial party committee between December 1936 and April 1937, praised Guanzhong in his *Summary of Work in Guanzhong*, saying that it was "the best soviet zone I have ever been to in Shaanxi and Gansu."

Xi Zhongxun recalled that the Guanzhong soviet zone, which now included Xinning, Xinzheng, Chishui and Chunyao, penetrated KMT-controlled areas and extended as far as the strategic city of Xi'an. The entire Guanzhong revolutionary base was recovered and the guerrilla groups

Shimen pass

were expanded. Although the KMT still exerted overt political power, "our political power was secretly established under the public guise of 'The Anti-Japanese National Salvation Association'".

After the Guanzhong revolutionary base was regained, it soon became an important foothold after the realignment of the three main forces of the Red Army and Taoqu plateau. It was situated on a direct route between Yan'an, where the CPC central committee was stationed, and Yunyang town, Jingyang county, which was the headquarters of the front line Red Army. This beautiful village had a habit of emerging into prominence in times of discord. Deng Xiaoping, who at that time was director of the political department of the first regiment of the Red Army, along with various Red Army generals including Nie Rongzhen, Yang Shangkun, Xu Haidong, Luo Ruiqing, Chen Guang and Wang Shoudao, had been stationed there for months, 'hosted' by Xi Zhongxun as secretary of the Guanzhong special party committee.

Taoqu plateau, where the Guanzhong special party committee was stationed (December 1936-April 1937)

On the eve of an expedition of the main forces of the Eighth Route Army (led at that time by the CPC) to fight the invading Japanese in August and September 1937, Xi Zhongxun selected more than 500 Red Army cadres and soldiers of high political and military calibre in Shaanxi and Gansu from Guanzhong special zone. They were tasked with organising a replacement regiment to head for the 120th Division stationed in Zhuangli town, Fuping county. It was the first group of replacement soldiers since the establishment of the Eighth Route Army, which profoundly impressed Zhu De, the commander-in-chief, Deng Xiaoping, deputy director of the General Political Department and He Long, commander of the 120th regiment of the Eighth Route Army. Forty-three years later, Deng Xiaoping and Xi Zhongxun, vice chairman of the CPC central committee and first secretary of the CPC Guangdong provincial committee respectively, discussed the first steps of China's reform and opening-up process. An unusual dialogue occurred between the two men but their shared history meant that neither of them ever forgot the turbulent years they experienced in the Shaanxi-Gansu-Ningxia and Guanzhong special zones.

Chapter 11

'Putting the Party's Interests First'

Xi Zhongxun was designated to serve in Guanzhong twice in 1936, and appointed as president of the northwest party school in August 1942. Over this six-year period, significant achievements were made in all areas of work under his leadership.

The party organisation in Guanzhong could be divided into two stages: the first lasted from September 1936 to October 1937, which was the period of the Guanzhong special party committee. The second period was one of

The former offices of the Guanzhong special party committee in Majia (April 1937-May 1940)

The former site of the Guanzhong branch of the party and government organs in Yangpotou (June 1940-July 1941)

party committee branches. Soon after becoming stationed in Taoqu plateau in December 1936, Xi Zhongxun explicitly commanded that "there should be party committee branches in all towns and party members in all villages". Two congresses of party representatives were held, in Majia village in October 1937 and Shangqiang village in September 1939. The number of party members and organisations at all levels soared. Five county party committees, 20 district party committees and 68 party branches had been set up by the foundation of the CPC northwest central office in May 1941.

It was a major feature of the party to train cadres in policy theory and culture in party schools and the like. Cadres at and above township and county level received the equivalent of a junior middle school education and most of those who had previously been illiterate were able to read newspapers and write letters by 1941.

Xi Zhongxun established a good model for implementing the policy of the anti-Japanese national united front, vigorously advocating negotiations with the KMT. The Guanzhong special party committee also set up two fund-raising and supplies offices in Chunhua and Xunyi counties and entered into mutual non-aggression pacts with Liu Tieshan's militia in

Ningxian and Sha Bingyan's militia in Yijun. Nevertheless, the able-bodied men of the Tuqiao militia took the opportunity of attacking the soviet zone to defect to the special party committee directly with their guns.

Two major elections were held in Guanzhong. The first took place in July-August 1937, when government representatives and members of all ranks were elected democratically; the second was held in the spring of 1941, to implement the requirements of the 'triangular organisation' regime. Votes could be cast in one of three ways: by putting a bean in a bowl behind the chosen candidate who was standing with his back to the voter; by burning a hole with an incense stick in a piece of paper carrying the name of the candidate; or, more conventionally, by using a mobile polling box. Voter turnout rates ranged from 70% to 80%. The 'enlightened gentry' took several governmental posts: Jing Tianyu from Chishui became financial section chief of the county government; Zhang Zhiping, a doctor of traditional Chinese medicine (TCM) from Xinzheng county and the famous hermit Xiao Zhibao from Xunyi county were elected as members of the Guanzhong branch; and Zhang Zhiping won a seat as a member of the Shaanxi-Gansu-Ningxia border region.

Xi Zhongxun (third from right) and comrades-in-arms in the Guanzhong soviet zone

Second party congress representatives in Guanzhong district

Under the leadership of Xi Zhongxun, the large-scale production campaign in Guanzhong was among the most successful in the entire border region. For example, Xinzheng county set up farms in Xiniu village and attained an annual grain output of more than 40 tonnes. The government of Xinzheng also contributed Rmb50,000 to establish consumer and producer cooperatives, set up affiliated textile mills, transport teams and commerce departments, and absorbed Rmb160,000-worth of share capital from the locals. Due to the unpredictable and prolonged nature of the struggle, party and government organs were transferred to Yaoqu plateau, Malan town and the villages of Majia, Changshetou, Liujia, Yangpotou and Leizhuang. To improve working conditions, Xi Zhongxun led soldiers and local people to excavate more than 300 caves in the high slopes to the northwest of the Malan river and built a hospital, clothing factory, machine maintenance factory and warehouses.

Guanzhong was also at the forefront of cultural education in the border region. In late autumn of 1939, Guanzhong opera troupe was founded in Majia. On 12 April 1940, *Guanzhong News* was published and distributed in Leizhuang.

Report on the election campaign of the Guanzhong special party committee in Chunyao county, page 3 of the *New China* newspaper (新中华报) on 3 August 1937

The number of primary schools and middle schools rose from 170 to 243 and student numbers exceeded 7,000; nine elementary schools were set up, catering for more than 400 students; secondary education was also established from a zero base. On 15 March 1940, the Second normal school of the Shaanxi-Gansu-Ningxia border region was established in Majia and Xi Zhongxun was appointed part-time headmaster. He proposed a "labour exchange and mutual help" arrangement, which involved students hoeing land for the masses one day and, in return, the masses furrowing school land on another. This helped to cement ties between the school and the local community. On hearing the news that more than 90 teachers and students were suffering from typhoid around the spring festival of 1941, Xi Zhongxun invited Zhang Zhiping to diagnose and treat them with TCM and sent two injection needles he kept with him to the school.

The Northern Shaanxi public school (July 1938-July 1939) and Lu Xun normal school (April 1938-July 1939) were moved to Guanzhong. He Zai, an alumnus of the Northern Shaanxi public school, remembered his time there with affection. "Whenever Northern Shaanxi public school encountered difficulties and even when we had no food to eat, we would turn to Xi Zhongxun for help and he would settle the problems for us," he said. "For this reason, the school enjoyed better conditions than those prevailing in Yan'an at that time."[1]

KMT supporters had coveted Guanzhong for quite a long time and began to make trouble in the winter of 1938. They precipitated the 'Xunyi incident', which involved the shooting of wounded personnel of the Eighth Route Army disabled soldier school in May 1939, and the 'Chunhua incident', when they besieged garrison troops of the Eighth Route Army in March 1940. In this period, Xi Zhongxun led the soldiers and civilians in Guanzhong to implement the policy of "meeting the enemy's local sector attacks with local sector guerrilla activities and meeting all-out enemy attacks with all-out guerrilla activities" and at the same time waged an anti-friction struggle ('friction' that led to infighting between the CPC and KMT in the face of their common enemy, the Japanese invaders) against the KMT diehards. In the spring and summer of 1940, more than 90 combat actions were conducted to wear down the enemy, involving the capture of 410 rifles and handguns, more than 8,000 bullets and 248 prisoners. The Guanzhong revolutionary base was consolidated and expanded, and Tongyiyao county[2]

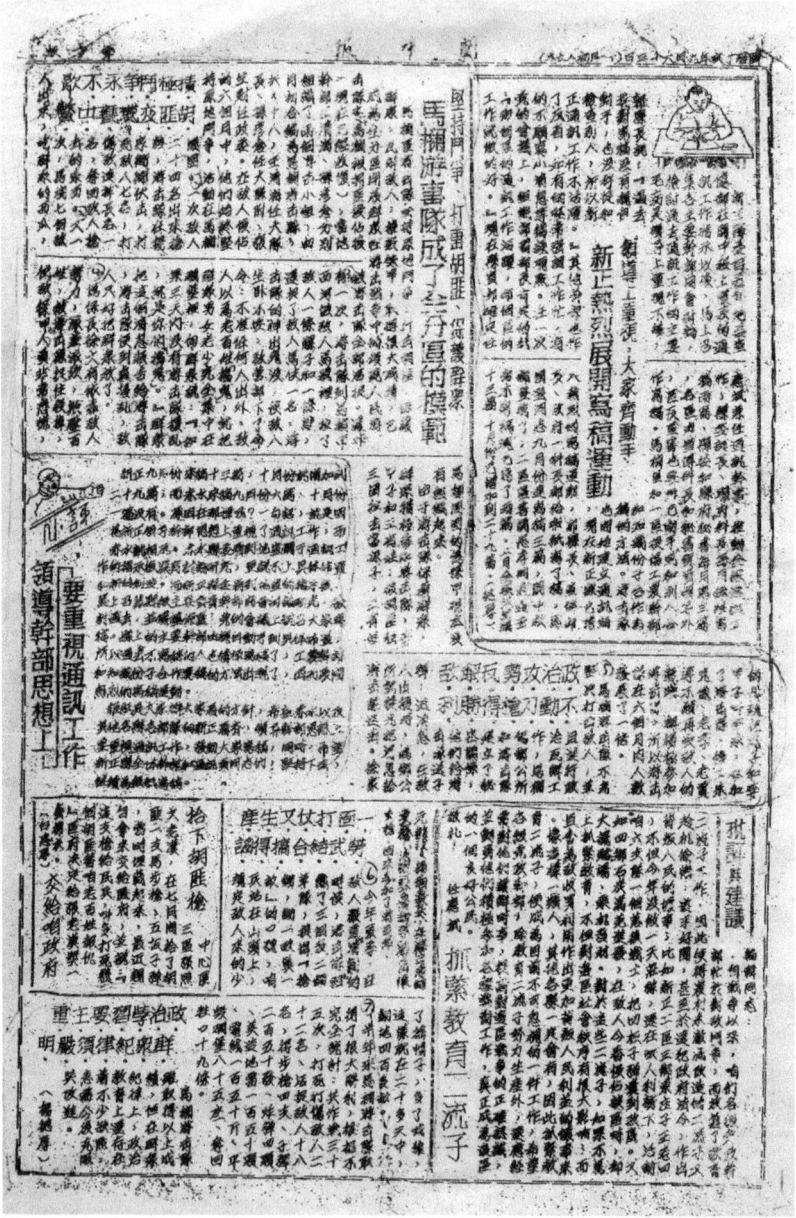

A page from *Guanzhong News*

was newly established in September 1940. It is estimated that, in 1940 alone, Xi Zhongxun wrote more than 100,000 characters in up to 27 reports about the anti-friction struggle for the Shaanxi-Gansu-Ningxia border region government.

In the summer of 1941, Xi Zhongxun and Wen Niansheng directed troops in fierce combat with the KMT army at Phoenix mountain, in Bin county. After three days of battle, the KMT forces were driven south to Tuqiao town in Chishui county and different parts of Xinzheng county. Not until then did the anti-friction struggle subside.

During these six years in Guanzhong, Xi Zhongxun immersed himself in the daily lives of residents. Whenever people faced a problem, they would commonly say: "Ask Zhongxun for help". An official testimonial in 1942 complimented Xi as being a "valuable leader of the masses of the party". When he was in Yangpotou, Xi held a meeting with a number of men including Zhang Zhongliang, commander of the security department of the sub-region. When they mentioned that troops paid less for trees than other people and that the locals did not dare complain, Xi flew into

The cave excavated by Xi Zhongxun in Malan

a rage. "Aren't we the army of the people?" he asked Zhang Zhongliang. "How dare you do it? Planting and growing trees is a painstaking business. You are the commander and I am the political commissar. What way is this to settle problems? Should we cut down their trees without paying adequate compensation?" That evening, Zhang Zhongliang confessed his shortcomings to Xi Zhongxun.

From 19 October 1942 to 14 January 1943, the CPC northwest central office held an 88-day conference for senior cadres in the Shaanxi-Gansu-Ningxia border region in the auditorium of the provincial assembly of the Yan'an border region. Mao Zedong regarded it as "an examination of the rectification of incorrect working style."[3] Ren Bishi was entrusted by the CPC central committee to chair the conference and Zhu De and Liu Shaoqi made speeches. The conference was the only one of its kind in the party's history.

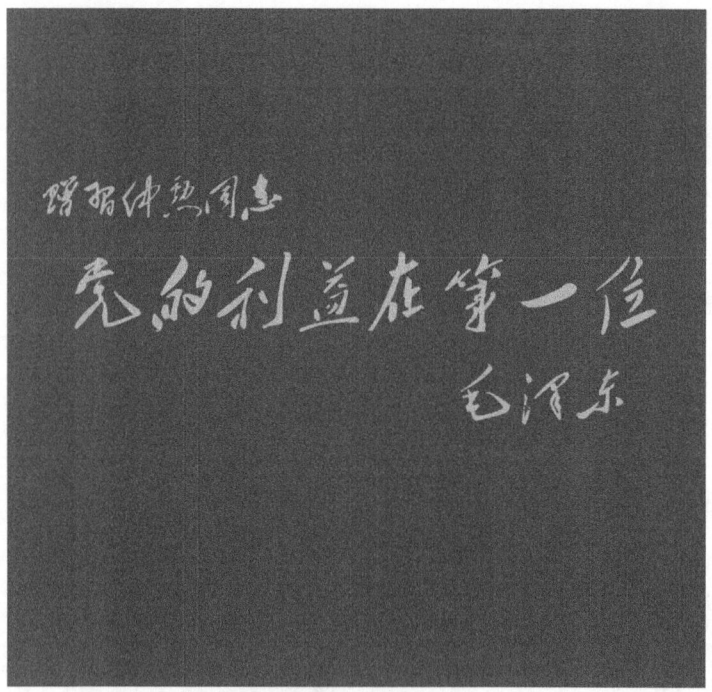

The calligraphy penned by Mao Zedong for Xi Zhongxun shown here reads: "Putting the party's interests first; a present for Comrade Xi Zhongxun; Mao Zedong"

The conference focused on rectification and discussions were held on the historical issues of the northwest revolutionary base, including the Shaanxi-Gansu border region and northern Shaanxi. In his speech to the conference on 11 November 1942, Xi Zhongxun reviewed the history of the Shaanxi-Gansu border region, the disagreements over various policies adopted by the party in the region, the disastrous impact of the crackdown on counter-revolutionaries in the Shaanxi-Gansu border region and northern Shaanxi, and concluded with criticism and self-criticism. On 8 January 1943, Xi delivered a speech entitled *A Brief Introduction to the Party's History in Guanzhong*, which was a comprehensive summary of the historical experiences of the party's history in the region. During the conference, on 12 December 1942, the CPC central committee made the *Decision to Re-examine the Issues on the 'Crackdown on Counter-revolutionaries' in Northern Shaanxi (including the Shaanxi-Gansu border region and northern Shaanxi) in 1935.*

Xi Zhongxun's speech was praised by Mao Zedong, who had got to know Xi much better during that period.

At the closing ceremony of the senior cadre conference on 14 January 1943, Mao Zedong wrote inscriptions for the 22 leaders, noting their remarkable economic achievements. The inscription for Xi Zhongxun was: "Putting the party's interests first", which was written on a piece of bleached cloth measuring about 30cm long and 17cm wide. "A present for Comrade Xi Zhongxun" was written at the top and at the bottom was Mao's signature.

Mao's message delighted Xi Zhongxun. "I kept the inscription with me for quite a long time," he said. "It served as a mirror, urging me to try harder to transform my world outlook."[4]

Chapter 12

Guarding the Northern Entrance to Yan'an

In mid February 1943, Xi Zhongxun was made secretary of Suide prefectural party committee and political commissar of Suide garrison headquarters. Before he departed to take up these new positions, Mao Zedong talked with him in a cave in Yangjia mountain. "If a person stays too long in one area, it's easy for him to become insensitive to his surroundings," Mao said. "A move to a new area is also good training."

Suide is situated in the north of the Shaanxi-Gansu-Ningxia border region, and its population of 520,000 accounted for one-third of the entire

The former site of Suide Normal University, previously known as No.4 Shaanxi Province Normal University

region. Due to long-term reactionary propaganda of the KMT, many of the inhabitants had a limited understanding of the CPC and their political awareness was generally low.

Xi Zhongxun proposed to make in-depth investigations, intensify publicity, educate the cadres and rank-and-file party members through propagating the party's tenets, guidelines and policies, and to ensure that no mistakes were made in rectification work and production. He hung Mao Zedong's inscription to him on the wall of his office to provide encouragement.

During this period, the rectification and interrogation work under the auspices of Kang Sheng[1] took a seriously wrong turn. The so-called 'salvation of those who have lost their way' campaign swept every corner of the Shaanxi-Gansu-Ningxia border region and led to a crackdown on counter-revolutionaries in institutions such as Suide Normal University. False confessions suddenly became the norm. Even students as young as 11 or 12 'confessed' to being 'little spies'. A majority of teachers and students were censored and suspected. The Anti-Japanese Military and Political University had 1,052 cadres above the military rank of platoon commander, 602 (57%) of whom were suspected and ordered to make confessions. Suide garrison headquarters and its subordinate regiments contained 425 members who were regarded as 'suspicious'.

Xi Zhongxun quickly recognised the severity of the problem. He took the opportunity to make speeches and hold informal discussions to remind everyone to tell the truth and to be loyal and frank with the party. He stressed that the crime of making irresponsible remarks was more serious than spying. He portrayed the true picture to the CPC northwest central office and the CPC central committee, conveyed his anxieties and advocated the prohibition of "obtaining confessions by compulsion and giving them credence" and rectifying 'leftist' deviation. He took something of a risk in repeating this message time and again. "We often talk about the party spirit," he said. "In my opinion, seeking truth from facts is the most important party spirit."[2]

When the central authorities decided to implement screening and rectifications, Xi Zhongxun invited representatives of the teachers and students, including Yao Xuerong and Bai Shuji, to hold discussions at the prefectural party committee. A 3,000-member conference was organised involving the participation of student parents, cadres and working people so as to publicise the CPC's anti-espionage policies of 'neither doing wrong to a good man nor letting go of a bad man'. He also gave instructions to invite parents to spend several days with their children on campus so that they could witness their daily lives and restore their faith in the party's policies.

The screening and rectifications policy protected a host of intellectual cadres who had come from outside and reviewed and redressed the unjust treatment of wronged comrades. Xi Zhongxun apologised to those who had been wronged, assumed responsibility on behalf of the prefectural party committee and solved a variety of problems that had resulted from the misguided campaign.

The most urgent task that faced Xi on taking office was how to stimulate production and achieve economic growth. In mid-April 1943, he led a group to stay with the villagers of Haojiaqiao, 10km west of Suide. After living there for one month, the group cited Liu Yuhou as a labour hero. Liu had encouraged the villagers to carry out intensive cultivation and to exchange labour for mutual benefit, which markedly boosted grain output and living standards. Suide prefectural party committee awarded him the titles 'model party member' and 'labour hero', encouraging each village

The 'model village' tablet awarded to Haojiaqiao, dated July 1944 and signed off by Xi Zhongxun, Bai Zhimin, Yuan Renyuan and Yang Heting

A report in *Liberation Daily* on 21 November 1943 on the production exposition in Suide

to learn from the example of Haojiaqiao and Liu Yuhou. They also gave Haojiaqiao a 'model village' tablet, signed by leaders such as Xi Zhongxun and commissioner Yuan Renyuan. *Liberation Daily* gave special coverage to the exemplary deeds of Liu Yuhou on 18 May 1943.

The great production campaign spread like wildfire in Suide. In that year, there was a bumper grain harvest and a number of model labourers were identified. Xi Zhongxun also worked out a plan to boost productivity in his own daily life: collaborate with the servants to plant cotton and Chinese cabbages; twist yarn for one hour each day; cut down the use of office supplies by two-thirds; avoid replenishment of clothes and bedding within one year; sleep on a cold bed, burning the stove rather than the kang (a heatable brick bed commonly found in north China) and turn off the heating in the 15 days before winter; take exercise and try hard to save medical expenses for the state.

Vice commissioner Yang Heting was highly appreciative of Xi Zhongxun's efforts. "The central government stipulated that we should till the land for three years in order to store enough grain to last one

The cave in Haojiaqiao where Xi Zhongxun once lived

Liu Yuhou and Xi Zhongxun talking cordially in Xi's house in Beijing on 11 February 1984

year. Nonetheless, Xi Zhongxun was so competent that we succeeded in reserving that amount in only one year."[3]

Given the acute shortcomings in the provision of cultural education, Xi Zhongxun led an educational reform programme in Suide. He advocated that the cultural education undertaking should serve all 520,000 people in the region's six counties and be integrated with every sector of society, oriented around the workplace, government and the family. Mao Zedong praised this course of action: there were many problems surrounding education, and how to resolve them in Suide with integrated measures. The way it was handled was not bad. It is a question of orientation.

By the autumn of 1944, 260 primary schools that were educating more than 11,400 students, along with 22 part-time schools for adults, had been built in Suide. Night schools and training classes were also set up. Various forms of educational and cultural activity were flourishing, including reading, 'blackboard newspapers', caricatures, yangko song and dance troupes (rural folk dancing popular in northern China), lectures, storytelling and clapper talk (a form of Chinese narrative chanting), and especially winter schools. On 11 March 1944, *Liberation Daily* published a comprehensive report entitled *National Education Reform in Suide* in order to encourage other places to follow Suide's example.

The upsurge of winter schools started in late 1943. In that year, 905 of them were established across the whole region, educating a total of 70,715 students. The following winter, Xi Zhongxun conducted special research in the Zhoujia hills of Zizhou county and wrote an article on the subject that was carried in *Liberation Daily* on 23 November 1944.

The Suide art troupe, which was built on the basis of the Suide people's opera troupe, was another beneficiary of the campaign to enhance cultural and educational life. Xi Zhongxun gave special instructions to improve the troupe's food and supply them with special shoes and socks for their performances in the countryside.

In a speech at the Suide judicial work conference in the autumn of 1944, Xi asked party members and cadres of all ranks to hold their ground and remember the party's tenets. He also stressed the requirement for them to "stand firmly on the side of ordinary people".

Suide was also a pilot zone for the construction of the 'triangular organisation' anti-Japanese democratic regime. As secretary of Suide prefectural party committee, Xi Zhongxun established contact with public figures from outside the party, listened to their opinions and invited them to offer advice and suggestions. He made friends and gained the confidence of many of them, including An Wenqin (Suide county), deputy chairman of the provincial assembly of the Shaanxi-Gansu-Ningxia border region, Li Dingming (Mizhi county), vice president of the border region government, Liu Jiesan and Liu Shaoting (both from Suide) and Ji Boxiong (from Mizhi), all assembly members of the border region.

In June 1943, Xi Zhongxun hosted a grand ceremony in Suide to welcome General Deng Baoshan, deputy commander of the 12th theatre of operations of the KMT army and commander-in-chief of Shanxi-Suide border region, who was on his way to attend a conference in Chongqing by way of Suide. They held amicable and intensive talks and forged a deep friendship that lasted decades.

Suide was something of a transport hub. In that period, many comrades inside the party would go to Yan'an from various anti-Japanese revolutionary bases by way of Suide. Whatever their rank, they received an enthusiastic reception in Suide. "All the comrades who passed by Suide praised Comrade Xi Zhongxun as the good secretary of Suide prefectural party committee,"[4] said Ren Bishi.

Chapter 13

Revolutionary 'Correspondence'

The simple and solemn wedding ceremony of Xi Zhongxun and Qi Xin took place on 28 April 1944 in Jiuzhen temple, the location of Suide prefectural party committee.

Qi Xin was born into a literary family in Gaoyang county, Hebei province, on 11 November 1923. Her father Qi Houzhi graduated from Peking University and went on to assume the post of county magistrate in Fuping county, Hebei province, and in Licheng city in Shanxi province. After the Lugouqiao (Marco Polo Bridge) incident[1] broke out on 7 July 1937, Qi Xin left Peiping (Beijing), led by her elder sister. She hurled herself into the revolutionary cause, joining up with the Taihangshan anti-Japanese revolutionary base in north China in March 1939. She became a CPC candidate member on 14 August 1939. According to the provisions of the party organisation, no one under 18 could be admitted to the CPC. This meant that the 16-year-old Qi Xin would normally have had to wait two years before she could become a regular party member. However, thanks to her outstanding performance in the intense struggles against the enemies' 'mopping-up operations', she became a full CPC member in less than one year. As a cadre college student, Qi Xin transferred from the middle school affiliated to Yan'an University to Suide Normal University; while studying, she also worked as a member of the university's general party branch.

Qi Xin was one month late arriving in Suide, but she soon noticed the name of Xi Zhongxun from a poster on the wall that read: "Welcome Comrade Xi Zhongxun to direct the work of Suide Prefectural Party Committee!" As she recalled: "Comrade Zhongxun personally came to deliver the university mobilisation report. It was only then that I was able to put a face to the name. It was in summer, with the sun shining brightly overhead, that we met each other for the first time. When I stepped out of the classroom, I suddenly saw Comrade Zhongxun walking down the slope of the garden of our head teacher, Yang Bin [a member of the general party branch of Suide Normal University]. I hurried to give him a military salute and he simply nodded and passed by, smiling."

Qi Xin and Xi Zhongxun in Yan'an in early 1947

They met at a time when the 'salvation of the delinquents' campaign was triggering panic in Suide Normal University. At the height of the campaign, more than 400 out of the 500-plus university students were subjected to 'salvation', which caused Xi Zhongxun to have serious misgivings and anxiety. He asked student representatives, including Qi Xin, to talk with him in the Suide prefectural party committee, and invited the parents of students to come to the university. Xi promptly suggested that the CPC central committee curb the practice of 'obtaining confessions by compulsion and giving them credence', rectified 'leftist' deviation, and apologised to those who had been wronged. Xi, himself, shouldered responsibility and reminded everyone of the principles of the party and the need to seek truth from facts. These actions left a profound impression on Qi Xin that summer.

The cave in Haojiaqiao where Qi Xin once lived

At around that time, Qi Xin saw Mao Zedong's inscription "Putting the party's interests first" hanging on the wall of Xi Zhongxun's office. "That inscription was written on a piece of bleached cloth using a writing brush," she recalled. With Li Huasheng, director of the publicity department of Suide prefectural party committee and Song Yangchu, secretary of the general party branch of Suide Normal University acting as go-betweens, Xi and Qi became better acquainted.

Xi Zhongxun asked Qi Xin to write an autobiography and to give it to him. "My elder sister Qi Yun said I was 'as innocent as an angel'," said Qi Xin, "so my autobiography was very easy." Qi Xin mentioned in her autobiography that she had twice escaped from home with the intention of joining the revolutionary cause, only to be caught and brought back by her father. Xi Zhongxun chuckled when he read this passage. "I had the same experience as you when I was young," he said. When He Changgong, vice president and director of education of the Anti-Japanese Military and Political University, wrote to Xi Zhongxun about Qi Xin's situation, he made special mention that "she did grow up in Yan'an".

The love that grew between Xi Zhongxun and Qi Xin was kindled through their correspondence. In one letter, Qi Xin discovered that Xi Zhongxun was the youngest leader to have set up the Shaanxi-Gansu border region revolutionary base. In another, Xi wrote: "Something important has come up and I am going to manage it well." Qi Xin responded that she "knew that he was considering the subject of our marriage".

The simple yet solemn wedding ceremony was held in a cave in Jiuzhen temple. He Changgong, Li Jingquan, political commissar of the Anti-Japanese Military and Political University headquarters, Wang Shangrong, commander of Suide garrison headquarters and commander of the First Brigade, Yang Qiliang, director of the political department, Yuan Renyuan, commissioner of the branch, Yang Heting, deputy commissioner and Bai Zhimin, deputy secretary of the prefectural party committee were all in attendance. The guests and newly-weds sat down to a simple dinner but,

Qi Xin returns to Haojiaqiao in the summer of 2000 to visit fellow villagers, accompanied by Li Zhanshu (fourth from left), then a member of the standing committee of CPC Shaanxi provincial committee

even so, this ranked among the grandest wedding ceremonies of those years. To mark the occasion, the so-called 'Red Sherlock Holmes', Bu Lu, director of Suide's security department, took photos of the happy couple.

Shortly after their marriage, Xi Zhongxun told his wife: "From now on, we should share our joys and sadnesses. But we cannot live in our own little world." In the summer of 1944, Qi Xin ended her study at Suide Normal University and worked as the correspondence officer in the 'first village' of Shatanping district (stationed in Haojiaqiao) and then as deputy secretary of Yihe district party committee. After that, and apart from a short period of time spent learning at the sixth branch of the party school, she was engaged in grassroots work in rural areas.

At a time when they were spending more time apart than together, each letter was especially valuable. In his letters, Xi Zhongxun expressed his greatest hope for Qi Xin was for her to keep close ties with the common people and strive to do her work well. He repeatedly likened the countryside to a large school, a source of inexhaustible knowledge. With his personal experience of performing mass work by going from one house to another when he set up the Shaanxi-Gansu border region revolutionary base, he encouraged his wife to value investigation and research. He told Qi Xin that, as long as she could properly handle village work, she could also deal with the demands of a district.

Wu Zhongxiu, a good friend of Qi Xin, occasionally saw these letters and was astonished at their content. "Where is the correspondence between husband and wife?" he asked. "These are more like the letters between two revolutionaries!" Even so, these letters helped to nurture their love and allowed it to blossom. In the words of Qi Xin, their marriage took root in "a sound political and emotional foundation".[2] It was for this reason that the revolutionary partners were able to repeatedly withstand the ordeals that followed and live together, without complaint or regret, for more than 50 years.

Xi Zhongxun came up with a celebrated dictum: "Fighting for a lifetime, happy for a lifetime, struggling every day and happy every day." After Xi passed away, Qi Xin signed the dictum and engraved it on the back of her husband's statue in Fuping cemetery.

What better way to depict the romance and lofty sentiments of these revolutionary lovers?

Chapter 14

Yetai Mountain Counterattacks

Having achieved victory in the war of resistance against Japan, the seventh NPC was convened in Yan'an. At the second congress of party representatives of the Shaanxi-Gansu-Ningxia border region in November 1939, Xi Zhongxun was elected as a representative of the seventh NPC. Between 23 April and 11 June 1945, Xi attended the congress and became the youngest person to be elected as an alternate member of the central government.

Xi Zhongxun during the war of resistance against Japan

During the CPC national congress, Mao Zedong memorably said: "We should go all out to strive for a bright future and a bright destiny and oppose the alternatives of a dark future and a dark destiny".[1] He also submitted a written political report entitled *On the Coalition Government*. At a panel discussion of the northwest bureau of the CPC central committee in Huashibian, Xi Zhongxun and other representatives agreed unanimously that Mao had not only stated the guiding principles and policies of the 'new democracy', but also established the future direction of revolution in China.

Xi Zhongxun also attended a symposium on the history of the party in northwest China, held between 26

June and 2 August 1945 under the direction of Zhu De, Ren Bishi and Chen Yun. During the symposium, on 11 July, Xi made a detailed summary of the history, experiences and lessons of the party's struggles in northwest China. He stated that truth counted for the most in history; it didn't matter whether history was fully understood or even if it was known at all; the greatest harm lay in the distortion and fabrication of history.

During the symposium, Xi received an emergency instruction that Mao Zedong had personally appointed him political commissar of the provisional Yetai mountain counterattack headquarters.

Yetai mountain is situated in the east of Chunyao county (now in Chunhua county), dominating the southern section of the Shaanxi-Gansu-Ningxia border region. Yetai was regarded as an altar. The Guanzhong people usually addressed God and Buddha respectfully as 'ye' (meaning God, heaven) and Yetai mountain was a place where the celestial being or the Buddha lived. It is one of a range of mountains in a region that is characterised by its varied topography. In July 1945, Hu Zongnan deployed his forces comprising nine divisions, splitting them to make a four-pronged

Yetai mountain

Zhang Zongxun   **Xi Zhongxun**

attack over a vast area of 500 sq km around Yetai mountain spanning 50km east to west and 10km north to south, and to build fortifications on the mountain itself.

The CPC central committee decided to stand firm against the invading enemy. In the Wangjiaping area of Yan'an, Mao Zedong, Zhu De and Ye Jianying gave personal orders to Zhang Zongxun[2] and Xi Zhongxun to immediately set up a makeshift base in Yetai mountain to launch counterattacks. Zhang was appointed commander, and Xi was made political commissar, with Wang Shitai, Wang Jinshan and Huang Xinting acting as deputy commanders, Tan Zheng as deputy political commissar, Gan Siqi as director of the political department and Zhang Jingwu as chief of staff. That was an 'impressive' array of elite warriors. In a commissioning ceremony in 1955, which was the first of its kind after the new China was founded, eight commanders were conferred military ranks, including Xi Zhongxun and Wang Shitai who did not attend the ceremony, one senior general (Tan Zheng), two generals (Zhang Zongxun and Gan Siqi) and three lieutenant generals (Wang Jinshan, Huang Xinting and Zhang Jingwu).

The temporary counterattack headquarters on Yetai mountain were located in Malan, and comprised the forces of eight regiments, including the newly organised Fourth Brigade, the First Pathfinder Brigade, the Second Pathfinder Brigade and the 358th Brigade. Since the enemy had not managed to establish a secure foothold in the area, the CPC forces decided to exploit this weakness by deploying their superior numbers. The Fourth Brigade was in charge of launching the main attacks, supported by the third regiment of the First Brigade. The 358th Brigade was stationed in Phoenix mountain and Zhaojin, tasked with violently repelling any counter-offensives by the enemy; the first and second brigades in Yulingwan and Shangzhenzi provided the rear guard.

Xi Zhongxun had pointed out before the war that enemy loyalists often stirred up friction by conducting 'field military exercises' or 'arresting deserters' and that they invaded and occupied 41 villages around Yetai mountain with the aim of wresting control of the Guandong branch region and provoking new civil wars. To combat this threat, Xi said that CPC troops must adhere to the principles of fighting "with good reason, to their advantage and with restraint", neither letting any enemy escape nor allowing them to breach their defences.

Xi Zhongxun and the comrades in charge of the Guanzhong prefectural party committee issued a document designed to support the army and the frontline through consultation. The committee's document, entitled *Urgent Instructions on Safeguarding Guanzhong and Preventing Civil War*, put forward the slogan "To give the army whatever it needs in the necessary quantities". The troops were fully equipped and the local population supported the front with "extraordinary enthusiasm". In Chishui county, for example, 1,400 or more members joined to support the front and locals supplied the troops with more than 400 stretchers, more than five tonnes of army provisions and more than 10,000 pairs of military footwear.

On 7 August 1955, the makeshift headquarters moved to Tulu village to the east of Taoqu plateau at the foot of Phoenix mountain, which was less than 10km from the highest peak of Yetai mountain. Later it was stationed on the Taoqu plateau.

The general offensive was timed to start at 11pm the following night, and went ahead as planned despite torrential rain. CPC combat forces launched a violent attack, while enemy troops mounted a desperate defence. In

The monument to the Yetai mountain counterattacks

order to quell the enemy and bring the fighting to a swift conclusion, the makeshift headquarters ordered the 358th Brigade to attack before dawn on 9 August. At 10am that day, the sixth company of the second battalion of the eighth regiment of the 358th Brigade stormed the trenches outside the enemy's fortifications and attacked at close quarters, using hand grenades and bayonets. The repeated charges created an extraordinarily intense scene. By 2pm, the CPC troops had managed to annihilate the enemy on the main peak. On 10 August, combat operations were concluded and the CPC troops retook the lost ground around Yetai mountain and defeated five companies and one battalion of the KMT army. Having made its way to the peak, the victorious sixth company of the Second Battalion became known as the 'hard-boned sixth company' after the battle.

Troops under the command of Zhang Zongxun and Xi Zhongxun needed just three days to rout the invading enemies and regain all the lost ground. In his article *The Current Political Situation and Our Guideline after the Victory of the War of Resistance Against Japan*, Mao Zedong stressed the significance of the battle. "A while back, the KMT designated the forces of six divisions to assault the Guanzhong branch region," he wrote. "Three of them succeeded and occupied an area of 500 sq km. We followed their methods and exterminated the KMT troops in that area." The victory in Yetai mountain boosted the confidence of the border region soldiers and civilians as they strived to secure the fruits of victory. For Xi Zhongxun, it was the prelude to a frenetic military campaign that took him across the vast northwestern battlefield.

On 12 August 1955, a US army investigation team carried out a so-called 'field survey' in its capacity as 'mediator'. However, the scattered cartridge cases, English writing on the ammunition boxes and captured American weapons exposed the survey team's bias towards the KMT side.

Soon after the clouds of smoke had dissipated from the battlefield, Xi Zhongxun received another promotion, having been appointed vice director of the organisation department of the central government.

Chapter 15

Nine Letters from Mao Zedong

In October 1945, Gao Gang was transferred to a post in northeast China. As proposed by Mao Zedong, Xi Zhongxun took charge of the work of the CPC northwest central office. When he introduced Xi to other party members, Mao said: "A young comrade should be selected as secretary of the CPC northwest central office. Xi Zhongxun is the best choice. He is a leader of the common people."

Xi Zhongxun merited the title "a leader of the common people",

Deputy Secretary Ma Mingfang and Secretary Xi Zhongxun talking cordially

according to the American scholar Sidney Rittenberg, who rushed over to Yan'an from Suide together with Xi. "Wherever he went, he seemed to know the people there," Rittenberg recalled. "He asked a man on his way: 'Has your wife got over her illness?' Then he asked another: 'Has your father recovered from his backache?'"[1]

Until that time, Mao Zedong had considered several different positions for Xi Zhongxun. The first was to lead the troops going to the south of China together with Wang Zhen;[2] the second was to work in northeast China with Gao Gang; and the third was to administer the affairs in east China with Chen Yi. At last, Mao Zedong told Xi Zhongxun: "On second thoughts, you'd better work in northern Shaanxi. Top priority should be placed on building up and consolidating the Shaanxi-Gansu-Ningxia border region. It is of the utmost urgency."

At 32 years old, Xi was the youngest secretary of all the major sub-offices. In September 1945, he was also deputy political commissar of the Shaanxi-Gansu-Ningxia-Shanxi-Suide joint defence militia, tasked with

Ma Mingfang, Wang Weizhou, Ulan-Fu and Xi Zhongxun in Yan'an

Nine Letters from Mao Zedong

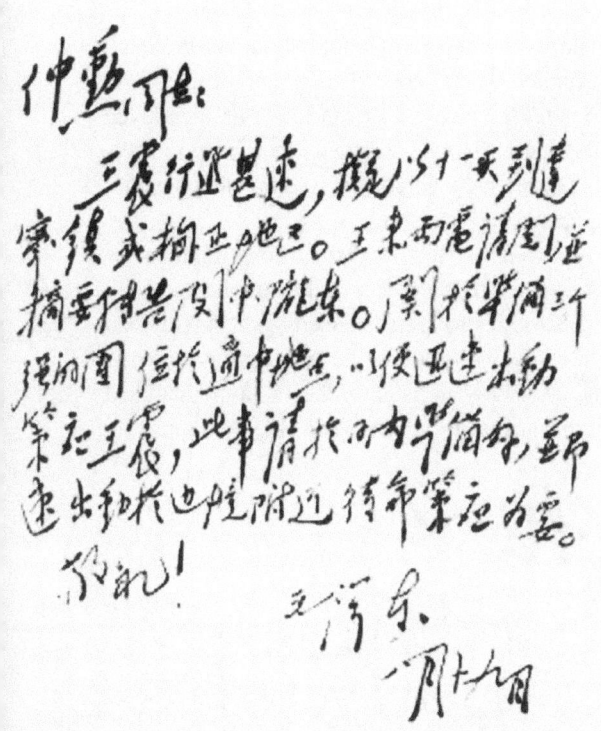

The letter Mao Zedong wrote to Xi Zhongxun on 19 August 1946

safeguarding the CPC central committee and the Shaanxi-Gansu-Ningxia border region.

In the early summer of 1946, less than a year after the signing of the Double Tenth Agreement, the KMT army broke the terms of the treaty by launching a large-scale attack on the Zhongyuan liberated area with a massive force of 300,000.

Mao Zedong monitored developments and made an appointment with Xi Zhongxun in Wangjiaping to ask his opinion about vital issues with regard to helping Wang Zhen's troops which had broken out of an encirclement in the central plains to return to the border region and repel the attacks of Hu Zongnan's troops against the border region. Mao wrote nine personal letters to Xi Zhongxun in less than two months.

On 26 July 1946, Mao wrote to Xi: "Please consider designating one or two high-ranking officials to assist the troops under Li and Wang, such as Wang Feng or others who are suitable."

One month earlier, Xi had dispatched Liu Geng, director of the mass movement section of the united front work department of the CPC northwest central office, to meet the troops that Mao Zedong mentioned in southern Shaanxi. On 10 August 1946, he assigned Wang Feng to leave Malan county and proceed to Shangluo where he arrived on 18 September to handle matters in Hubei, Henan and Shaanxi.

Mao wrote two letters to Xi on 10 August 1946. In one of them, he suggested: "Please consider dispatching several guerrilla detachments with construction and logistics capabilities to act in concert with Li Xiannian and Wang Zhen in establishing the guerrilla base for future development." In the second letter, he wrote: "The 84th division of the 17th army marched to Foping county in southern Shaanxi to attack Wang Zhen's troops. Do

The letter Mao Zedong wrote to Xi Zhongxun on 23 August 1946

we have comrades or sympathisers in the 84th division? How about the situation now? Please find out and report back."

The next day, Xi Zhongxun cabled Li Hebang, secretary of the Longdong prefectural party committee, Sun Zuobin, secretary of the Gansu working committee, Huang Luobin, commander of the Third Police Brigade and Guo Bingkun, political commissar of the Third Police Brigade. He instructed them to dispatch armed forces of 150-160 men to Longnan to set up a guerrilla zone there and to assign several military work teams to Haiyuan, Guyuan, Jingning and Zhuanglang. No one was allowed to divulge this confidential information. Meanwhile, he transferred more than 300 servicemen from two reinforced companies of the First Police Brigade to form the Xifu guerrillas. They were detailed to march to the

The letter Mao Zedong wrote to Xi Zhongxun on 29 August 1946

Linyou mountain region under the leadership of Zhao Bojing to keep Hu Zongnan's troops at bay and reduce the pressure on the 359th Brigade.

On 19 August 1946, Mao Zedong wrote to Xi Zhongxun and commanded him to "prepare three powerful regiments", and to "immediately dispatch troops to the frontier and stand by to provide active support".

At 10pm that evening, Xi Zhongxun, Wang Shitai, deputy commander of the joint defence troops, and other leaders cabled orders that the New Fourth Brigade and the seventh regiment of the Third Police Brigade should prepare for fighting in two days, equipped with light backpacks, and to stand by for action.

Twenty-four hours later, Xi Zhongxun and Wang Shitai issued an order to launch attacks from the southern front, with the New Fourth Brigade on the left flank responsible for breaking through from an area between Changwu and Binxian counties; the seventh regiment of the Third Police Brigade were on the right flank, tasked with breaking through from an area between Pingliang and Jingchuan counties; the First Police Brigade were in charge of a small group of guerrillas, and their role was to hide by day and launch attacks on the enemy at night in Chunhua and Xunyi counties.

On 22 August, Xi Zhongxun ordered Zhang Zhongliang and Li Hebang to take immediate action. That night, a sleepless Mao Zedong wrote to Xi Zhongxun to enquire about the military strength and deployment of the enemy in the counties of Changwu, Binxian, Pingliang, Longde, Jingning, Zhengning, Ningxian, Xifeng, Zhenyuan and Guyuan.

On 23 August, the attacks on the southern flank broke through and the 359th Brigade travelled a circuitous route, via Longxian county and then northwards. Xi Zhongxun reported the attacks on the southern front and the deployment of the enemy to Mao Zedong. Mao replied later that same day. "I learnt from your letter that the deployment was effective and I've relayed that information to Wang Zhen," he wrote.

On 24 August, Xi Zhongxun and Wang Shitai cabled an order to the troops, pointing out that the main objective of the attack was to protect Wang Zhen's forces on their journey to the border region and to make utmost efforts to attack and annihilate the pursuing enemy. Having helped Wang Zhen's troops reach safety, the troops were then tasked to gradually wind down their offensives and withdraw to the border region.

Nine Letters from Mao Zedong

Wang Zhen heads the 359th Brigade on its return to northern Shaanxi in September 1946

On 29 August, the 359th Brigade crossed the Xilan highway in Changwu and Jingchuan counties, crossed the Jinghe river and triumphantly met up with the Third Police Brigade in the town of Tunzi, Zhenyuan county. On hearing the news later that day, Mao Zedong couldn't conceal his happiness. "The main forces of Wang Zhen's troops have arrived at the edge of the Shaanxi-Gansu-Ningxia border region," he wrote to Xi Zhongxun. "They are going to stay in Longdong for rest and recuperation. Please tell the Longdong party, administrative and military officers to welcome them and provide them with help."

On 1 September, Mao again wrote to Xi: "Hu Zongnan seemingly intends to attack Longdong. Please make plans and preparations to cope with the attack and report to me."

On the following day, and having received Xi Zhongxun's assessment of the opposing forces and the battle plans, Mao Zedong wrote to Xi Zhongxun once more. "I have received your letter. Please take actions according to the guidelines you've made. During the fighting, pay attention to deploying our superior forces to annihilate the first troop of the enemy and pool together six or seven regiments to defeat a regiment of the enemy, as you stated in your letter."

Xi Zhongxun had strong recollections of the nine letters he received from Mao Zedong during this period. "Chairman Mao asked me about the route, where to cross the Weihe river, and instructed me to dispatch troops to come to [Wang Zhen's] aid. During this period, Chairman Mao was in regular correspondence with me, sometimes sending a letter every other day. In a little more than one month, he wrote me nine letters in total."[3]

Chapter 16

Instigating the Hengshan Uprising

After victory in the war of resistance against Japan, the KMT army quickly adjusted its military deployment and reinforced the troops stationed in a line from Hengshan county to Yulin county in an attempt to mount an attack on the Shaanxi-Gansu-Ningxia border region from both the north and south. Xi Zhongxun responded by leading the Hengshan uprising, disrupting the strategic deployment of the KMT army, liberating a vast area to the south of the Wuding river and vigorously maintaining the safety of the northern border region.

Xi Zhongxun in Yan'an

In June 1946, Mao Zedong made an appointment with Xi Zhongxun and listened to his report on the work of the CPC northwest central office and the border region. Xi's proposal to instigate the uprising of Hu Jingduo's[1] troops stationed in Boluo fort in Hengshan caught the attention of Mao Zedong, who at once pointed out the importance of liberating Yulin and Hengshan and expanding their room for manoeuvre.

The expansive land at the foot of the Great Wall and along the Wuding river has always been a hotly contested area in Chinese history. As one of the 36 Great Wall forts built in the Ming dynasty (1368-1644), the military fortress of Boluo has guarded a vital communication line on the southern and northern banks of the Wuding since ancient times.

Hu Jingduo was a younger brother of Hu Jingyi. Xi Zhongxun, Hu Jingduo and Hu Xizhong, who was the son of Hu Jingyi, were classmates in Licheng middle school. They formed an unbreakable bond at the school and maintained a secret united front relationship.

As early as the spring of 1946, Xi Zhongxun appointed Shi Yuan, who was also a compatriot

Hu Jingduo

and classmate of Hu Jingduo, as deputy director of the united front work department of Suide prefectural party committee. Xi ordered Shi to go to Boluo fort to contact Hu Jingduo and despatched 30 or more crack fighters to join Hu's troops, which laid a solid foundation for the uprising. On his second trip to Boluo, Shi Yuan declared to Hu Jingduo that, thanks to Xi Zhongxun's introduction, his membership of the CPC was approved by the CPC central committee with effect from 1 July 1946. In the meantime, the CPC northwest central office approved Zhang Yaxiong and Xu Xiuqi, two of Hu Jingduo's troops, to become CPC members. So far, the uprising was going through its implementation phase.

In August 1946, Xi Zhongxun and Wang Shitai analysed their battle tactics for the campaign on the northern front. They appointed Wang Shitai as director general and Zhang Zhongliang as political commissar of the northern front operational command, which was meant to assist in

The historic site of Boluo fort

the uprising. In late August 1946, Mao Zedong met with Xi Zhongxun and Wang Shitai and stressed the tactical imperative of concentrating their superior forces in order to annihilate the enemy. On 28 August, Xi Zhongxun published an article *Raise vigilance and safeguard the border region* in *Liberation Daily*.

In mid September 1946, Xi Zhongxun designated Fan Ming, head of the united front work department of the CPC northwest central office, to go to Boluo fort with his signed letter on white silk to consult with Hu Jingduo about the planned uprising. Before his departure, Xi held three separate discussions with Fan Ming on how to implement the uprising. After his arrival in Boluo, Fan consulted with Hu Jingduo about the uprising plan. "I told him openly who I was and that it was Xi Zhongxun who had sent me and told me to pass on the instructions for revolt," recalled Fan. "That's it. They knew about our relationship and that I would not betray them. They invited me to come in right away."[2]

Fan Ming returned to Yan'an and reported to Xi Zhongxun the preparations for the uprising. Xi, together with Wang Shitai and Fan Ming, left directly for Zaoyuan to report the news to Mao Zedong.

Monument to the Hengshan uprising

As dawn broke on 13 October 1946, the northern battle began. A bright-coloured red flag rose slowly on top of the city wall of Boluo fort. Hu Jingduo, in charge of more than 2,100 officers and men from five military units of the Ninth Security Regiment initiated the uprising. On the same day, more than 1,400 men from the same regiment stationed in Shiwan and Gaozhen town joined the uprising. Hu Jingduo wrote to the Independent Cavalry Regiment of the 22nd KMT army stationed in Hengshan county urging it to revolt, and on 16 October, up to 2,000 soldiers did so. On 24 October, the border region troops captured Xiangshui village, bringing the northern battle to an end. The Hengshan uprising represented a milestone on the revolutionary path for the 5,000 officers and men involved, liberated a vast area of more than 5,000 sq km to the south of the Wuding river, and marked a turning point in the future fighting in northern Shaanxi.

At the same time, KMT troops under Hu Zongnan had also been gathering and attempted to attack the border region. Mao Zedong wrote to Xi Zhongxun on 6 November 1946, informing him that "the First Army and the 90th Army of Hu Zongnan's troops have begun to cross the river from Yumenkou and advance westwards in an attempt to attack Yan'an directly". At the border region government cadre mobilisation conference on 13 October 1946, Xi Zhongxun mobilised all military personnel and civilians to safeguard Yan'an, the border region and Chairman Mao. On 21 October, Xi Zhongxun and Wang Shitai issued a jointly-signed order *On Resisting the Attack on Yan'an*.

Xi Zhongxun gives a speech at the safeguarding Yan'an mobilisation conference

On 16 December 1946, Xi Zhongxun and Peng Dehuai, who was vice president and chief of staff of the Central Military Commission, attended a senior cadre conference of the Shaanxi-Gansu-Ningxia border region, Shanxi-Suide military region and Taiyuan in the village of Gaojiagou, Lishi county, Shanxi province. They researched issues concerning the deployment of a united front and collaborative fighting in the two liberated regions on both banks of the Yellow river and took sufficient funds to pay for the replenishment of military supplies for troops on the east bank. Hu Zongnan's plot to attack Yan'an in a lightning strike failed to materialise.

On 24 October 1946, Xi Zhongxun accompanied leading cadres of the central committee, such as Liu Shaoqi, Zhou Enlai, Zhu De and Ren Bishi, to interview officers and men who had participated in the uprising, including Hu Jingduo, in the auditorium of Zaoyuan, about 8km northwest of Yan'an. That evening, Mao Zedong attended a reception banquet. He commented: "Comrade Jingduo, you made the right choice to step out of

Deng Baoshan's boat into Xi Zhongxun's under the circumstances where the enemy was stronger than you."

Xi Zhongxun in northern Shaanxi in 1946

Chapter 17

All Border Region Forces 'Under the Unified Command of Peng Dehuai and Xi Zhongxun'

On 3 March 1947, Commander Zhang Zongxun and Political Commissar Xi Zhongxun of the Shaanxi-Gansu-Ningxia Field Army ordered their troops to annihilate more than 1,500 soldiers of the 48th Brigade in Xihuachi, Heshui county, and shot and killed brigade commander He Qi. This came to be known as 'the first battle of Xihuachi'.

At that time, Hu Zongnan had mustered 34 brigades, comprising some 250,000 men, and launched attacks from six directions against important targets in Yan'an in an attempt to destroy the base.

Mao Zedong and the central military commission (CMC) realised the seriousness of these attacks. After careful consideration, they decided to dispatch Peng Dehuai and Xi Zhongxun to carry out the formidable and glorious task jointly. Peng, as vice president of the CMC, had abundant experience of directing large military formations in combat. Xi, as one of the founders and leaders

Xi Zhongxun during the liberation war
(August 1945-June 1950)

of the Shaanxi-Gansu revolutionary base and the northwest Red Army, was familiar with the geography and conditions of the people in that part of China. He also enjoyed the respect and support of the officers and men of the border region and was well acquainted with the ideological and political work in the army. The collaboration between Peng and Xi facilitated the mobilisation of all forces in the border region to fight against the enemy and repel their attacks, and engulfed the invading enemy forces in an ocean of people's warfare.

On 13 March 1947, the first shots rang out in the battle for the defence of Yan'an.

The next day, the CMC cabled Xi Zhongxun, ordering him to "immediately return to Yan'an to oversee work in the border region together with Peng Dehuai".

On 16 March, Xi Zhongxun travelled back from the southern front at breakneck pace for two days and two nights to return to Wangjiaping where the CMC office and Mao Zedong were based. On seeing Xi Zhongxun,

Peng Dehuai and Xi Zhongxun study troop deployments in the spring of 1947

All Border Region Forces 'Under the Unified Command of Peng and Xi'

Xu Liqing, Peng Dehuai, Xi Zhongxun and Zhang Wenzhou look over Qinghuabian[1]

Peng Dehuai handed him a CMC presidential decree drafted by Mao. The decree ordered him to make battle ready the militia on the right flank (led by Zhang Zongxun and Liao Hansheng), the militia on the left flank (led by Wang Zhen and Luo Yuanfa) and the Central Committee militia (led by Zhang Xianyue and Xu Liqing). "From 17 March 1947, all the above militias and troops should operate under the unified command of Peng Dehuai and Xi Zhongxun," the decree went on to state.[2] That was the last order of Mao Zedong and the CMC before they left Yan'an. It was at this time that the term Northwest Field Corps began to be used, although it was not yet officially known as such.

Three days after the evacuation from Yan'an, on 21 March, Peng Dehuai and Xi Zhongxun jointly sent a telegram to the CMC. "The movements of the enemy are uncertain after they occupied Yan'an," it read. "All our forces will strive to conceal themselves and stay hidden for seven days of rest and recuperation from 22 March 1947. Instructions for the deployment of the border forces will be issued to all the regions with the approval of the central government." This was the first cable jointly signed by Peng

The historic Yangma river battlefield site

Dehuai and Xi Zhongxun. Hu Zongnan, seeing that "the CPC army could not withstand even a single blow", became increasingly overconfident. He ordered 10 brigades to be stationed to the south of Yan'an and dispatched 10 brigades to confront the main forces of the Northwest Field Corps for a final battle.

On 23 March, the Northwest Field Corps deployed 'pocket' tactics in Qinghuabian, whereby enemy forces were isolated into small pockets before being attacked by superior numbers. At 10am on 25 March, the enemy's 31st Brigade completed their occupation of the 'pocket'. Before engaging in combat, the brigade was holed up in a ravine measuring 7km long and 200-300 metres wide in a state of some confusion. In just one hour and 47 minutes, 2,993 enemy soldiers were killed, brigade commander major general Li Jiyun was captured, and almost 300,000 bullets were seized. Li Jiyun was shocked by this unexpected turn of events: "Is it already over? It's too fast! Too fast!"

On 10 April, the Northwest Field Corps held a meeting for cadres above brigade rank in Yunshan temple, Zichang county, with the emphasis on rectifying the troops' discipline. Xi Zhongxun seriously criticised the erroneous attitude and behaviour of the scouting troops, based on the false assumption that "it's better for us to appropriate property from the common people rather than for the enemy to do so" and he proposed to set up a disciplinary inspection system. He said the bond between the people and the army was fundamental to conquering the enemy. The more they were united, the more victories they would achieve.

On 14 April, the Northwest Field Corps prepared another ambush to the north of the Yangma river. At about 10am, the enemy's 135th Brigade was drawn into its trap and the Corps used its numerical advantage to eliminate the brigade with four brigades of its own. The main forces of Dong Zhao's army and Liu Kan's army consisting of Hu Zongnan's troops were only a few kilometres away, but they were closely contained by CPC troops and were unable to come to the rescue. After bitter and intense fighting that lasted six hours, the Northwest Field Corps had killed more than 4,700 enemy soldiers and captured deputy brigade commander major general Mai Zongyu. Moreover, they had succeeded in annihilating an entire

Xi Zhongxun (second from left), Liao Hansheng (third from left) and Zhang Zhongliang (fourth from left) in the spring of 1947, during a lull in the fighting

brigade and earning the reputation of being able to "snatch food from the lion's den".

In recalling the scene of combat, Xi Zhongxun said: "The main forces of the enemy on the mountain stronghold had no alternative but to watch anxiously as our troops captured their guns and comrades in arms. This battle took place less than 20 days after the success at Qinghuabian."

Xi Zhongxun asked the troops to openly discuss several specific issues when they weren't engaged in battle, including: the political work in wartime; how to let all party members know their tasks before, during and after battle; how to quickly restore the party's grassroots organisations once they had been destroyed; how to direct the activities of each cook and livestock attendant; and how to replenish the troops of the liberation army.

Chiang Kai-shek, leader of the KMT, urgently ordered the main forces of Hu Zongnan to march northwards and Deng Baoshan's troops southwards, in an attempt to defeat the Northwest Field Corps in Jiaxian county and Wupu village. After Hu Zongnan's main forces set off, the 7,000 troops defending Panlong were unable to escape, caught like rats in a hole. Panlong was a pivotal supply depot of the KMT army in northern Shaanxi.

The Northwest Field Corps launches an attack in Panlong

All Border Region Forces 'Under the Unified Command of Peng and Xi'

Soldiers and civilians read the news of victory

Peng Dehuai and Xi Zhongxun were determined to seize the opportunity to win the battle in Panlong. At dusk on 2 May 1947, they launched an attack against the heavily fortified positions.

The attack involved repeated setbacks. Peng Dehuai and Xi Zhongxun commanded the troops to apply democratic principles and held a conference of company-level and platoon-level cadres and a meeting of each squad to summarise their experiences and draw conclusions. Several good suggestions were made, for instance, digging trenches in order to get close to the barbed wire and fortifications, blasting a way through with explosives and launching feint attacks in order to draw enemy fire. These discussions became known as 'A meeting of Zhuge Liangs — a meeting to pool the collective wisdom'.

On the afternoon of 3 May, another general attack was launched. Between then and midnight on 4 May, Peng Dehuai and Xi Zhongxun's troops wiped out all the defending troops and captured Brigade Commander Major General Li Kungang, along with 40,000 military uniforms, more than 10,000 bags of flour, more than 1m bullets and a huge quantity of medicine.

A military correspondent of Xinhua news agency was moved to write the following verse: "Hu Zongnan's troops tragically served no use, / Couldn't break through the Yan'an-Yulin highway, / Lost Panlong and Suide one after the other, / Failed to score success for ever and ever, / Six thousand officers and men were taken prisoner, / The nine and a half brigades were cowards, / Calamity befell Deng Baoshan of Yulin, / Left hanging in space with nowhere to go."

On 14 May, the Northwest Field Corps held a victory celebration conference in Zhenwu cave, Ansai county. To facilitate a meeting between Qi Xin and Xi Zhongxun before the conference, the party organisation specially arranged for Qi to join the Shaanxi-Gansu-Ningxia border region goodwill mission to go to the cave. Unexpectedly, Xi Zhongxun was sharply critical of his wife when they met. "Why have you come?" he asked. "It's so arduous here! If the war were to last 10 years, I'd rather not see you for 10 years."

Qi Xin did not argue. She knew Xi Zhongxun's responsibilities, but was at least glad to have had the opportunity to meet with him during wartime.

On 20 May, Xi Zhongxun chaired a political work conference in Dugou village, the location of the political department, to discuss discipline among the masses, the liberation of army soldiers and their political work activities. He suggested that, for a certain period of time, the focus of political activities should be on working with the liberation army soldiers.

In a telegram sent that day, Mao Zedong wrote: "Peng Dehuai and Xi Zhongxun's troops [comprising just six depleted brigades] repelled the attacks of Hu Zongnan's 31 brigades and demoralised their forces in two months. In the months ahead, the troops are sure to kill many more enemy soldiers and seize more territory."[3] In stark contrast, Hu Zongnan had to confess to Chiang Kai-shek that his troops were "in an inferior position and faced an even deeper crisis than they did in the war of resistance against Japan".

On 30 May 1947, the Northwest Field Corps launched the battle of Longdong, in which, over 19 days, more than 4,300 enemy troops were killed and the counties of Huanxian, Quzi and Qingyang were recaptured, along with an extensive area to the west of Heshui county. In between the fighting, some of the officers and men were unsure about how to treat enemy captives, especially Ma Bufang's soldiers who had been captured in the battle in Heshui. Xi Zhongxun immediately held a meeting and made it clear that Ma's troops were labourers forced into fighting, and that they fought recklessly in the battle of Heshui with no regard for the consequences simply because they were deceived by the propaganda that no prisoners would be taken alive. We must treat the captives well, he argued, set them free and give them travel allowances in order to undermine Ma Bufang's propaganda.

The Northwest Field Militia marching towards Jingbian, Dingbian and Anbian

On 25 June, the Northwest Field Militia advanced from Huanxian to Jingbian, Dingbian and Anbian to attack Ma Hongkui's forces. Xi Zhongxun knew that the local river water was unfit to drink, so he commanded the troops to bring with them field rations and water rather than drink the water from the cellars of the local people. Otherwise, the locals would be deprived of drinking water themselves. In early July, the militia successively conquered Anbian and Yanchi counties and regained all the territories of Jingbian and Dingbian.

Between 21 May and 7 July 1947, the Northwest Field Militia fought in a territory measuring 370km from south to north and 180km from east to west between Longdong, Jingbian, Dingbian and Anbian. They defeated the troops of Ma Bufang and Ma Hongkui in Qinghai and Ningxia, which significantly boosted the confidence of party cadres and the masses.

The militia then moved to fight in northern Shaanxi. Xi Zhongxun and Peng Dehuai forged a closer relationship, while the Northwest Field Militia's strength grew in battle. They initiated eight battles, killing 26,000 enemy soldiers. Their own forces had swelled over this period from a little over 26,000 at the beginning to about 45,000, giving them the strength to engage in a people's war, repel the KMT's attack on Yan'an and transform the situation on the northwestern battlefield. In four months, there were 96 telegrams between Peng Dehuai and Xi Zhongxun and the CPC central committee, the CMC and Mao Zedong. Mao genially referred to the Northwest Field Militia as "the troops of Peng Dehuai and Xi Zhongxun". Peng and Xi also forged a close friendship through their shared military experience.

Chapter 18

Rectifying 'Leftism' in Land Reform with the 'Total Approval' of Mao Zedong

From 21-23 July 1947, Xi Zhongxun attended an enlarged session of the CPC central committee in Xiaohe village, Jingbian county (historically known as the Xiaohe conference).

The Xiaohe conference discussed the issue of strengthening the northwestern battlefield and came up with the objective, for the first time, of overthrowing the KMT government in five years. The conference decided

The Xiaohe conference

He Long and Xi Zhongxun

to reincorporate the Shanxi-Suide military region into the Shaanxi-Gansu-Ningxia-Shanxi-Suide joint defence army, with He Long[1] as commander and Xi Zhongxun as political commissar. The Northwest Field Corps was to be renamed the Field Army of the Northwest People's Liberation Army with Peng Dehuai as both commander and political commissar, and Xi Zhongxun as deputy political commissar. It was also agreed to set up the CPC Northwest Field Army front committee, composed of Peng Dehuai, Xi Zhongxun, Zhang Zongxun, Wang Zhen and Liu Jingfan, with Peng holding the position of secretary. It was further decided that He Long should be responsible for the unified rear work in an area to the east of the Yellow river (Shanxi and Suide) and to the west of the river (Shaanxi, Gansu and Ningxia), and that the CPC northwest central office should go back to deal with work in the rear.

With regard to the strategic offensive, Xi Zhongxun coordinated with the two noted generals, Peng Dehuai at the frontline and He Long in the rear, which was a vital decision taken by Mao Zedong and the CPC central committee in order to strengthen the northwestern battlefield.

On 18 August 1947, Xi Zhongxun, He Long and Lin Boqu led the

Rectifying 'Leftism' in Land Reform with the Total Approval of Mao Zedong

CPC northwest central office, the border region government and the Joint Defence Army office to go eastwards across the Yellow river and along Xili valley, and to temporarily set up base in the counties of Linxian and Lishi in Shanxi province. At that time, Hu Zongnan's troops were pursuing the main forces of the Northwest Field Army on the west bank of the Yellow river for a decisive engagement, which offered the Northwest Field Army a naturally advantageous position for fighting. Peng Dehuai directed the main forces to win a famous victory in Shajiadian on 20 August. "It quickly annihilated the enemy's reorganised 36th Division, which was one of the 'three main forces' on the northwestern battlefield" and "transformed the momentum of the entire war in northern Shaanxi".[2] From then on, the northwestern battlefield entered a counter-offensive stage. On 21 August, Xi Zhongxun and He Long jointly gave instructions to collaborate with the main forces of the field army in counter-offensives.

In mid October 1947, Xi Zhongxun, He Long and Lin Boqu returned to northern Shaanxi and were stationed in Yihe town, Suide county. The CPC northwest central office was located in the town's Xuejiaqu district.

The courtyard in South Geduo in Linxian county, Shanxi province, where Xi Zhongxun once lived

The cave dwelling (centre) in Xuejiaqu where Xi Zhongxun once lived

On 1 November, the CPC northwest central office convened a conference for cadres of the Shaanxi-Gansu-Ningxia border region in Yangwan Square opposite Xujiaqu village to convey the spirit of the national land conference and to carry out land reform and party rectification work. It later became known as the Yihe conference. Xi Zhongxun became very aware of certain 'leftist' emotions that were apparent during the conference. He explicitly ordered a revision of the case of An Wenqin, a democrat and deputy councillor of the border region, who was wrongfully "swept out of the door". As early as the Xiaohe conference, Xi had put forward proposals to immediately rectify the erroneous tendency to damage the interests of middle (middle-income) peasants and national industrial and commercial entrepreneurs, the practice of indiscriminate struggle and beatings, and to seize "changeling landlords" (landlords masquerading as something else).

After the Yihe conference, 'leftist' sentiment spiralled out of control. In Jiaxian county, where the problem was most serious, the belongings of all middle and poor peasants were expropriated. Some members of a revolutionary martyr's family were expelled and even the horsekeepers struggled against their squad leaders. The policy was referred to as the

Rectifying 'Leftism' in Land Reform with the Total Approval of Mao Zedong

emancipation of the poor peasants and farm labourers. "It was really cruel," recalled Zhang Guang, a former war correspondent at *Liberation Daily*. "Nobody dared to intervene because anyone who did so would be driven out right away. At that time, only Xi Zhongxun was bold enough to report it to Chairman Mao. I was profoundly impressed by his spirit of seeking truth from facts."[3]

From 25-28 December, Xi Zhongxun attended an enlarged session of the CPC central committee held in Yangjiagou village, Mizhi county, subsequently known as the December conference or the Yangjiagou conference.

At the preliminary meeting, Mao Zedong instructed Xi to deliver a keynote speech on land reform. Xi spoke from personal experience for no less than three hours. Mao's expression became increasingly intense. Then he grabbed a chair, sat directly facing Xi Zhongxun and listened to his speech intently. It was the first time he had heard so many facts about the land reform movement. While others regarded Xi Zhongxun's speech as being too bold, Mao stood up abruptly and exclaimed: "Good! I feel content in having you handle the affairs in northwest China."

After the conference, Xi led a working group to Suide and Jiaxian county to convey the spirit of the conference and to review land reform work there. He wrote three telegrams to report prominent issues to the CPC central committee, the CPC northwest central office and Mao Zedong himself between 4 January and 8 February 1948, specifying his objection to 'leftist' sentiments and proposing to rectify 'leftist' deviations without delay.

On 4 January 1948, Xi wrote a letter from Suide to the CPC northwest central office, which was forwarded to the CPC central committee. He said: "If the old revolutionary base areas continue to work on the basis that landlords and rich peasants account for about 8% of the population, it will result in serious errors." Continuing in this direct manner, he went on to write that "to mobilise the masses in old revolutionary base areas, measures should be taken to fight firmly against 'leftist' doctrinairism". He also made it clear that "these sort of 'leftist' sentiments do not originate from common people but have been brought in by cadres. It is still a very arduous task to steer things in the right direction."

Mao Zedong replied on 9 January 1948: "I totally agree with Comrade Zhongxun's suggestions. We should look at carefully applying these

Site of the December conference

opinions to land reform work at branch and county level so that work in the border region can get back on the right track and errors can be minimised."

On the same day, Mao issued instructions on Xi's *Report on the Breach of Discipline by Our Army in the Battle of Gaojia Village*, which was written one week earlier. "Those who committed a breach of discipline in Gaojia should be called to account," Mao said. "The whole army should receive education on policy and disciplinary matters."

During the nine days from 5-13 January, Xi Zhongxun conducted research and surveys in Zizhou county. On 8 January, he wrote a letter that included preliminary survey results to the CPC northwest central office. On 10 January, the office forwarded it to the CPC central committee. In the report, Xi highlighted nine aspects of land reform that needed to be overturned, such as beating all landlords and rich peasants and carrying out corporal punishment and executions. Liu Shaoqi, in charge of the CPC working committee in Xibaipo, gave this advice: "This letter should be held by the central government and read by all its members. The central government has reviewed it."

Rectifying 'Leftism' in Land Reform with the Total Approval of Mao Zedong

On 19 January, Xi Zhongxun wrote another telegram to Mao Zedong. He pointed out that, due to the influence of 'leftism' in land reform in Shanxi and Suide and the negative mood apparent at the Yihe conference, land reform in the border region focused on "the poor peasants and farm labourers line" and opposed "the middle peasants line". This led to protests by a minority of people who could not genuinely be counted among the masses, and to a general feeling of anxiety and tension in villages. He also summarised the nine issues that everyone needed to pay attention to. He acknowledged that "one should not be afraid to have middle peasants in power in old revolutionary base areas. Genuine, basic and good people exist among both middle and poor peasants."

Mao Zedong replied to Xi Zhongxun in a telegram on 20 January. "In full agreement," he wrote, adding that "'leftist' deviation should be firmly rectified". He went on to write: "I completely agree with Xi Zhongxun's

A group photo taken in 1947 of some party, administrative and military cadres from the Shaanxi-Gansu-Ningxia border region. Back row, from left to right: Wang Weizhou, Jia Tuofu, Yang Mingxuan, Ma Mingfang, Ma Wenrui and Huo Weide. Front row: Lin Boqu, He Long, Zhao Shoushan, Xi Zhongxun, Zhang Bangying and Cao Liru

suggestions. If 'leftist' errors are also apparent in the old revolutionary base areas in north and central China, close attention must be placed on rectifying them."

On 6 February, Mao Zedong wrote a telegram to Xi Zhongxun and others, asking for their views about the implementation of land reform in different regions.

Two days later, Xi replied to Mao and made some original suggestions about implementing different types of land reform in three different regions according to local conditions. "The area liberated before the surrender of Japan can be regarded as the 'old' liberated area," he wrote, "while 'semi-old' liberated areas are those that were liberated after Japan surrendered and during the two years of nationwide counter-offensives. Those liberated after the counter-offensives are the new liberated areas. This sort of classification conforms to reality. Consequently, the approach of land reform should differ." He also proposed that the poor peasant league should not dominate all matters in old liberated areas.

Mao Zedong highly valued Xi's suggestions. He personally revised a telegram from Xi Zhongxun and made the following instructions: forward it to Shanxi, Suide, the central working committee, the CPC Handan office, the CPC east China office, the East China Working Committee and the northeast office.

In the Shaanxi-Gansu-Ningxia border region, Xi energetically highlighted the experience of Huangjiachuan village. This old revolutionary base area regulated land on the basis of taking it from the haves and giving to the have-nots and in the approach of 'evening up'. On 12 March, Mao Zedong gave instructions to promote the typical experiences of the liberated areas of Huangjiachuan, Pingshan county in the Shanxi-Chahar-Hebei border region and Guoxian county in the Shanxi-Suide border region.

Xi Zhongxun reported the practical experience of land reform to the CPC central committee and Chairman Mao suggested rectifying 'leftist deviations' and wrote articles such as *On Land Reform and Party Consolidation in 1948* and *Several Issues on Leadership in Land Reform and Party Consolidation*. His proposals to differentiate between new and old liberated areas and to rectify 'leftist' practices captured the attention of Mao and the central government, and played a pivotal role in steering prevailing and future land reform in China.

Chapter 19

"All for the Front and All for the Development of the New Zone"

In February 1948, the Shaanxi-Gansu-Ningxia-Shanxi-Suide Joint Defence Army was renamed the Shaanxi-Gansu-Ningxia-Shanxi-Suide joint defence military region of the Chinese People's Liberation Army (PLA), with He Long as commander and Xi Zhongxun as political commissar. At that time, the history of the liberation of northwest China gradually began to unfold.

He Long, Ma Mingfang, Xi Zhongxun, Lin Boqu, Jia Tuofu and Wang Weizhou pictured in Suide in 1948

On 3 March, the Northwest Field Army recorded an important victory in Yichuan, Shaanxi province. One week later, 10,000 people from all walks of life in the border region gathered in Yangjiagou village in Mizhi county to celebrate the victory and to commemorate women's day. In a speech, Xi Zhongxun said that the Yichuan triumph showed that the CPC would soon recover the whole border region and liberate the whole of northwest China.

On 21 April, troops under the jurisdiction of the joint defence military region recovered Yan'an, where the CPC northwest central office would later be based. War correspondent Zhang Guang and Comrade Qi Xin recalled that Xi Zhongxun handled office affairs in the same room in Wangjiaping where Mao Zedong had once lived.

Since the Xiaohe conference, Xi Zhongxun, He Long and Lin Boqu attended garrison duty, directed local troops to combine their fighting forces and transport grain for the army, expanded the army and collected military supplies. All these activities provided a solid foundation for the liberation of northwest China.

Around the time when KMT forces attacked Yan'an, more than 20,000

The People's Liberation Army retake Yan'an

"All for the Front and All for the Development of the New Zone"

A donkey caravan on its way to support the front

guerrillas and more than 100,000 militiamen were organised in the Shaanxi-Gansu-Ningxia border region. From trenches and mountain tops, they were active in blocking traffic, attacking KMT strongholds, ambushing motorcades and checking for enemy spies, coordinating with the main fighting forces and disrupting the enemy day and night.

In those years, there were more than 80,000 border region troops and office staff and they needed about 800 tonnes of grain a month. From July 1947 to the spring of 1948, the CMC, Mao Zedong and Peng Dehuai wrote more than 20 telegrams to Xi Zhongxun and He Long to urge them to collect and transport grain for the army. The CPC northwest central office formulated the *Outline of Grain Transportation and Disaster Relief in the Shaanxi-Gansu-Ningxia Border Region* and set up a grain transportation and disaster relief headquarters with Xi Zhongxun acting as political commissar. Military depots were set up in all corners of the region so that the field army could be supplied with grain in a timely manner. Incomplete statistics indicate that 12,300 tonnes of public grain was collected in the Shaanxi-Gansu-Ningxia border region in 1947, up by 4,150 tonnes over the previous year. More than 60,000 tonnes of grain for the army, 60,000 tonnes of firewood and 920,000 pairs of military footwear were collected and transported in just a single year.

Xi Zhongxun saw at first hand the eagerness of the common people to support the front line. "In October 1947," he later recalled, "I witnessed many fellow villagers collect immature sorghum and black-eyed peas, fry them dry that very night and give them to the troops in Suide, Mizhi and Qingjian."[1]

On 8 February 1948, Xi Zhongxun wrote instructions to Yu Jie, who was manager of the Northwest Commercial Company and also president of the Northwest Peasant Bank. "Imported materials are allowed to be exchanged for soap in the main inland strongholds strictly pursuant to the rules and regulations designed to limit the scope of such exchanges inland and to combat smuggling." This was an example of the care that was taken to ensure that the onerous work undertaken to support the front line was conducted in an orderly manner.

Xi Zhongxun and He Long streamlined internal departments of the joint

Xi Zhongxun delivers a speech at the second plenary session of the front committee conference of the Northwest Field Army

"All for the Front and All for the Development of the New Zone"

defence military region to replenish fighting troops, issued repeated orders for mobilisation and recruited more than 42,000 young men to join the army.

Xi Zhongxun also dispatched cadres to remind troops that they must protect cultural relics. On 26 March 1948, Xi, He Long and Lin Boqun jointly issued *The Notice to Protect Cultural Relics and Historic Sites.*

During this period, Xi also participated in making vital operational decisions for the Northwest Field Army, attended the front committee conference and assisted Peng Dehuai in the ideological and political work of the troops.

On 26 May, Xi was present at the second plenary session of the front committee of the Northwest Field Army held in the town of Tuji, Luochuan county (known historically as the 'Tuji Conference'). The conference reviewed and summarised the experiences and lessons of the battle of Western Shaanxi. Xi pointed out flaws in battle strategy and was highly critical of column leaders for liberalism, non-intervention, reluctance to engage the enemy, failure to obey orders and even squandering military opportunities.

Xi Zhongxun delivers a report *On the Question of Taking Over Cities* at the first congress of the CPC Northwest Field Army

Despite these failings, the pace of victories quickened. Xi Zhongxun put into practice the guideline of the work of the CPC northwest central office: "Everything is done to support the front line and develop the new zone."

In the spring and summer of 1948, the CPC northwest central office convened three meetings to discuss the work for the new zone. Between 19 July and 4 August, it held the Shaanxi-Gansu-Ningxia border region prefectural party committee secretary conference. Xi Zhongxun delivered the opening and closing reports and came up with three new concepts: basic zones, zones bordering enemy territory and new zones. He explained that land reform would be suspended in zones bordering enemy territory and new zones, where waging war against the enemy would be the priority; basic zones, which covered old zones and most of the semi-old zones, would no longer concern themselves with land reform, but instead would focus on determining land ownership, granting land certificates and promoting the big production campaign as the fundamental task.

In November 1948, in line with the CMC's order, the Shaanxi-Gansu-Ningxia-Shanxi-Suide joint defence military region was renamed the northwest military region with He Long as commander and Xi Zhongxun as political commissar.

The dawn of the great northwest China was coming closer. It was a new and urgent issue to assume control of cities. From 11-23 January 1949, the first congress of the CPC Northwest Field Army was held in Wuzhuang county, Weibei. On 17 January, Xi Zhongxun delivered a report *On the Question of Taking Over Cities*. He put forward the basic guideline that the first priority was to become familiar with prevailing conditions and to become proficient, and then to carry out gradual and reasonable reforms. He highlighted a specific policy "to break up organisations and make use of materials", meaning that vestiges of old political power should be destroyed and placed in the hands of the people while, at the same time, protecting equipment and infrastructure. Ordinary officials, having undergone reform, could regain access to the equipment under certain circumstances.

On 24 January, the front committee conference of the Northwest Field Army, in accordance with the order of the CMC, decided to rename the Northwest Field Army as the First Field Army of the Chinese People's Liberation Army with effect from 1 February. Later in the year, on 30 November, the First Field Army and the Northwest Field Army were

"All for the Front and All for the Development of the New Zone"

The permanent members of the Shaanxi-Gansu-Ningxia border region provincial assembly and government members on 15 February 1949. Xi Zhongxun, deputy chairman, is standing in the middle row, fifth from the left

amalgamated with Xi Zhongxun as political commissar.

From 5-13 March 1949, Xi Zhongxun attended the second plenary session of the seventh central committee of the CPC in Xibaipo, Pingshan county in Hebei province.

On 10 May, Xi gave a speech at the marching towards Xi'an cadre mobilisation assembly in Yan'an's Taolin Square. He said they must be disciplined and keep close contact with the common people, and only in that way could they complete the tasks of taking over and constructing Xi'an. "We don't fear those who know little, but those who refuse to learn," he said. "As long as we have the spirit of primary school students, we can become college students; by contrast, if we are afraid to learn like primary school students, we will always remain primary school students."

On 4 June, the Xi'an edition of *Qunzhong Ribao* (群众日报 *The Masses Daily*) released some important news: Xi Zhongxun, the leader of the people of northwest China, the comrade in charge of the party, administrative and political affairs and secretary of the CPC northwest central office, had arrived in Xi'an along with He Long, commander of the PLA northwest military region and director of the Xi'an military control committee, Ma Mingfang, Liu Jingfan and Zhao Shoushan. After entering Xi'an, Xi temporarily lived in Xincheng (Newtown) Courtyard, which was the former site of the KMT provincial government and is today occupied by the Shaanxi provincial government. Later on, he moved to handle office affairs in the residence of Wang Youzhi, the former KMT mayor of Yan'an, in Xi'an's Xiaochai Market (which is today Jianguo Road).

On 8 June, the CPC central committee decided to set up a new CPC northwest central office, with Peng Dehuai as chief secretary, He Long as second secretary and Xi Zhongxun as third secretary. At that time, Peng commanded the First Field Army on its march northwestwards (towards Gansu, Ningxia, Qinghai and Xinjiang), He Long was preparing to lead troops into Sichuan and Xi Zhongxun was in charge of routine work of the CPC northwest central office.

On 30 September, the first plenary session of the CPPCC closed in

Xi Zhongxun delivers a speech at the defending Xi'an mobilisation assembly in June 1949

"All for the Front and All for the Development of the New Zone"

He Long, Liu Bocheng, Deng Xiaoping, Chen Yi, Xi Zhongxun and Wang Weizhou in Beijing's Summer Palace in the autumn of 1949

Beijing. Xi Zhongxun was elected as a member of the central people's government (CPG) commission and was later appointed as a member of the CPG people's revolutionary military committee.

On 1 October 1949, Mao Zedong stood in Tiananmen Gate Tower and solemnly declared to the world: "The central people's government of the People's Republic of China (PRC) was founded today!" The Chinese nation had initiated a new chapter in its great history and the new China began to appear on the oriental horizon like the rising sun.

Chapter 20

Managing and Developing the Great Northwest

Under the leadership of Peng Dehuai and Xi Zhongxun after the new China was founded, rapid progress was made in the establishment of a government. Xi held standing committee meetings of the CPC northwest central office on 31 October, 2 November and 10 November 1949, to discuss a plan to set up the northwest military and administrative committee. He proposed that the committee should accept non-party members and that they should account for one-third of the committee membership in each province. Xi specifically proposed that 'democratic figure' (a member of a non-CPC political party) Ma Dunjing could serve in the Ningxia provincial government and Ma Hongbin in the Gansu people's government as vice chairman. In just a few months, all the people's governments in northwest China were successively founded.

Xi Zhongxun also selected Shaanxi's Chang'an county as the pilot for the establishment of a government. On the morning of 8 October, Xi attended the opening ceremony of Chang'an's first farmers' representative assembly. In his speech to cadres from all levels, he said: "We must bear in mind that we are the people's labourers, we are the people's servants. We must be humble in learning from the people and follow the direction of our masters."

On 19 January 1950, the northwest military and administrative committee was officially established in Xi'an, with Peng Dehuai as chairman, and Xi Zhongxun and Zhang Zhizhong as vice chairmen. The committee comprised 44 members, one-third of whom were not party members. It was the institution representing the CPG responsible for implementing military control in northwest China on behalf of the northwest people's government.

Xi demonstrated his desire for inclusiveness during his inauguration ceremony on 19 January 1950. "I will join hands with party and non-party members of all nationalities and from all walks of life, encouraging everyone to be loyal in serving the people of northwest China."

Before leaving for a meeting in Beijing in March 1950, Peng Dehuai said at a standing committee meeting of the CPC northwest central office: "After I go to Beijing, Xi should act on my behalf in government. He can also carry out orders for internal and external affairs as the acting chairman."[1]

On 4 October 1950, Peng Dehuai boarded a private plane in Beijing. A few days later, Xi Zhongxun learned that Peng was taking command of the Chinese people's volunteers to fight in north Korea. The historic burden of managing and developing the great northwest fell onto the shoulders of Xi Zhongxun.

Xi Zhongxun reviews documents with his secretary and research director Huang Zhi in 1950

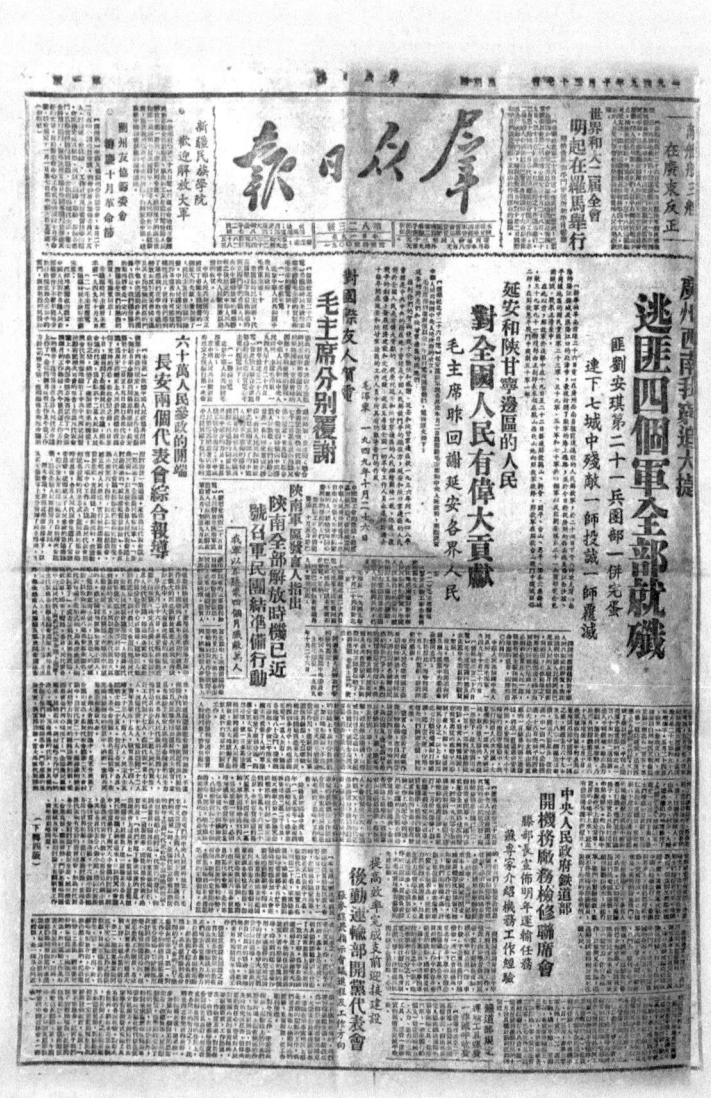

The Masses Daily (群众日报 Qunzhong Ribao) on 27 October 1949 reported the NPC and CPPCC meetings held in Chang'an

On 19 January 1950, Xi Zhongxun (sixth from left), Peng Dehuai (fifth from left) and Zhang Zhizhong (fourth from left) accept silk banners offered by representatives of all nationalities at the inaugural meeting of the northwest military and administrative committee

The great northwest is a vast territory that contains mighty mountains and rivers. Since ancient times, it has been inhabited by people from various ethnicities and it has also been characterised by socio-economic imbalance.

National unity was a top priority in northwest China. Xi Zhongxun proposed that national unity should underpin all work and that the guideline of "stable progress and prudent action" should be followed. The indispensable priority was to win over all nationalities and important religious figures and then to mobilise the people. In those years, meetings of the northwest military and administrative committee were held twice a year and required the participation of people from all nationalities and from various socio-economic groups as well as all democratic parties. Their participation doubled or even tripled the number of committee members.

Doing a good job of land reform in the regions inhabited by ethnic groups was an important test for the newly formed people's regime. Xi Zhongxun took on the post of director of the northwest land reform committee, starting with cropland and then pastureland. The issue of land reform was

The chairman, vice chairman and members of the northwest military and administrative committee pictured on 19 January 1950

inextricably linked with the treatment of ethnic minorities given the vast areas of land they deployed for pasture and raising livestock, so Xi came up with the original idea of "uniting with the feudal to fight against the feudal". It was a method referring to uniting with a minority of the feudal forces to fight against the majority of the feudal forces, properly carrying out united front work to win over the upper levels of society and religious figures, then mobilising the masses and exterminating the feudal forces in a top-down manner in order to foster peace and stability.

Jiang Ping, who was once the director of the united front work department of the CPC northwest central office, had clear recollections of this important initiative. "It would have been exceedingly difficult for Xi Zhongxun to carry out this policy against the background of a class struggle if he had not thought through the theoretical issues or if he had lacked courage," he said. "That report won the approval of Chairman Mao. Uniting with a small part of the feudal forces won over the big chiefs and big landlords to the democratic cause, which was the objective of our united front work."[2]

In February and March 1951, a visiting group of land reformers directed by Beijing went on an inspection visit to northwest China. On 18 March, "Wu Jingchao and Zhu Guangqian investigated land reform in Xi'an", stated Mao Zedong, "and they were favourably impressed. This practice should be applied in training our cadres. We should do away with the mentality of closed-doorism."[3] By late 1953, land reform had been completed in northwest China.

To develop the economy and industrial capacity in backward northwest China was a real challenge for the CPC northwest central office. They had no alternative other than to tackle the problem head-on. Xi Zhongxun proposed to improve corporate management and make progress on the economic front using the combined efforts of the workers and capitalists. In a speech in April 1950, he indicated that, on the one hand, the capitalists should be told to acknowledge the involvement of workers in assisting with the production management process and their consciousness of complying

Central government members and candidate members attending the third plenary session of the seventh CPC central committee held in Beijing in June 1950. Xi Zhongxun attended the conference

Xi Zhongxun, Jia Tuofu, Zhang Zhizhong and Peng Dehuai at the second session of the northwest military and administrative committee in July 1950

with labour discipline; on the other hand, the workers and the masses should realise that it is also the responsibility of workers in privately-owned factories to be productive, and to come up with positive suggestions and settle problems together with the capitalists without interfering with their administrative rights and power to promote or demote staff.

At the first northwest transport conference in March 1950, Xi Zhongxun set out his proposals on infrastructure construction. "The work of the transport sector should be based on the positive joint efforts of all staff," he said. "Repairs to roadbeds and the maintenance of bridges and roads should be undertaken with the widespread participation of the peasants." On 23 August 1952, the Tianshui-Lanzhou railway was completed. On 11 September, Xi Zhongxun wrote the following inscription: "Congratulations on the completion of the Tianshui-Lanzhou railway! The long-held wishes of the people of all nationalities in northwest China have been realised three years after the liberation. This is a great joy. We must move ahead and continue to struggle for all the railway trunklines and all the indispensable railway projects in northwest China."

A Soviet expert pictured in 1950 flanked by Xi Zhongxun and Lü Zhengcao (left), vice minister of railways, who had come to northwest China to direct the planning and construction of the Baoji-Lanzhou railway

Xi Zhongxun paid considerable attention to agricultural production. Before the spring ploughing each year between 1950 and 1952, he issued instructions on the granting of loans for agricultural production in the name of the northwest military and administrative committee and required 'agricultural loan committees' to be established at all levels in order to use valuable state capital to "support the development of agriculture, launch water-conservancy projects, increase output of grain and cotton, and accelerate reproduction of livestock in a focused and planned manner".

Xi encouraged 47 mutual-aid teams such as the Zhang Mingliang mutual-aid team of Xingping county, Shaanxi province to initiate a summer harvest competition to select the best variety of wheat seed. The PRC's ministry of agriculture also called on wheat-producing areas nationwide to focus on "organising mutual-aid teams on the basis of completing spring ploughing and production". Some 3,300 teams in Shaanxi and 8,500 teams nationwide joined the competitions enthusiastically. Furthermore, competitions in cotton yield, afforestation, water conservancy and livestock breeding were carried out in northwest China.

In the spring of 1951, the northwest military and administrative committee issued an order to "implement afforestation over an area of 38 sq km, to plant 26.76m trees and to promote the forestry industry" throughout the year. In 1952, it initiated a 'one-tree-per-capita-per-year' campaign and advocated the planting of trees along railway lines, roads, rivers and on barren mountains. On 3 September 1952, Xi Zhongxun was present at the first northwest forestry work conference. "What we are doing now is not only getting to know China," he said, "but also reforming China and building a better, more beautiful China."[4] He went on to make an appeal to the northwestern people: "We should build a great wall of forests on tens of thousands of metres of shifting sands and plant trees everywhere along both banks of the rolling rivers and on the red soil of the mountains."[5]

Pictured at the first northwest education conference, held in Xi'an between July and September 1950, are Peng Dehuai, Xiao San, Ai Qing, Zhao Zhongchi and Xi Zhongxun

Xi Zhongxun and representatives of the northwest Chinese people's volunteers group who marched to north Korea in March 1951

Xi Zhongxun, Zhang Zhizhong and Jia Tuofu attend a military parade held by the northwest military and administrative committee on the national day holiday in 1951

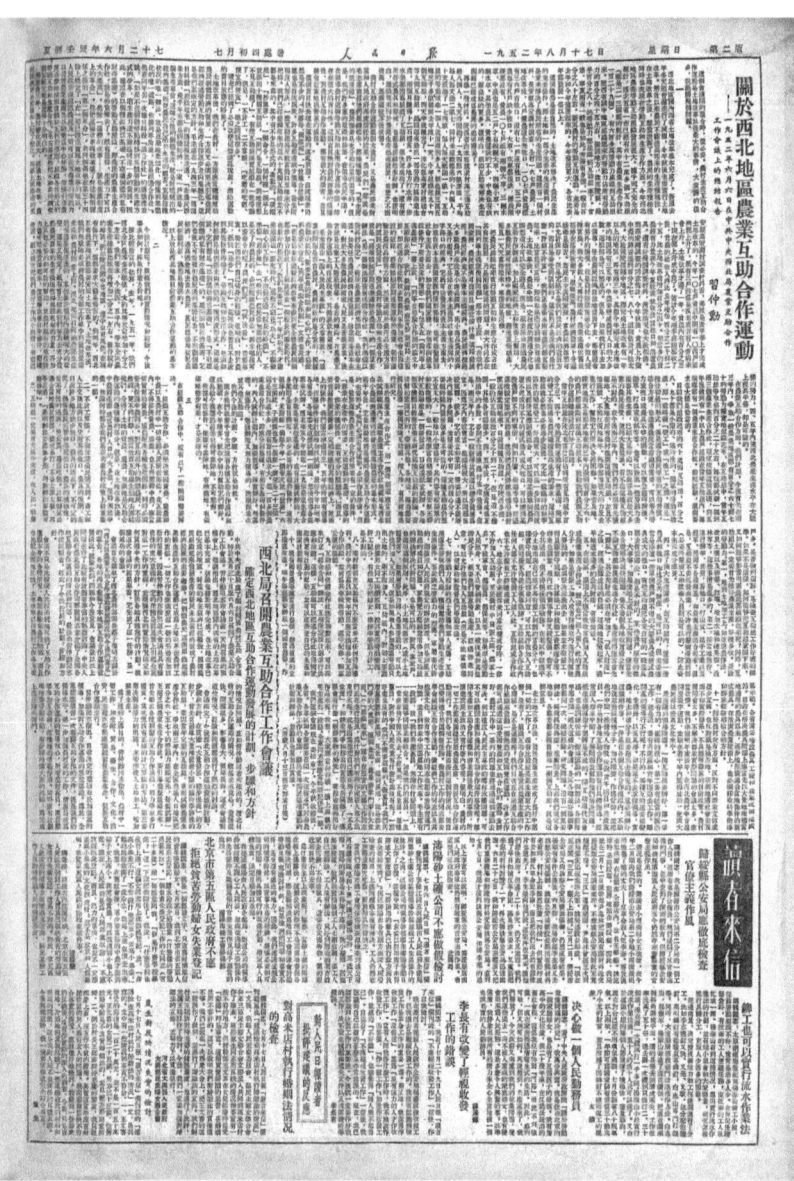

On 17 August 1952, *People's Daily* carried Xi Zhongxun's summary report at the agricultural mutual-aid team conference of the CPC northwest central office

On 27 May 1951, Xi Zhongxun wrote to Mao Zedong and the CPC central committee, suggesting developing the oil industry in northwest China as soon as possible and dispatching Kang Shi'en, director of the northwest petroleum administration bureau, to Beijing to undertake research with the fuel industry department. The northwest petroleum industry achieved tremendous growth and gave impetus to the economic expansion of northwest China in the initial stage of the PRC.

Xi Zhongxun rigorously followed the policy of struggling against the 'three evils' and the 'five evils', a campaign carried out between late 1951 and October 1952 in the northwest to tackle corruption, waste and bureaucracy among party members and administrative institutions and to clamp down on bribery, tax evasion, stealing and cheating state property, overcharging customers for labour and materials and theft of state economic information from private businesses. Especially in the final phase of "fighting top officials", he advocated "close scrutiny, strict control, avoidance of wronging suspects and preventing the extraction of forced confessions and giving them credence". Mao Zedong recognised his "good advocacy" and gave instructions "to remind comrades of this point in the climax of the campaign".

In early 1952, Mao Zedong reviewed Xi Zhongxun's report *On the Plenary Session of the CPC Northwest Central Office Committee* sent from Xi'an. He spoke highly of the report and told comrades in the party that Xi Zhongxun had "attained a high degree of proficiency".

Xi Zhongxun, his wife Qi Xin and their daughter Qiaoqiao in Xi'an in 1950

Chapter 21

Plenipotentiary Appointed by the Central People's Government

On 22 April 1951, the 10th Panchen Lama Erdeni Choekyi Gyaltsen[1] headed a group of officials from the Khenpo chamber[2] to Beijing via Xi'an. Xi Zhongxun went to meet them at Xi'an airport on behalf of the CPC northwest central office and the northwest military and administrative committee. At the airport, the handsome young 'living Buddha' and the amiable Xi Zhongxun got on well at their first meeting and acted like old friends. Xi was full of praise for the Panchen Lama, saying that a man's will does not depend on his age! The 10th Panchen Lama was just 13 years old at the time.

Xi Zhongxun meets the 10th Panchen Lama Erdeni Choekyi Gyaltsen at Xi'an airport

Plenipotentiary Appointed by the Central People's Government

Xi Zhongxun and the 10th Panchen Lama stand side by side in this group photo

Due to complicated historical reasons and the invasion of Tibet by imperial forces in the 1920s and their interference in its affairs, the ninth Panchen Lama Qoigyi Nyima was forced to leave Tibet and could not return to the Tashilhunpo monastery where generations of Buddhist abbots lived even after he passed away.

As the PLA began its advance into Tibet, the Khenpo chamber lodged a request to return to the region as soon as possible. For this reason, Xi Zhongxun wrote to the central government after discussions with other officials of the CPC northwest central office. "Only after Tibet is completely liberated or the central government and the Dalai Lama's government have negotiated an agreement can they return to Tibet," he said. "Allowing them to return to Tibet too early would have an impact on our strategy for Tibet's liberation and our policy of uniting the whole of Tibet." The judgment of the CPC northwest central office coincided with the central government decision. To ensure the safe return of the 10th Panchen Lama to Tibet, Xi Zhongxun dispatched Wang Feng and Fan Ming to Kumbum monastery to communicate the detailed arrangements for his return to Tibet in the divine office of Panchen Lama.

On 23 May 1951, *The Agreement on the Peaceful Liberation of Tibet Between the Central People's Government and the Tibetan Local Government*, also known as *The 17-Articles Agreement*, was officially concluded. On 21 June, the 10th Panchen Lama returned to Qinghai via Xi'an and met with Xi Zhongxun for the second time. On 24 June, he wrote Xi a letter from Kumbum monastery. "We should continue to treat each other sincerely in the future," he wrote. "I wish to focus my efforts on establishing a prosperous and happy new Tibet under the leadership of Chairman Mao and you." The conditions for the 10th Panchen Lama to enter Tibet gradually became more favourable. On 11 November 1951, the CPC central committee wrote a telegram to the CPC northwest central office, which in turn forwarded it to the Qinghai provincial party committee: "Please review and expedite the issue of the Panchen Lama's entry into Tibet and help him overcome the difficulties that cannot be ignored." It went on to say: "Please ask Comrade Zhongxun to convey our best wishes

Xining, Qinghai province, December 1951. On behalf of the CPC central committee and Chairman Mao, Xi Zhongxun sends off the 10th Panchen Lama, who is about to return to Tibet

to the Panchen Lama and explain central government policies related to the accompaniment of Tibetan and Chinese personnel on behalf of Chairman Mao and the central people's government before they depart."

On 14 December 1951, Xi Zhongxun went to Kumbum monastery to meet the 10th Panchen Lama. "I came to Xining to escort the young Buddha to Tibet on behalf of the CPC central committee and Chairman Mao," he said. The 10th Panchen Lama replied gratefully: "Without the CPC or Chairman Mao, it would be impossible for us to return to Tibet."

On 16 December, Xi Zhongxun attended a grand farewell ceremony for the 10th Panchen Lama to return to Tibet in the auditorium of Qinghai provincial government. He pointed out in his speech that: "I hope and believe, after the Panchen Lama returns to Tibet, he will be more closely united with the Dalai Lama under the leadership of Chairman Mao and the CPG, faithfully implement the *17-Articles Agreement* with the assistance of the PLA and make efforts to eradicate the influence of imperialism, consolidate frontier defence, build on the political, economic and cultural development and progress of Tibet and create a flourishing new Tibet!"

The 10th Panchen Lama said in an emotional acceptance speech that: "Only when we follow the leadership of the CPC and Chairman Mao and closely unite with all the fellow nationalities can Tibet be thoroughly liberated. There is no other way forward!"

At noon on 17 December 1951, Xi Zhongxun talked with the 10th Panchen Lama and his retinue and asked him to unite with the Dalai Lama and Kashag (cabinet) officials after they returned to Tibet, to evaluate possible difficulties, to foster confidence and courage to patiently overcome the difficulties and to implement the agreement step by step.

Officials from the Khenpo chamber requested some guns and silver dollars in addition to a car for the Panchen Lama in Xigaze. Xi Zhongxun responded promptly. "As long as the Buddha needs them, we will make every endeavour to meet his satisfaction," he said. "The request can be honoured tomorrow." He personally approved the decision to dismantle a car and tie it to the back of a yak for transportation to Tibet.

On 18 December, Xi Zhongxun spent a whole day delivering a report on realising an agreement for the peaceful liberation of Tibet to more than 300 field headquarters personnel and Han Chinese cadres in a small meeting room in Qinghai province. A policy of "cautious and steady progress" should be applied in Tibet, he argued. "Impatience should be avoided. 'Steady progress' does not mean standing still but more deliberation on what is needed to achieve the best outcome. The achievements of the work can be consolidated. This is the principle of managing the work in Tibet. More haste, less speed. It doesn't matter if it is handled slowly. Otherwise, we will end up going round in circles."[3]

On that day, the working team of the divine office of the Panchen Lama, who arrived in Lhasa together with the CPC northwest Tibet working committee on 16 December, wrote a telegram to Xi Zhongxun. "We fully appreciate that this victory was granted by you and the glorious CPC," it stated. "We really appreciate it."

On 19 December, the 10th Panchen Lama set out for Tibet. Before departure, he said goodbye to Xi Zhongxun and presented him with a pure white Hada, a traditional ceremonial silk scarf used as a greeting gift. Clutching the hands of the 10th Panchen Lama, Xi Zhongxun said: "May you have a smooth trip!"

On 28 April 1952, after a journey of more than four months, the party

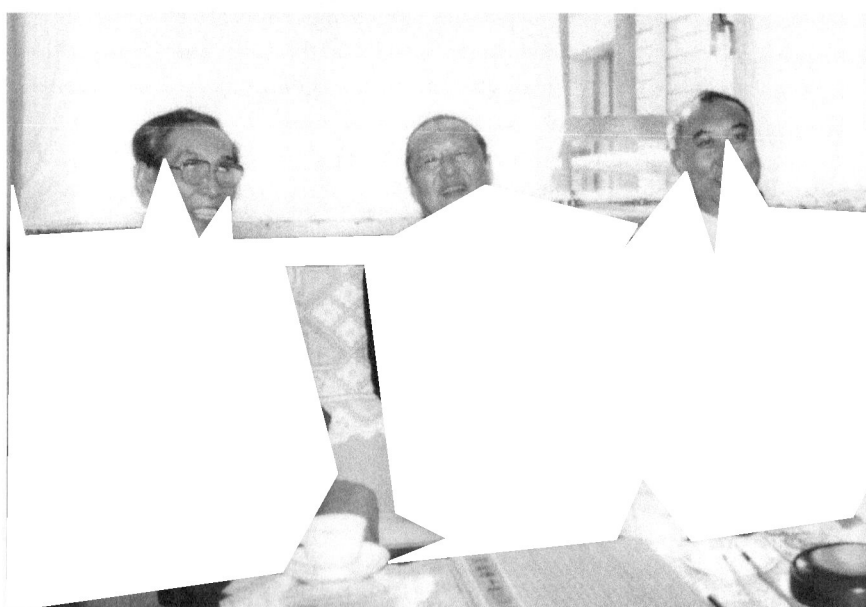

Ngapoi Ngawang Jigme, Xi Zhongxun and the 10th Panchen Lama

headed by the 10th Panchen Lama reached Lhasa and then travelled to the revered Tashilhunpo monastery, arriving on 30 June.

Afterwards, entrusted by the central government, Xi Zhongxun and the CPC northwest central office assumed the responsibility of keeping in contact with the 10th Panchen Lama. They treated one another like family. After Xi Zhongxun was assigned to work in the central government, whenever the 10th Panchen Lama travelled to Beijing during the decade from the early 1950s to the early 1960s, Xi would be there to meet or send him off at the airport or railway station.

In 1962, the 10th Panchen Lama was condemned due to the so-called '70,000-Word Report'[4] incident, in which Xi Zhongxun and Li Weihan were implicated. Xi Zhongxun was also investigated because of events arising from 'the *Liu Zhidan* novel' incident. After 1962, both men encountered years of extreme hardship. They didn't meet again for another 16 years. The occasion was the first session of the fifth CPPCC held in the Great Hall of the People, where they simply embraced each other, without speaking.

In later years, when Xi Zhongxun returned to work in the central government and was administering Guangdong province, the 10th Panchen Lama paid him a special visit. In the 1980s, Xi's family spent a day celebrating the spring festival or the Tibetan New Year with the 10th Panchen Lama, who sent two sheep to Xi Zhongxun. "We would say farewell before departure and hold close talks after meeting again," Xi recalled. "It was an established habit of our long relationship."[5] In the eyes of the 10th Panchen Lama, Xi Zhongxun was a mentor and trustworthy friend.

In the 1980s, Xi Zhongxun and the 10th Panchen Lama often discussed the '70,000-Word Report' incident. At that time, Xi Zhongxun and Li Weihan were entrusted by Zhou Enlai to discuss with the 10th Panchen Lama his criticism and suggestions concerning the work in Tibet in the '70,000-Word Report'. He admitted that a large part of the report was good but that it went too far in places. Xi praised the 10th Panchen Lama's commendable spirit in voicing his honest opinion without reservation, but advised him not to speak in anger. "I accept what you say," the 10th Panchen Lama replied. "You have witnessed my growth since childhood and helped me along the way, both on behalf of the CPC and as a personal friend. You have my best interests at heart, for which I am very grateful. But angry

Xi Zhongxun and the 10th Panchen Lama pay a visit to the Tibetan Thangka art exhibition in Beijing's Cultural Palace of Nationalities, 15 June 1986

words have been said already that should never have been spoken. I will watch my step from now on. But I must declare that I am genuinely on the party's side."

Sometimes, it is only after experiencing hardship that one sees the truth. The friendship between Xi Zhongxun and the 10th Panchen Lama endured, surviving all difficulties. On 28 January 1989, the 10th Panchen Lama passed away in Tashilhunpo monastery. On hearing the news, Xi Zhongxun felt deep sorrow. He shed tears while holding the last hada given to him by the 10th Panchen Lama. Soon afterwards, he wrote a touching and sincere article for *People's Daily* in memory of his friend.

Chapter 22

Mao Zedong Says: "You are More Formidable than Zhuge Liang"

In the early years after liberation, banditry plagued northwest China. There were 130,000 members of more than 470 major bandit gangs, of whom 90,000 were coerced into joining. However, by the middle of 1953, insurrections in Xiji county, Amuquhu town and Osman had been quelled, the bandits eliminated and people from all ethnic groups were living in unity and harmony. The Xi Zhongxun-led defeat of Xiang Qian,[1] the battalion commander of the Angla tribe in Qinghai province, was an important step in suppressing the bandits, shoring up opposition against local despots and solving the ethnic minority issue. Xi Zhongxun's leadership in this regard was highly valued by Mao Zedong.

On 29 June 1950, Xi delivered a speech to an enlarged session of the CPC northwest central office. "Any issues concerning bandits, including armed riots led by spies, should be treated from the context of the masses," he said. "Only in that way can we adopt prudent attitudes, policies and tactics in addressing problems and avoid mistakes." He went on to say: "Any issue relating to bandits should follow the principles of defence before assault, figuring out what the problem is before attacking, and political persuasion before suppression. If necessary, the method of suppression mixed with conciliation should be implemented."

The Angla tribe lived in the Jianzhatan (Jianzha Beach) region of Guide county (now Jianzha county) in Qinghai, approximately 150km from the provincial capital of Xining. In those years it contained seven lamaseries, eight villages, more than 1,000 households and 8,000 inhabitants. Xiang Qian was the 12th battalion commander of the Angla tribe, giving him religious, clan and political power. Following liberation, Xiang Qian paid

Beautiful Jianzha

allegiance to the people's government and was recruited as a member of the CPPCC Qinghai committee. In the early 1950s, instigated by the remaining bandits of Ma Bufang's troops and KMT spies, he organised the second 'anti-communist national salvation army' to harass and attack the people's government, the masses and even the PLA. In August 1950, as a result of political persuasion, Xiang travelled to Xining to surrender but broke his word after returning to Angla. During the armed rebellions, Xiang Qian was both reactionary and open to persuasion. The 10th Panchen Lama and the Buddhist Sherab Gyatso[2] tried to win him over by writing letters and dispatching special representatives.

Having failed to win Xiang round politically on eight occasions, the comrades in charge of the task in Qinghai province advocated military suppression. Xi Zhongxun wrote a telegram on 30 September 1950 to Qinghai provincial party committee, advocating a more conciliatory approach. "We haven't done well in our dealings with all the Tibetan tribes in the pastureland," the message stated. "It is premature to say that we have gained a firm foothold. We haven't entered the Tibetan areas of Sichuan, Tibet, Gansu and Qinghai frontiers or the Tibetan tribes in Qinghai. We haven't even shaken hands with the people there. What worries us is the influence of these gigantic Tibetan areas." He went on to say: "If our political work has not been carried out thoughtfully – and, of course, there are still military preparations to be made – then military suppression should be postponed. If we create a big fuss about the likes of Xiang Qian, it will only serve to further isolate them."

However, the Qinghai authorities insisted on taking military action. Xi Zhongxun immediately called up Qinghai provincial party committee secretary Zhang Zhongliang to protest. "It is inadvisable to start a fight arbitrarily," he said. "Military action should not be considered until political persuasion fails. Action should not be taken without the approval of the central government. Before that, the Buddhist Sherab Gyatso should be invited to persuade them."

The mansion of the Angla battalion commander

Between December 1949 and April 1952, Xiang Qian surrendered and went back on his word on a number of occasions. Under the instructions of Xi Zhongxun, more than 50 senior figures including the Tibetan Buddhist Sherab Gyatso, Zhou Renshan, director of the Qinghai united front work department, along with Tibetan tribal chiefs and prominent Buddhists travelled to Angla region and negotiated with Xiang Qian on 17 occasions.

In the spring of 1952, the armed rebels of Xiang Qian launched repeated assaults on the PLA. Some Tibetan headmen wavered and took

Xiang Qian, the 12th Angla battalion commander

their forces to Angla. The situation became increasingly serious and the opportunity was ripe for military suppression. On 9 April 1952, the Qinghai provincial party committee sent a telegram to the CPC northwest central office asking for permission to launch a military attack.

"If political persuasion is successful, the rebellions will disappear by themselves; without first evaluating the situation, both lenient policies and rigorous guidelines would be futile," noted Xi Zhongxun who, after repeatedly considering the situation, conditionally agreed with the suggestions of the Qinghai provincial party committee and Qinghai provincial military region to launch military suppression in late April 1952. He sent telegrams on 22 and 25 April to the Qinghai provincial party committee. "It is advisable to distinguish between Xiang Qian and other spies and bandits during the suppression," he wrote. "We should try to persuade him to neutralise his position. It would be more beneficial.

For the time being, it would be better to use any means to win him over politically." This proved to be sound advice in the eventual winning over of Xiang Qian.

The battle started at 6.30am on 2 May 1952. It took just four hours to defeat the armed rebels. Xiang Qian led a small number of followers to flee from the battlefield for the dense forest of Nanhujiagai, about 35km southwest of Jianzha. The Qinghai provincial party committee, as instructed by Xi Zhongxun and the CPC northwest central office, set up an Angla region resettlement committee, held rallies to propagate and implement the lenient policies of the party and to set free the captured armed leaders. The Qinghai provincial people's government appropriated relief funds of Rmb200m and provided 40 tonnes of relief grain to Jianzha region. It also dispatched cadres in charge of medical care, culture and education, trade and ethnic work to work with the Angla tribe and provide them with

Descendents of Xiang Qian, the Angla battalion commander

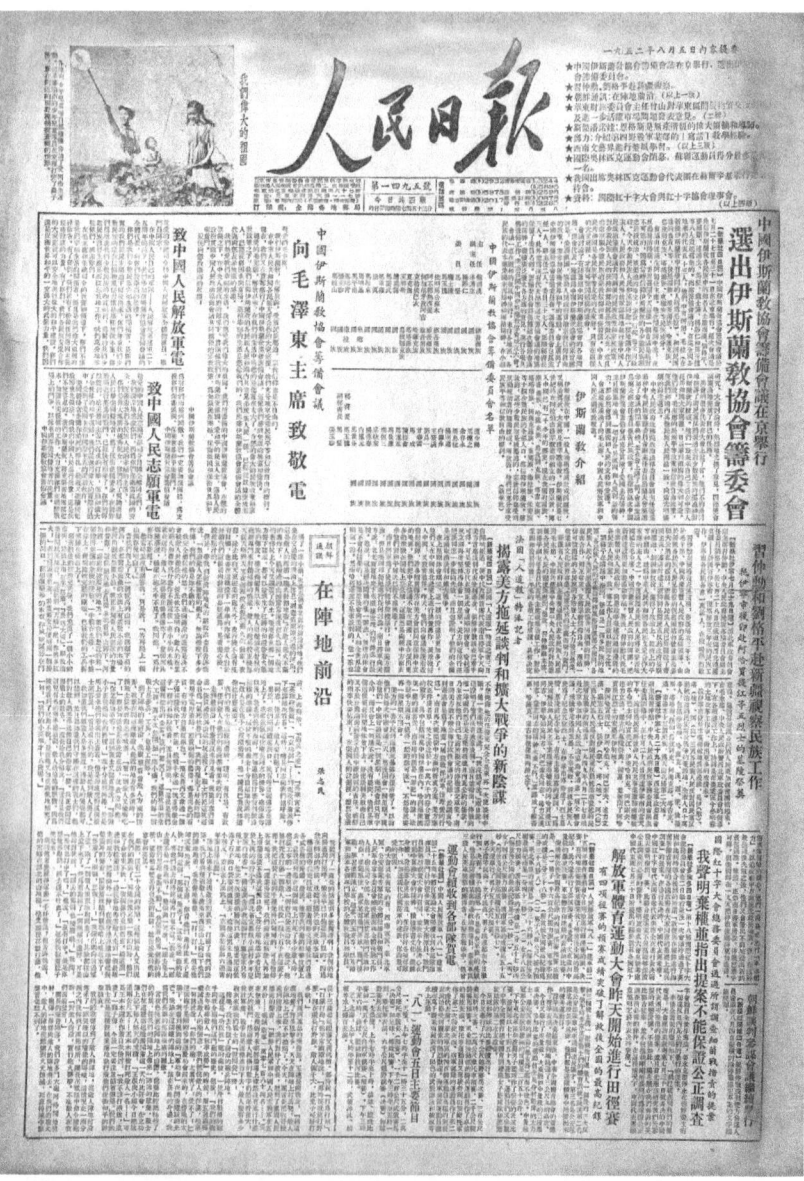

People's Daily reports Xi Zhongxun's investigation into ethnic work in Xinjiang on 5 August 1952

clothing, salt, tea, medicine, movies and publicity materials written in Tibetan. Significantly, they cured Xiang Qian's mother of a disease.

Moved by the sincerity of the people's government, Xiang Qian emerged from the Nanhujiagai forest to surrender on the afternoon of 11 July 1952. Five days later, Xi Zhongxun, who was in Xinjiang, received the news in a telegram from the Qinghai authorities and promptly sent telegrams to the CPC northwest central office and the Qinghai provincial party committee. "Maybe Xiang Qian had scruples and made a tentative return," he wrote. "No matter whether or not he surrendered sincerely, we should treat him earnestly and with kindness in the hope that he changes. I think that would be the best policy. But we must keep in mind that Xiang Qian has been extremely frightened. Any carelessness on our part might cause him to escape again. If he does decide to flee, we should keep alert and be prepared to keep on catching and releasing him until we have completely won him over."

Deeply moved by the policy of political persuasion led by Xi Zhongxun, Xiang Qian finally returned to the people's government in the summer of 1952 and published an article entitled *Feelings on Returning to the People's Government*, which shocked northwestern China.

On 11 August, Xi Zhongxun arrived in Lanzhou. He welcomed Xiang Qian and held a banquet for the "last battalion commander" to yield to the people's government. He encouraged Xiang Qian to develop the Jianzha region under the leadership of the government. Xiang Qian presented a Hada to Xi Zhongxun and rendered services as the governor of Huangnan district. He lived up to Xi's expectations and carried out his work with diligence.

The campaign of political persuasion of Xiang Qian went on for two years and seven months. After listening to a detailed report on this subject by Li Weihan, director of the united front work department of the CPC central committee, Mao Zedong said: "Zhuge Liang captured Meng Huo and set him free seven times. Xi Zhongxun did more. He captured Xiang Qian and set him free 10 times."

When he met Xi Zhongxun later, Mao Zedong said jokingly: "Zhongxun, you are really formidable! Zhuge Liang captured Meng Huo and set him free seven times. You are more formidable than Zhuge Liang!"

Chapter 23

'An Accomplished Head of the Central Publicity Department'

In August 1952, the central government decided to transfer the major regional leaders Gao Gang, Deng Xiaoping, Rao Shushi, Deng Zihui and Xi Zhongxun to work in the central government. Some people jokingly referred to this as "five horses entering Beijing". Xi Zhongxun was 39 years old at the time, 17 years younger than the oldest, Deng Zihui, and eight years younger than Gao Gang.

Xi Zhongxun as director of the CPC central committee publicity department and vice chairman of the culture and education committee of the state council

Xi Zhongxun at work

On 7 August 1952, the 17th session of the CPG commission appointed Xi as vice chairman and party secretary of the culture and education committee of the state council. On 22 September, he took over the work of Lu Dingyi as director of the publicity department of the CPC central committee. On 16 November, Xi also became a member of the SPC.

Before Xi assumed these duties, some comrades from the publicity department of the CPC central committee heard that Mao Zedong would appoint someone of high calibre to be director. A couple of days later, they realised that this person was Xi Zhongxun.

Xi was scrupulous in carrying out the duties of director of the publicity department. His predecessor before the seventh NPC was Lu Dingyi. He was the party's 'senior director of publicity' and Xi Zhongxun respected him highly. So it was natural that Xi was somewhat embarrassed to be now working as director with the former director as his assistant. Moreover, Xi was mentally unprepared to take on the role. When he accompanied Mao Zedong on an investigation of the Juyongguan railway, Xi told Mao about his concerns. Mao responded by telling him a story about a snake charmer: snakes often frighten people but they are very tame in the hands of snake charmers because they have mastered the behavioural patterns of snakes. You have never handled affairs concerning publicity. But if you master the rules, you can go on to perform the work better.

Lu Dingyi and other leaders and comrades of the publicity department were sincere in welcoming Xi Zhongxun to enhance the department's work and fully cooperated with him.

In the autumn of 1952, Mao Zedong began to push forward his ideas for the transition to socialism. In September 1953, the central government officially released the party's general line for the transitional period: "Over the medium- to long-term, the state will gradually realise the socialist transformation of agriculture, handicrafts and capitalist industry and commerce." Under the leadership of Xi Zhongxun, the publicity department of the CPC central committee drafted *Struggle to Mobilise All Forces to Build Our Country into a Great Socialist State — Outline of Learning and Publicising the General Line of the Party During the Transitional Period* which was approved by the central government, modified by Mao Zedong in person and issued to and implemented by all the regions nationwide. From then on, the publicity work of the CPC made the historic transition from publicity and education of the programmes, guidelines and policies of the 'new democracy' to those of the general line of the party for the transitional period.

In May 1954, the CPC central committee held the second national publicity work conference. The conference summarised the experiences of the three years since the first national publicity work conference in 1951, and established the main tasks of propagating the principles of "educating the whole party and the people with Marxist-Leninist socialist ideology and mobilising the whole party and the people to struggle to materialise the general line of the party and complete the first five-year plan for state construction". It also passed *The Resolution to Improve Newspaper Work* and *The Instructions to Strengthen the Publicity Work of the Party in Rural Areas*.

In encouraging Xi Zhongxun to carry out his cultural and educational duties well, Mao Zedong asked him to make good use of the publicity department's allocation of 100m tonnes of millet in the first five-year plan.

'An Accomplished Head of the Central Publicity Department'

Xi Zhongxun in Zhongnanhai in 1953

From 1953, China implemented its first five-year plan and initiated large-scale economic construction. As vice chairman of the cultural and educational committee and secretary of its executive party committee, Xi Zhongxun assisted Guo Moruo, vice premier and chairman of the committee, in leading the work of a number of ministries and departments, including the ministry of culture (with Shen Yanbing as minister), the ministry of education (Ma Xulun as minister), the ministry of higher education (Yang Xiufeng as minister), the ministry of health (Li Dequan as minister), the general administration of press and publications (Hu Yuzhi as director) and the writing system reform committee (Wu Yuzhang as director). To adapt to the requirements of large-scale economic construction and further straighten out the basic ideology of cultural and educational work, Xi Zhongxun suggested convening a conference of the chairmen of the cultural and educational committees of all major regions in China. His suggestions were supported by the central government.

The conference was held from 13-21 January 1953. The guidelines of "rectification, consolidation, development priorities, quality enhancement and stable progress" proposed by Xi Zhongxun were applauded by the central government and other comrades present at the conference. The

Representatives of the second national publicity work conference held in May 1954. Front row, from left to right: Xi Zhongxun, Lin Boqu, Zhu De, Mao Zedong, Liu Shaoqi, Wu Yuzhang and Deng Xiaoping

guidelines gave firm directions for the practical work of culture and education in the early stages after liberation.

With the upsurge of construction, the blind and misguided pursuit of bureaucratism started to rear its head on the cultural and educational front. In a campaign to eliminate rural illiteracy, people in the countryside were pressured to organise classes of 40 students and to complete 250-300 hours of study, which triggered widespread falsification of statistics relating to the number of classes held and the graduation results achieved. Institutions of higher learning tried to complete the five-year Soviet curricula in four years, involving an average of 70-90 study hours a week. Translators, teachers and students could not cope with the workload.

On 2 March 1953, Xi Zhongxun reported this problem to the CPC central committee and Mao Zedong and came up with five viewpoints: first, to integrate the work of anti-bureaucratism with all other work practices and to adopt a more genial, less confrontational manner; second, to appreciate

'An Accomplished Head of the Central Publicity Department'

and analyse the realities of bureaucratism, to prioritise specific issues and tasks, to resolve cases of people being wronged arbitrarily and to attend to "big and small matters simultaneously"; third, to give priority to party members and to allow non-party members to voluntarily learn through studying documents rather than force them to make self-criticisms; fourth, to fight against bureaucratism on the one hand and to advocate a working style that addresses the realities and makes direct contact with the masses; fifth, to concentrate on strongly opposing bureaucratism and at the same time to avoid proposing too many slogans and questions to be solved.

On 3 March 1953, Mao gave instructions to the CPC central committee, all departments of the CMC and the party organisations of the CPG. "Comrade Xi Zhongxun's report is good," he said. "You should take it as a reference in the struggle against bureaucratism."[1]

On 13 March, at the invitation of the deputy director of the publicity department of the CPC central committee, vice minister and party secretary of culture Zhou Yang, Xi Zhongxun made a two-hour report at the first film and art work conference. He held the view that culture and art should not be led in an oversimplified or crude way. It is unwise to require all works to conform to uniform standards or demand that writers finish their work at an appointed time as if they were delivering goods to meet a deadline. He

Xi Zhongxun

exemplified this point through *The History of Entrepreneurship* and *The Impregnable Fortress* created by Liu Qing. The report generated a strong reaction among arts and literature workers and it had a positive impact on literary and artistic creativity in the new China.

Chapter 24

'Majordomo' of the State Council

In September 1953, Xi Zhongxun took over the work of Li Weihan as secretary general of the government administration council, which became known as the state council in September 1954. In this post (in April 1959, he was appointed vice premier as well as secretary general of the state council), Xi worked with Premier Zhou Enlai for a period of 10 years. He was one of Zhou's right-hand men during this time and was

On 18 September 1953, the 28th conference of the CPG commission appointed Xi Zhongxun as secretary general of the government administration council

known as the 'housekeeper' of the state council. In the beginning, Zhou Enlai arranged Xi Zhongxun's office in the courtyard of Xihua Hall in Zhongnanhai, the central headquarters of the CPC in Beijing. Zhou was accustomed to working at night and always busied himself until the early hours. Therefore, the few hours left for sleep were especially valuable. Xi Zhongxun was in charge of many specific affairs. He was used to getting up early, holding meetings or asking others to report their work. To avoid disturbing Zhou Enlai's rest, Xi proposed moving out of Xihua Hall to the less salubrious office of the state council and shared this work space with several deputy secretary generals.

In addition to his role as vice premier, Xi Zhongxun was also responsible for the other 12 institutions directly affiliated to the state council. At the second plenary session of the state council on 31 October 1954, Zhou Enlai suggested that major issues should be centralised and settled at the

From 19-25 March 1959, Xi Zhongxun and Zhu De (middle of front row), vice chairman of the CPC central committee and vice chairman of the PRC, headed a government and party delegation to Hungary

In the summer of 1959, Xi Zhongxun accompanied Zhou Enlai (wearing cap) to the construction site at Beijing's Miyun reservoir

plenary sessions and executive meetings of the state council and that other issues should be reported to him, Chen Yun, Chen Yi and Xi Zhongxun.[1] On 10 May 1955, Zhou Enlai chaired a state council report meeting and decided that Xi should be responsible for affairs beyond the jurisdiction of institutions directly affiliated to the state council and other routine work; Xi Zhongxun should report comprehensive affairs to Zhou Enlai or directly instruct the departments concerned to handle such affairs.

The office of the secretary general was the operational hub of the state council. In accordance with Zhou Enlai's wishes and the working realities of the state council, Xi Zhongxun formulated a series of rules and regulations to standardise the activities of government offices to ensure their effective operation. On 16 November 1954, Xi chaired the first state council secretary general meeting to establish systems for the official organs of the state council. He determined to hold secretary general office meetings each Friday and set up a confidential office in charge of receiving, dispatching, classifying, circulating, filing and printing telegrams and documents of the premier, vice premiers and secretary general.

From 1954 until early 1956, Xi Zhongxun chaired 35 secretary general meetings, made practical and feasible regulations and formulated various rules and regulations concerning the functional spheres, organisation, leadership coordination, work plans, inspections and summaries of more than 10 units – including the secretariat, the national government offices administration, the state administration of foreign experts affairs, the legislative affairs office, the state archives administration, the state administration of press, publications, radio, film and television, the state personnel bureau, the state administration for religious affairs, the state meteorological bureau, the national administration of surveying, mapping

Between 27 August and 11 September 1959, Xi Zhongxun, vice premier of the state council, headed a Chinese government delegation to the Soviet Union and Czechoslovakia. This picture shows the party at Kiev airport

Xi Zhongxun heads cadres of the state's central organs to harvest wheat with members of the Red Star people's commune in the outskirts of Beijing, June 1960

and geoinformation, the advisory office, the research institute of culture and history, the confidential communications bureau, the bureau for external cultural relations, the state language reform committee, the organisation and wage committee office and the administration of workers going abroad – so as to ensure the precise, effective, standard and orderly operation of the routine work of the state council.

To mark the 10th anniversary of the new China, the state planned to construct 10 major buildings in the capital. In 1958, the relevant state council department selected a site in Fuyou Street. After seeing the programme, Zhou Enlai put the idea to Xi Zhongxun. "The Great Hall of the People is a place for the people's representatives to discuss state affairs," said Xi. "It is necessary to build it. Zhongnanhai used to be the office of Yuan Shih-kai and Tuan Chi-jui.[2] We can use it as an office building after some refurbishment.

So there is no need to build a new one. Furthermore, building a new office block would require the demolition of people's homes." Zhou Enlai was in agreement, adding later that he would not build an office building for the state council in his tenure.[3]

In those years, Xi Zhongxun was extremely busy with his work. Arrangements for meetings and activities, checking name lists of visiting delegates, optimising departmental structures, formulating the national economic plan and handling important foreign events all involved the direction and participation of Xi Zhongxun. Managing human resources was another of his duties. In the three years of natural disasters, he instructed the national government offices administration to select wasteland in the suburbs of Beijing and turn it into farmland for the ministries and commissions. By turning this land to productive use, for cultivation and raising livestock, the ministries and commissions won the support of both cadres and workers. The approach of having farms run by offices was quickly promoted in the ministries and commissions of the central government, the provinces and the cities. Afterwards, however, when Xi discovered that the practice impaired the interests of farmers in some areas, he suggested the central government terminate this provisional measure.

Chapter 25

Premier Zhou Enlai's 'Minister of Internal Affairs'

In assisting Premier Zhou Enlai for a decade, Xi Zhongxun poured most of his energy into united front work. When Xi took office in the government administration council, Premier Zhou planned for him to also take on the post of minister of foreign affairs. Unexpectedly, Xi firmly refused, saying half-jokingly and half-seriously: "I wouldn't work as minister of foreign affairs even if you expelled me from party membership." He told Zhou, cordially: "However, I can serve as minister of internal affairs and assist you in the united front work." Zhou Enlai knew that Xi Zhongxun was experienced in united front work and had profound insight into ethnic and religious affairs. So he asked Xi Zhongxun to contact 'democratic figures' and do more work.

Going back to the days of the war of resistance against Japan, Xi Zhongxun was fond of telling an anecdote to explain the united front work. One day, when he had a meal with cadres in charge of the united front work, Xi talked about the principle of this work in the context of the stories in the historical novel *The Romance of the Three Kingdoms*. He said, the fact that Zhuge Liang, a brilliant military strategist and statesman in the Three Kingdoms period, dispatched Guan Yu to block Cao Cao's path even though he had known that Guan Yu would set Cao Cao free, was actually a united front problem because if Cao Cao were killed, the Kingdom of Wu would conquer the weak Kingdom of Shu. He went on to say that Liu Bei failed because he persisted in sectarianism and trusted only in his sworn friends, meaning that there were no senior generals in the Kingdom of Shu to help him, thereby leaving him with no choice but to dispatch the mediocre Liao Hua as the vanguard.

Xi Zhongxun was one of the first party leaders to study ethnic and religious issues. From the eve of the liberation of northwest China, he began to research the organisation and political power structures in regions inhabited by ethnic groups.

In managing the fight in northwest China, one of Xi's greatest contributions was to cope with various complicated national problems and bring about a national unity that had never been achieved for thousands of years.

A number of ethnic minorities, including Kazaks, Tibetans and Mongolians, lived at the foot of the Altun mountains, on the borders of Gansu, Qinghai and Xinjiang. For historical reasons, many large-scale clashes and even wars broke out to contend for the pasturelands. After conducting research to understand the situation, Xi Zhongxun proposed the creation of the Kazak autonomous county of Aksay in Gansu province in accordance with the situation of the nationality and population distribution so that longstanding ethnic conflicts could be resolved and allowing the

Xi Zhongxun, Deng Baoshan (back row, second from right) and Yu Xinqing (back row, far right) stay with local cadres and ordinary people in Gansu's Aksay Kazak autonomous county, September 1958. Third from left back row is the county magistrate Shahai Dula

Kazak people to live and work in peace in this beautiful area. In 1954, Gansu established the only ethnic minority autonomous county where Kazaks were the main nationality. During a visit to northwest China in 1958, Xi started out purposefully from Lanzhou and came to the far-off Aksay to meet Kazak compatriots. The county magistrate Shahai Dula was moved to tears.

In the 1950s, Xi Zhongxun participated in research programmes on the establishment of ethnic minority autonomous regions. In 1953, the central government authorised Deng Xiaoping, Li Weihan, Ulan-Fu, Xi Zhongxun, Burhan Shahidi and Seypidin Eziz to research a programme on setting up an autonomous region in Xinjiang. Ultimately, the question was whether to create one, two or three autonomous regions in Xinjiang, which covered one-sixth of the national land area. They disagreed on issues including territorial scope and name. Mao Zedong asked Xi Zhongxun to air his view

Xi Zhongxun, Chen Yi (fifth from left), Li Weihan (third from right), Wang Feng (far left) and the 10th Panchen Lama Erdeni Choekyi Gyaltsen (fifth from right) attend a banquet, January 1960

on the question of autonomy of northwestern regions inhabited by ethnic groups. A consensus was reached thanks to the joint efforts of Xi Zhongxun and other leaders in this project resulting in the successful establishment of Xinjiang Uygur autonomous region in 1955.

The central government designated Chen Yi, Li Weihan, Ulan-Fu and Xi Zhongxun to research, formulate and implement the creation of Ningxia Hui autonomous region, which was eventually founded in 1958. With careful and meticulous work, the administrative division of Ningxia was finally settled.

As Premier Zhou Enlai's 'minister of internal affairs', Xi Zhongxun participated in united front work policy research and in the settlement of many vital issues. Xi was good at uniting and working with non-party people. They treated each other like sworn brothers, working together through both good times and bad.

Xi Zhongxun and Zhang Zhizhong were "a model of relationships between party and non-party members". Xi showed great respect for Zhang and often sought his opinion when they worked together in the northwest military and administrative committee. Not only did Xi Zhongxun fully delegate responsibility to Zhang Zhizhong for his designated tasks, but whenever they returned to the northwest after attending CPG meetings together, on each occasion Xi asked Zhang to convey important decisions or thinking of the central government. Whenever Zhang departed from or returned to Xi'an, Xi was there to meet him or see him off at the airport or railway station. At that time, whenever mentioning Chiang Kai-shek in compiling reports or publishing articles, Zhang Zhizhong would refer to him as "Mr". Once, a comrade in charge of *The Masses Daily* took a final proof of the newspaper to ask Xi Zhongxun what needed to be changed. Xi made explicit instructions to respect the will of Mr Zhang Zhizhong and not to change a single word. After working in Beijing, Zhang would talk with Xi about his suggestions for the party and the government.

Fu Zuoyi and Xi Zhongxun also had mutual respect and established close contact. Whenever Fu's peaches ripened in early summer, he would pick a basketful and send them to Xi. At the weekend, Xi often took his children to visit Fu. Qi Qiaoqiao, Xi Zhongxun's daughter, can still remember the happy times she spent in Fu Zuoyi's home. In 1957, Fu was hospitalised due to a heart attack, and Xi went to visit him frequently and asked him to

Xi Zhongxun, Zhang Zhizhong (third from right), Zhang Zhizhong's wife Hong Xihou (far right), Jia Tuofu (second from left), Yang Mingxuan (far left), Zhang Jiafu (fifth from left) and Wang Yixia (third from left) visit the mausoleum of the first Qin emperor in the spring of 1952. The girl in the arms of Xi Zhongxun is Qi Qiaoqiao

keep calm, concentrate on the treatment and forget about his work at the ministry of water resources. Whenever comrades from the ministry came to report to the state council, Xi always enquired after Fu Zuoyi's health. In early 1962, Xi made a report to Zhou Enlai and arranged for Fu Zuoyi and his family to recuperate in Conghua, Guangdong province, which is famous for its hot springs.

General Deng Baoshan was a loyal friend of the CPC. He met Xi Zhongxun in Suide during the war of resistance against Japan. They trusted each other and were candid in their conversations. In Zhongnanhai's Fengze garden in 1956, Deng commented to Mao Zedong that Xi was generous, good at bringing teams together and very trustworthy. Mao agreed, saying:

Ulan-Fu and Xi Zhongxun attend a celebration gala to mark the 40th anniversary of Inner Mongolia autonomous region, held between 29 July and 5 August 1987

"Your opinion is accurate. Xi's greatest attribute is to unite people from various sectors in society. He is broad-minded and can take on greater responsibilities."[1]

Years later, during the period when Xi Zhongxun was ostracised due to events arising from the novel *Liu Zhidan*, Deng Baoshan and Zhang Zhizhong spoke out boldly in his defence.

Xi Zhongxun and Ulan-Fu first met in Yan'an. Xi highly admired Ulan-Fu's outstanding contributions to the establishment of Inner Mongolia autonomous region. Before the spring festival of 1961, Ulan-Fu invited Xi Zhongxun and his wife to celebrate the holiday in Hohhot. In the early 1980s, they were both in charge of the united front work and work among the ethnic minorities.

From July to August 1987, Ulan-Fu and Xi Zhongxun, respectively as head and deputy head, led a CPC central committee delegation to participate in a series of activities celebrating the 40th anniversary of the establishment of Inner Mongolia autonomous region. Initially, the central government decided to appoint Xi Zhongxun as head, but Xi recommended that Comrade Ulan-Fu lead the delegation.

Premier Zhou Enlai's 'Minister of Internal Affairs'

Qu Wu was the mayor of Dihua (now Urumqi) when a peaceful uprising broke out in Xinjiang. Both he and Xi Zhongxun came from Shaanxi and they often joked with each other in Shaanxi dialect. They established a lifelong friendship. Once, when visiting Xi, Qu Wu said: "It's difficult to enter such an imposing dwelling!" It turned out that Qu Wu was turned away by a new guard at the gate. Xi Zhongxun lost no time in apologising to him. Years later, Xi wrote the preface for *The Collected Works of Qu Wu* entitled "The maple leaf is redder than flowers in February", in which he praised the patriotism of this revolutionary veteran.

Yu Xinqing was an assistant to the renowned patriotic general Feng Yuxiang. He once served as director of the bureau of ceremonies at the government administration council and deputy secretary general of the state council. He participated in the design and implementation of many important events such as the founding ceremony of the PRC. He worked with Xi Zhongxun for many years. During the anti-rightist movement, Yu Xinqing was not categorised as a rightist under the protection of Zhou Enlai and Xi Zhongxun but he felt very despondent about the attacks he endured. In the autumn of 1958, Xi Zhongxun made an inspection tour to northwest China. He asked Deng Baoshan, who was also a 'democratic personage', to talk with Yu Xinqing so that he could unburden himself of his troubles. However, during the Cultural Revolution (1966-1976), Yu Xinqing could not bear the humiliation and committed suicide. Xi Zhongxun was distraught. "Yu Xinqing is a senior intellectual who followed

Xi Zhongxun in Mongolian robes

Xi Zhongxun, Wang Feng (fourth from right), Wang Bingnan (far right), Qu Wu (fifth from right) and Yu Xinqing (fourth from left) in 1959

the leadership of the party. He is upright and outspoken. 'A scholar prefers death to humiliation'. How could he bear that humiliation? If I had been in Beijing and had the opportunity to reason with him, he might not have committed suicide."

The famous social activist and educator Zhang Xiruo and Xi Zhongxun were compatriots and bosom friends. In 1957, Zhang, who was noted for his outspoken comments, bluntly criticised Mao Zedong for "craving greatness, seeking quick success and instant benefits, disdaining the past and having blind faith in the future".[2] Many people were seized with anxiety for him during the anti-rightist movement, but he miraculously escaped the fate of being categorised as a rightist. It was Zhou Enlai and Xi Zhongxun who stood up for him. When Xi recollected this episode, a variety of emotions welled up in his mind. "Whenever I went to see [Zhang], he would treat me to local dishes," he recalled. "The decorated archways and walls in Beijing were dismantled. Zhang Xiruo could not accept it. Premier Zhou asked me to work on him and the only way I could console him was by saying that at least we managed to save the ancient city walls in Xi'an."

Renowned democratic personage Chen Shutong was 37 years older than Xi Zhongxun. To exchange views and ideas, Chen went to Xi Zhongxun's home. Xi was deeply moved. "I can go to see you if you want to talk with me so as to avoid the trouble of you having to come here." But Chen Shutong persisted in visiting Xi Zhongxun. "He still came to me frequently."

Sherab Gyatso, an eminent Tibetan Buddhist and a Tibetan master, and Xi Zhongxun kept a friendship despite their age difference. Xi was one of the few people to admire Sherab Gyatso during his lifetime. In trying to win round Xiang Qian, Xi entrusted Sherab Gyatso on four occasions to persuade and placate the Angla tribe. Whenever he encountered any difficulty or problem, Sherab Gyatso always consulted with Xi Zhongxun directly. Xi listened to his opinion with patience, helped him solve specific problems and praised him as "an admirable friend giving forthright advice to the CPC".

Huang Zhengqing was a brother of the fifth Living Buddha Jamyang. He served as commander of the Tibetan army in Xiahe, Gannan prefecture, was appointed by the KMT as 'major general in command of public

Xi Zhongxun, Sherab Gyatso, chairman of the Chinese Buddhist association (second from right) and Zhao Puchu, vice chairman of the association (far right) talking cordially on 18 February 1962

Huang Zhengqing and Xi Zhongxun greet each other warmly in the Shenzhen Guesthouse orchid garden, 25 January 1997

security' during the war of resistance against Japan and was later elected as candidate member of the KMT central committee. Before Lanzhou was liberated in 1949, Huang led his troops in revolt, treated Xi Zhongxun like an old friend at their first meeting in Lanzhou and regarded Xi as "a family member in the mind of Tibetan compatriots".[3] Xi knew Huang well and completely trusted him. In the spring of 1953, the Taiwan authorities parachuted a certificate of appointment to major general Huang Zhengqing and urged him to participate in the armed rebellions of Ma Liang's troops, the remnants of the defeated troops of Ma Bufang in Linxia. Xi Zhongxun still trusted Huang and appointed him as deputy general of the bandit suppression headquarters. When Huang left Xi'an and rushed to the front, Xi presented a valuable handgun given by He Long to Huang Zhengqing and said to him: "We have worked together for years. I know you well and trust you. Hereafter, let me know if anything happens at any time. No matter what happens or what others say, you don't need to worry about it." Huang lived up to Xi's expectations, commanded the troops in the military region of Gansu province and quickly quelled the rebellions. Huang Zhengqing

Shang Xiaoyun, Tian Han, Mei Lanfang and Xi Zhongxun (from left to right, front row) and young actors of Shaanxi opera research institute, November 1958

was appointed governor of Gannan Tibetan autonomous region in 1950 and was awarded the military rank of major general in 1955. He made a great contribution to ethnic unity in Gannan and the socialist construction of Gansu province. Their friendship was renewed and cherished increasingly as the years went by. In his twilight years, when he knew that his days might be numbered, Huang travelled all the way to visit Xi Zhongxun, saying it was "his life's greatest wish".[4]

Xi Zhongxun attached importance to culture and art and he was a close friend of many literary figures and artists. Famous Beijing opera artists Mei Lanfang, Shang Xiaoyun, Cheng Yanqiu and Xun Huisheng, Shaoxing opera artist Yuan Xuefen, Yu opera artist Chang Xiangyu, Cantonese opera singer Hung Sin-nui, Shanxi opera singer Wang Tianmin, singers Guo Lanying, Wang Kun and Wang Yuzhen and playwrights Cao Yu and Ouyang Shanzun all established deep friendships with Xi Zhongxun.

In the early summer of 1956, Mei Lanfang was invited to perform in

Japan. But he was resolutely opposed to performing for the Japanese during the war of resistance against Japan and was scrupulous about visiting the country. Entrusted by Premier Zhou Enlai, Xi Zhongxun succeeded in persuading Mei to help heal relations between the two peoples by putting on an opera performance and helped him set up a high-calibre Beijing opera delegation.

After the Cultural Revolution, Mei's family unsuccessfully claimed the return of his paintings, calligraphy and antiques that were taken from him during those years; more than 200 letters of appeal went unanswered.

Xi Zhongxun (second from right, middle row), his wife Qi Xin (third from right, front row), Yang Mingxuan (fifth from right front row), Zhao Shoushan (second from right front row), Huang Zhengqing (far right, front row), Yu Xinqing (third from right, middle row), Zhao Boping (fourth from right, middle row), Pan Zili (far right, middle row), Wang Bingnan (fifth from right, middle row), Shen Yanbing (far right, back row), Zhou Erfu (second from right, back row), Cao Yu (third from right, back row) and Qu Wu (fourth from right, back row) at the Summer Palace in the spring of 1960

Later on, the Mei Lanfang memorial hall was set up at the suggestion of Xi Zhongxun and many of Mei's paintings, calligraphy and antiques were displayed there.[5] On 27 October 1986, Xi Zhongxun personally inaugurated the memorial hall.

Shang Xiaoyun, one of the four biggest Beijing opera stars of that era, was celebrated for his generosity in aiding the needy and for investing his assets in running schools. At the suggestion of Xi Zhongxun in 1959, Shang Xiaoyun moved his family to Shaanxi, which caused a sensation in arts circles.[6] Shang took on the role of general arts director of Shaanxi Opera School and the first principal of Shaanxi Opera House and made vital contributions to the cause of Shaanxi opera. He donated 66 paintings, calligraphic works and jade pieces that he had collected over a number of years to Shaanxi museum and gave practical support to the cultural development of western China. Xi Zhongxun also instructed the Shaanxi authorities to shoot a film about opera. Regrettably, Xi Zhongxun was unable to watch the art film with Shang Xiaoyun because of Xi's disappearance from public life as a result of events arising from the novel *Liu Zhidan*. By the time Xi resumed public duties 16 years later, Shang had passed away.

Xi Zhongxun watching children at play

Xi Zhongxun proposes a toast to foreign guests at a banquet to celebrate international working women's day in Beijing, 8 March 1962. The woman on the left is Cai Chang, chairperson of the All-China Women's Federation

The art film was to prove the swansong of the opera master.

In the early stages of the war to resist US aggression and aid Korea, Xi Zhongxun enthusiastically supported Chang Xiangyu's idea to 'donate' an airplane. In a letter to Xi, Chang wrote: "These glories are the result of the education and help given by the party and you. On the eve of national day, I convey my sincere thanks to you and assure you that we will definitely redouble our efforts to complete the glorious task of making this donation." Whenever Chang went to Beijing, Xi Zhongxun and his wife Qi Xin would invite her home to dinner and cook her favourite spinach soup and congee.

When he was snowed under with work, Xi would ask his wife to take care of and visit some 'democratic figures' and old artists on his behalf. "When their families needed help while Comrade Zhongxun could not spare the time," Qi Xin recalled, "he would ask me to give a hand. For instance, when Xun Huisheng's wife became ill, Comrade Zhongxun asked me to see her on his behalf."

Xi Zhongxun's daughter Qi Qiaoqiao can still remember her father's busy days and frequent conversations when she was young. She once asked him whether it was revolutionary work to talk with others. "Revolutionary work is to unite others," Xi Zhongxun told her.[7]

Qi Xin meets Mei Baojiu, the son of Mei Lanfang and Tu Zhen, wife of Mei Shaowu, who was the second son of Mei Lanfang, in 2006

Chapter 26

Declaration of Endowed Military Commands

On the afternoon of 27 September 1955, the PLA military rank and medal-conferring ceremonies were held in Zhongnanhai's Huairentang hall and the auditorium of the state council.

The title-conferring ceremony began at 2.30pm. The secretary general of the state council, Xi Zhongxun, read out the order of the premier of the PRC's state council to confer military titles on military officers of the

Xi Zhongxun confers military titles on PLA officers and generals

Declaration of Endowed Military Commands

PLA. Premier Zhou Enlai conferred the order certificates of senior general, general, lieutenant general and major general on the generals and officers in Beijing, one by one.

The ceremony to confer military titles and medals on the supreme commanders was held afterwards in the Huairentang hall. Mao Zedong personally conferred the commissioning certificates and three class-one medals on the supreme commanders, including Zhu De and Peng Dehuai, who attended the commissioning ceremony.

Xi Zhongxun read out the commissioning order on behalf of the state council. It was his responsibility to do so as secretary general of the state council, but was particularly appropriate because of his deep contacts with the people's army. He threw himself into military affairs at 17, led and launched the Liangdang mutiny at 19, participated in establishing the Northwest Red Army and was one of the founders and leaders of the Shaanxi-Gansu border region revolutionary base.

In establishing the Shaanxi-Gansu border region revolutionary base, Xi Zhongxun personally led the creation of the first, third, fifth, seventh, ninth and 11th branches of the region's guerrilla force and the guerrillas in the counties of Ansai, Heshui, Bao'an, Zhongyi and Pingzi. He also fought in scores of battles and was wounded on a number of occasions. The main forces of the Red Army, namely the interim general headquarters of the Shaanxi-Gansu border region Red Army, redesignated as advocated by Xi Zhongxun as the 26th Red Army rebuilt on this basis, formed part of what would later become the 11th PLA infantry division.

During the agrarian revolutionary war (July 1927-July 1937), Xi Zhongxun was appointed political instructor of the second branch of the Weibei guerrilla forces, political commissar of the first branch of the Weibei guerrilla forces, secretary of Shaanxi-Gansu border region CPC special military committee, political commissar of the headquarters of the Shaanxi-Gansu border region guerrilla forces and team party secretary of the general headquarters of the second guerrilla forces. During the war of resistance against Japan, he served as political commissar of Guanzhong security headquarters, political commissar of Suide garrison headquarters, political commissar of the interim headquarters of Yetai mountain counterattacks and deputy political commissar of Shaanxi-Gansu-Ningxia-Shanxi-Suide joint defence troop. In the war of liberation, he was deputy political commissar of the Northwest Field Army and the First Field Army, and political commissar of Shaanxi-Gansu-Ningxia-Shanxi-Suide joint defence forces, the joint defence military region and the First Field Army (northwest military region). As a result of his abundant experience of battle, he grew to be an outstanding ideological and political leader and an excellent political instructor. He played a key role in various historic achievements, such as the founding and rectification of the Shaanxi-Gansu guerrilla forces, the restoration and rebuilding of the main forces of the Northwest Red Army, the attrition struggles, the northern Shaanxi campaign and the liberation of the great northwest.

During the war of liberation, Xi Zhongxun, together with Zhang Zongxun, Wang Shitai, Peng Dehuai and He Long, commanded a substantial number of cavalry and infantry to fight in northern Shaanxi, safeguard Chairman Mao and the CPC central committee, retake Yan'an, liberate Xi'an and Lanzhou, advance to Xinjiang and achieve brilliant victories in defeating enemy troops with forces inferior in both number and strength.

Xi Zhongxun chats with officers and soldiers, 1980. Fourth from left is Wu Kehua, commander of Guangzhou military region

Declaration of Endowed Military Commands

Xi receives representatives of the national security guard work conference, December 1983

After the founding of the new China, leaders who had served with distinction in the revolutionary wars, such as Xi Zhongxun, Deng Xiaoping, Deng Zihui, Zhang Dingcheng and Tan Zhenlin, were not conferred military titles because they did not hold military posts at the time. But history offered Xi Zhongxun the special honour of reading out the order to confer military titles on PLA officers and soldiers on behalf of the state council.

On the occasion marking the 100th birthday of Xi Zhongxun in October 2013, a docudrama reflecting his epic revolutionary life was broadcast. People were astonished to watch these previously unseen historical film archives in colour. The film was salvaged by chief choreographer Xia Meng from video footage that had been collecting dust in a central government building for 58 years. Viewers were able to witness the heroic achievements of Xi Zhongxun in those years and to witness these solemn moments as bright as shining stars.

Chapter 27

Establishing the State Council Petition System

Xi Zhongxun always retained the qualities of a real working person. He valued the letters and visits of the people and regarded it as an important task of the party and the government to listen to their appeals and keep close ties with them.

In 1954, the complaint letter and request handling office was set up under the leadership of Premier Zhou Enlai with Xi Zhongxun in charge of day-to-day operations. Its purpose was to handle the complaint letters and requests of the people. From its inception, the work of complaint processing by the state council started to be put on the right track and formalised.

Ma Yongshun, director of the state council's complaint letter and request handling office, recalled that "Xi Zhongxun attached great value to the problems reflected by the people through their complaint letters and visits. We sent him the 'summary reports' of important complaint letters, the 'contact reports' of visiting complainants, and the composite reports, which he then either instructed the relevant departments or the relevant provincial or municipal authorities to deal with, or instructed us to handle directly. He never treated the problems reflected by the people as 'trifling' or turned his back on them."[1]

Even if he was very busy, Xi Zhongxun would spare the time to handle important complaint letters and personal visits and set a good example in how to receive people. On 30 December 1954, Xi wrote special reports to Mao Zedong and Zhou Enlai on the problems concerning rural work that were raised in the complaint letters and visits of people from northwestern China. When he drew up the report, he asked his secretary to include the real examples of everyday people. When he reviewed one report, he frowned unconsciously and asked why the secretary did not mention the

Establishing the State Council Petition System

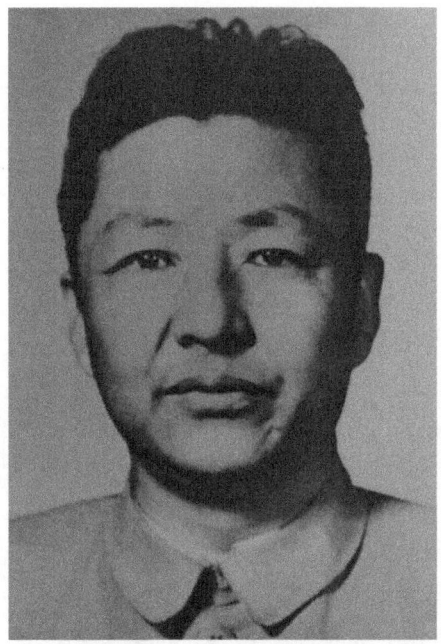

Xi Zhongxun when he was vice premier and secretary general of the state council

dissatisfaction of the people facing inadequate supplies of edible oil. The secretary replied awkwardly that the people had originally spoken in a vulgar manner and asked whether the specific cases could be omitted. Xi Zhongxun insisted on "reporting the realities to Chairman Mao".[2] In one case, a farmer mentioned a jingle, "200g of edible oil reminds me of Chiang Kai-shek"; in another case, a farmer ran a transportation business with a fleet of wooden-wheeled vehicles whose axles squeaked endlessly for lack of lubricating oil. The driver became angry and cursed: "I have no edible oil for eating. And yet you want lubricating oil!" After uttering these words, he relieved himself against the wheels of the vehicle. The report received the attention of the central government. Mao Zedong and Zhou Enlai personally approved and forwarded the report to relevant departments.

From start to finish, Xi Zhongxun was always mindful of the common people. Some wrote letters stating that they didn't earn enough to save any money, while others knelt in front of cadres and beseeched them bitterly; several even committed suicide by throwing themselves into wells because they were unable to purchase a government loan. After reading such letters, Xi Zhongxun pounded the table, jumped to his feet and shouted angrily: "If we party cadres stand opposed to the people, you should expect the people to whip you with their shoulder poles!"

At the suggestion of Xi Zhongxun, the first national complaint letter and request-handling working conference was convened on 31 May 1957 jointly by the general office of the CPC central committee and the state council secretariat. Xi seriously criticised instances of poor practice among central organs and the localities, including the negligence of cadres, serious bureaucratism, the blind copying and forwarding of complaint letters, the mismanagement of miscopied letters and the hasty and evasive handling of letters. He blamed the changing ideology of cadres, their distance from the people and their indifference to their plight. As an example, he cited a plan by the state bureau of surveying and mapping to build houses in Xi'an and demolish nearly four hectares of ripening wheat. Even though the land was bought, the people were still angry about the acquisition and even cursed: "What sort of a party is the communist party!" He believed that the work of complaint letters and request handling reflected the internal conflicts of the people and that "it was an important political task rather than trifling, ordinary work".

He came up with six requirements to properly handle complaint letters and visits:

1) Every provincial, municipal and autonomous region party and government leadership must have one person dedicated to handling complaint letters and requests; 2) those responsible should address the problems proactively rather than passively; 3) practice the method of combining the efforts of professional institutions with 'everyone lending a hand' and some cadres from institutions should be willing to devote their spare time to the task; 4) complaint letters and requests should be treated by the central government or local institutions according to the nature of the problems highlighted in order to

Xi Zhongxun in Zhongnanhai in the 1950s

Establishing the State Council Petition System

Xi Zhongxun delivers a speech at a state council conference, 1958

avoid blind copying and forwarding; 5) some cadres should be dispatched to make a breakthrough in resolving longstanding cases that were either not forwarded or remained unsettled after forwarding; 6) penalties should be imposed on cadres in line with the cadre management authorities.

The six requirements became the fundamental criteria of the complaint letter and request-handling system of the state council, which vigorously promoted systemised and standardised working procedures that are still relevant today.

Chapter 28

Keeping a Clear Head Amid the Frenzy of the Great Leap Forward

In May 1958, the second session of the eighth NPC passed the general line of "Going all out, aiming high and doing more, faster, better, cheaper to build socialism". As a consequence, the 'Great Leap Forward' campaign came into being. The practices of setting unrealistic production targets, issuing confused orders and egalitarianism in the name of communism as well as the tendency to boast and exaggerate prevailed throughout society.

Xi Zhongxun and Peng Dehuai (left) visit the suburbs of Zhengzhou, April 1958

In late April 1958, Xi Zhongxun and Peng Dehuai accompanied Zhou Enlai to investigate the realities of industrial and agricultural production in Henan province. In the upsurge of the Great Leap Forward, and entrusted by Zhou Enlai, Xi Zhongxun headed a team to carry out two grassroots surveys. They reflected the realities and problems to the CPC central committee and the state council and provided a valuable basis for the central government to rectify 'leftist' practices and adopt measures to overcome the difficulties.

The first survey was conducted between September and October 1958, when Xi Zhongxun led an investigation team to survey five provinces and regions in northwest China. On the one hand, he saw the enthusiasm of the masses to eradicate poverty and backwardness. On the other hand, he discovered serious problems with the Great Leap Forward. For example, the land in Liquan county, Shaanxi province, was covered in mounds. "What are these for?" he asked. He was told it was the "invention" of scientists from Beijing, who had come up with a new method of cultivation

Xi Zhongxun makes a speech to state council cadres transferred to work in Pucheng county, Shaanxi and to local students, 5 September 1958

Xi Zhongxun returned to his hometown in Fuping county, 6-7 September 1958. This photo shows Xi surrounded by cadres of county-level institutions on the morning of 7 September

Xi Zhongxun returns to his home village of Dancun, Fuping county, 7 September 1958

Keeping a Clear Head Amid the Frenzy of the Great Leap Forward

Xi Zhongxun flanked by Deng Baoshan (right), governor of Gansu province, and Yu Xinqing, deputy secretary general of the state council, in Dunhuang's Mogao Grotto, September 1958

to boost productivity by increasing the surface area of earth exposed to the sun. He squatted on the ground, pushed the mound aside with his hands and saw the extremely weak roots of the grain seedlings. He frowned and asked: "How can you boost productivity with sunshine but without soil and manure?"

Xi Zhongxun was very apprehensive about a project to divert water from the Taohe river to the mountains in Gansu province, which was started during the Great Leap Forward. The project planned to divert water a distance of more than 1,000km from the Taohe in Minxian county, Longnan, to Qingyang in Longdong. At that time, senior Gansu leaders suggested irrigating the land by building the world's first canal in a mountainous area on which boats could sail. As a by-product, electricity could be generated by making use of the locks that would be needed to regulate water levels over such an undulating terrain. Xi saw tens of thousands of farmers dig the mountains with pickaxes and transport stones and rubble with wheelbarrows; the only advanced tool they used was an iron-chain pulley used to transport heavy materials up the mountain. The workers toiled hard day and night but productivity was extremely low. Xi realised that, given the large workforce devoted to this construction project, agricultural production would be severely affected in an area where the harvest was not good even in bumper years. What worried him more was that the Gansu authorities falsely stated a grain output increase of 1.5m tonnes. "It won't do!" he told comrades in charge of Gansu provincial party committee. "Ordinary people will suffer losses from it in future!"

In Dunhuang, Gansu province, Xi Zhongxun expressed clear doubts about a policy to give away free supplies of 10 essential products and services within the county covering 'food, clothing, shelter, transportation, birth, old age, illness and death, kindergartens and schools'. However, the comrades in charge of Gansu provincial party committee insisted on following this course of action. A heated argument broke out. Xi Zhongxun also discovered similar problems in Qinghai and Ningxia.

Xi Zhongxun and his old friend Deng Baoshan, who was the governor of Gansu province, held an in-depth talk. Deng was frank about the many problems that existed, including the tendency of farmers to beg. He was also worried about the Taohe river water diversion project. Looking at Deng, whom he knew deeply, Xi Zhongxun encouraged him to speak out. "You have direct access to the highest authorities," he argued. "You can directly report your misgivings to the Chairman!"²

Xi Zhongxun visits Ningxia Hui autonomous region, October 1958

Xi Zhongxun with miners on a visit to Shizuishan, Ningxia province, in October 1958

Xi Zhongxun was deeply worried about many aspects of the Great Leap Forward on his trip to northwest China. After returning to Beijing, he reported to Premier Zhou Enlai and the CPC central committee on 6 November 1958: "At present, most of the main forces of the party committees at all levels are busy with iron and steelmaking," he said. "What remains in question is how best to formulate the new production plans and how to ensure a doubling of agricultural production next year. On these issues, we are in a race against time. Otherwise, agricultural production next year could be seriously affected." He also offered his advice on industrial production. "As the iron and steelmaking campaign develops, the labour forces of these industries should be gradually professionalised. Provinces or special regions should set up iron and steel industry bases step by step in favourable locations, with abundant supplies of iron ore deposits, coal and water so that backward, traditional Chinese furnaces can be replaced by advanced Western ones and other industries can be driven by the steel industry. This is the way to reduce waste in the workforce, enhance technology, quality and labour efficiency, and foster the logistics to support large-scale industry."

Between November and December 1958, Xi Zhongxun attended the plenary session of the political bureau of the CPC central committee and the sixth session of the eighth NPC in Wuchang. In discussing the *Resolution on Issues Concerning People's Communes*, he considered his visit to northwest China and delivered a speech. "The so-called 'large in size and collective in nature' of the people's communes should not lead to communes becoming so big that there is only one commune in each county, and nor should they offer free supplies for everything, turn collective ownership into ownership by the entire people, leap forward from socialism to communism or replace distribution according to one's work with distribution according to one's needs."

His concerns proved justified. In the spring of 1959, temporary grain shortages occurred and became severe in Gansu province, which led to starvation. On the instructions of Zhou Enlai, Xi Zhongxun immediately

Xi Zhongxun and cadres from Anyang (Henan) municipal authorities, May 1959

Xi Zhongxun inspects a steelmaking plant in Jiaozuo, Henan province, May 1959

called on comrades in charge of the ministries of food, internal affairs, railways and communications to hold a meeting and urgently dispatched food aid from Shaanxi, Ningxia and Sichuan.

After asking Zhou Enlai for instructions in mid- and late April 1959, Xi called on the comrades in charge of the 11 provinces stricken by serious disaster to attend a meeting in Beijing in the name of the state council. "Delegates from all provinces made reports at the meeting and voiced their different viewpoints," recalled Ma Yongshun. "The representatives of most provinces verified that problems such as edema (a swelling that is caused by fluid trapped in the body's tissues) and death did occur... The reporting continued all day long. When the meeting was about to end, Xi Zhongxun asked them to promptly make an abstract of their reports by the end of that day. After this had been done, Xi handed the abstracts to the premier, who issued prompt instructions. The premier had shown the reports to Chairman Mao and forwarded them to these disaster-stricken provinces. From then on, the premier asked us to write a report every 10 days. Xi Zhongxun also instructed us to reflect the conditions and make summaries frequently. Much attention was paid to such problems! At that time we felt that if these leaders had relaxed their vigilance even a little bit, there could have been even more deaths."[3]

At the first session of the second NPC in April 1959, Xi Zhongxun was appointed as vice premier and secretary general of the state council.

A month later, confronted with evidence of increasingly serious problems, Xi Zhongxun led an investigation team to Henan and Shaanxi provinces. In late May, 1959, they fully acquainted themselves with the problems related to the quantity and quality of pig iron production in Henan. In early June, they transferred from Henan to Shaanxi and inspected working conditions in Zhouzhi, Huxian, Tongchuan, Lintong and Weinan counties. They familiarised themselves with the details of the conditions in rural areas, held two symposiums with leaders of Shaanxi provincial party committee, delivered reports to cadres of above bureau level and convened

Xi Zhongxun makes a visit to Anyang, Henan province, May 1959

Xi Zhongxun hosts the naming ceremony of the Sino-Czech Friendship factory in Shenyang, 4 May 1960

a symposium of 'democratic figures'. That was the second special survey on the Great Leap Forward.

After returning to Beijing, Xi Zhongxun immediately arranged for the secretariat to summarise and classify the survey results in combination with the complaint letters and requests of the people. He found that the problems related to several points: the conditions to establish people's communes were immature and their development advanced too urgently and too intensely; the practice of eating for free did not conform to the principle of distribution according to work; the slogan 'steelmaking by the whole people' was incorrect and there needed to be political and economic accountability; the principle of 'simultaneously developing five things' was changed to 'simultaneously fixing a hundred broken things'; the policy of 'walking on two legs' was changed to the guideline of 'walking on more legs'.

Between 2 July and 16 August 1959, the plenary session of the political bureau of the CPC central committee and the eighth plenary session of the eighth NPC were convened in Lushan, Jiangxi province. They became known as the Lushan conference. Materials classified by the secretariat and arranged by Xi Zhongxun were delivered to Zhou Enlai, forwarded to Mao Zedong, and distributed as brief reports of the conference. Xi Zhongxun had hoped that the original 'discussion meeting' would unify the whole party in wanting to rectify 'leftism' but it backfired due to a letter written by Peng Dehuai to Mao Zedong. The second half of the conference focused on criticising the 'anti-party clique headed by Peng Dehuai'. Xi Zhongxun's heart was weighed down with anxiety.

As the Great Leap Forward gathered momentum, Xi Zhongxun maintained his concern for the real lives of the people. In June 1959, many in Gansu province continued to write letters about the problem of food scarcity. On 26 June, Ma Yongshun presented a letter with a 'food' package mailed by one of the masses to Xi Zhongxun. Xi read the letter, carefully examined the contents, exerted great effort in breaking the

Xi Zhongxun heads a central government inspection team to Changge county, Henan province, between April and May 1961. Xi is pictured with cadres of the Changge county authorities

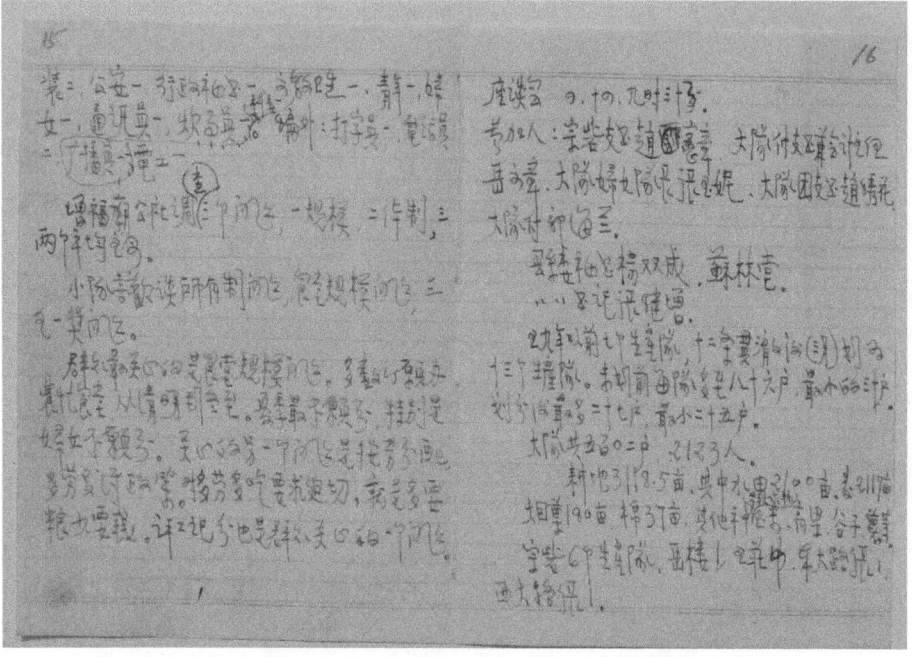

Excerpts from Xi Zhongxun's notes on the visit to Changge county

food with his hands and tried to taste it. "How is this food fit for human consumption?!" he said disgustedly. The first thing the next morning, he dispatched two cadres to undertake a field survey in Gansu and deal with the problem.

To implement *The 60 Articles on Agriculture* and rectify the tendency towards exaggeration triggered by the Great Leap Forward, Xi Zhongxun headed an inspection team under the unified deployment of the central government to Changge county, Henan province, in early April 1961. He made elaborate written reports to the general secretary of the CPC central committee, Deng Xiaoping, and to the CPC central committee on 23 April and 9 May 1961. "The present situation shows that the canteen can no longer be run and that grain should be distributed directly to each household," he stated. "It is an effective measure to rapidly turn around the difficult situation in the rural areas."

Changge county had been praised by Mao Zedong for deeply turning

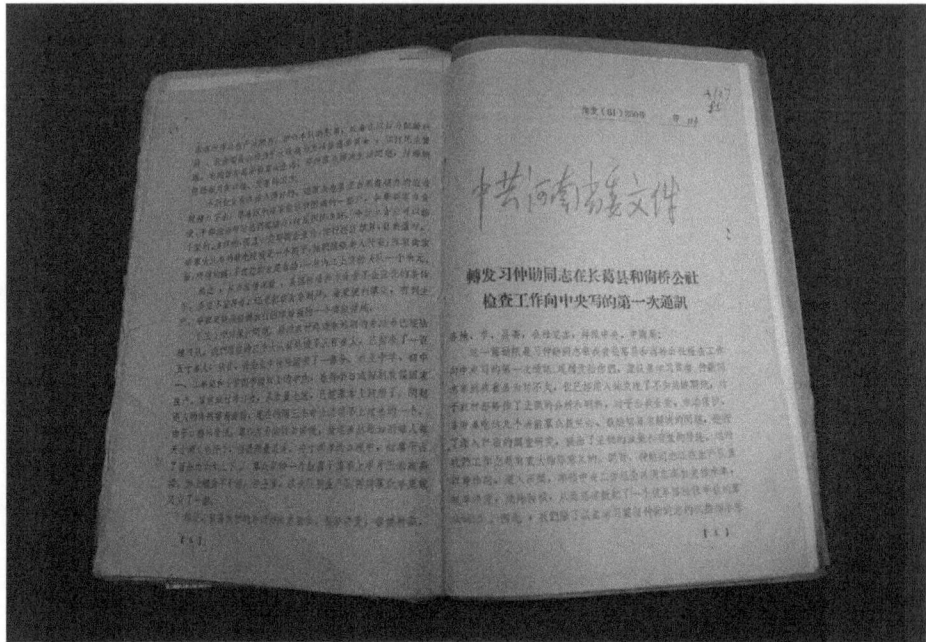

The documents submitted to the Henan provincial party committee regarding Xi Zhongxun's inspection reports on Changge county and Shangqiao commune on 25 April 1961

over the soil. Due to the 'tendency towards boasting and exaggeration', the newly constructed county was inspired by the example of Chang'an Street in Beijing to build an auditorium that was as magnificent as the Great Hall of the People. But it meant that local people had to live on dried sweet potatoes, edible wild herbs and leaves. Xi Zhongxun was sharply critical of the situation at the plenary session of the county party committee. "It is absolutely unnecessary and better to avoid building on such a large scale and build everything new from the ground up. Can't the old county town house the county office? Comrade Mao Zedong was able to handle important affairs and rendered many services without large buildings in Yan'an." He continued: "Party members who only look after their personal interests rather than the interests of the masses are completely incompatible!"

Xi Zhongxun's two investigation reports on Changge county were

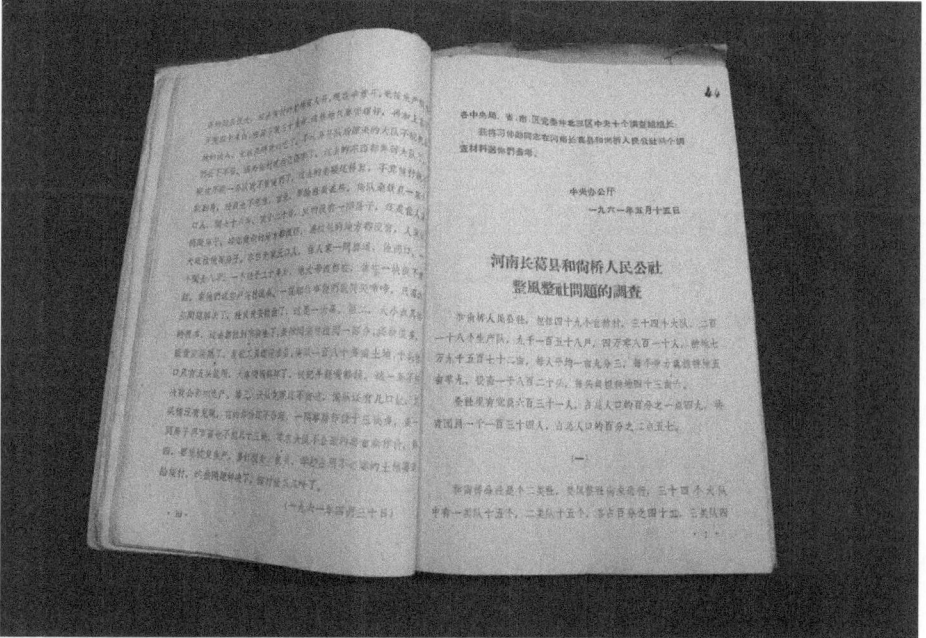

Xi Zhongxun's two inspection reports on Changge county and Shangqiao commune in Henan province submitted to the general office of the CPC central committee on 15 May 1961

highly appreciated by the CPC central committee. The general office of the CPC central committee added their own comments to the two reports and forwarded them to all party members.

Chapter 29

Protecting the Ancient City Walls of Xi'an on Three Occasions

The ancient city walls of Xi'an were expanded during the reign of Emperor Hong Wu in the Ming dynasty on the remains of the former Chang'an imperial city in the Sui and Tang dynasties (about AD1374-1378). Boasting a history of more than 600 years, the walls are the world's largest and most complete defensive structure in the cold weapons era. From the founding of the new China to the period after the Cultural Revolution, Xi Zhongxun prevented the destruction of the historic 'echo wall' on three occasions. Especially during the Great Leap Forward, he played a decisive role in protecting the city walls.

Xian's ancient city walls

A corner of Xi'an's city walls

As early as 1950, the Xi'an authorities came up with plans to dismantle the city walls. At the third collective meeting of the northwest military and administrative committee that he chaired, Xi Zhongxun said that the city walls should not be dismantled, arguing that doing so "would trigger chaos". Afterwards, the committee issued *The General Order to Prohibit Dismantling and Transporting the Masonry of the City Walls* in the name of Peng Dehuai, Xi Zhongxun and Zhang Zhizhong so that the ancient city walls of Xi'an were saved from destruction.

During the Great Leap Forward, there was growing pressure to dismantle city walls across the country. Xi'an municipal government delivered a report to dismantle its city walls to the provincial government, which approved the proposal. At that time, the city walls in Beijing, Nanjing and Kaifeng were being dismantled in quick succession. The crenels of the ancient city walls in Xi'an were almost levelled and the exterior bricks of the western part of the southern city walls had all been removed. Zhao Boping, then secretary of Shaanxi provincial party committee, called up Xi Zhongxun and advised him to prevent the Xi'an authorities from dismantling the walls.

Almost simultaneously, five figures, including Wu Bolun, a celebrated archaeologist and deputy director general of Shaanxi provincial department of culture, and Wang Hanzhang, a cadre of Shaanxi provincial documentation committee, campaigned and made appeals but without success. So they decided to bypass their immediate bosses and sent a telegram to the state council, earnestly requesting Xi Zhongxun to intervene in the dismantling of Xian's ancient city walls.

Receiving this message, Xi immediately arranged for the state council secretariat to send a telegram to the Shaanxi and Xi'an authorities ordering them to stop demolition work. He approved and forwarded the telegram to the ministry of culture to work out plans to protect the walls. On 1 July 1959, the ministry of culture submitted the *Report of the Ministry of Culture to Protect the City Walls of Xi'an.* "The city walls measure more than 3.5km from east to west and 2.5km from south to north, with a perimeter of 12.5km, a height of 10 metres, a foundation thickness of 20 metres and a width of 10 metres at the top," it stated. "In the past, it had four gates. The gate towers, ramparts and watchtowers are well preserved. The magnificent and grand architectural style is typical of a large-scale city wall in feudal society. The wall is well preserved and provides important physical evidence and a reference to researchers of urban planning, military history and of ancient building works and the arts. It is known that the city walls in Xi'an are not a hindrance to the growth of industrial construction. For this reason, the ministry of culture thinks

The Xi'an city wall ruins

Protecting the Ancient City Walls of Xi'an on Three Occasions

Xi Zhongxun visits Huaqing hot springs in Lintong, Shaanxi province, in September 1981

the city walls in Xi'an should be preserved and protected." On 22 July 1959, the state council officially issued *The Notice to Protect the City Walls of Xi'an* and made clear regulations to preserve them. On 4 March 1961, the ancient city walls in Xi'an were among the first group of national key cultural relics to be listed for protection. From then on, there was a legal basis for the protection of the ancient city walls of Xi'an.

Despite this protection order, the ancient city walls of Xi'an were severely damaged in the turmoil of the Cultural Revolution. In the winter of 1981, Xi Zhongxun read an internal reference document reporting severe damage to the walls and asked his secretary to call up the state bureau of cultural relics to deal with the matter without delay. The bureau formulated *The Advice to Enhance the Protection of the City Walls of Xi'an* on 31 December 1981 and wrote a letter to Shaanxi provincial government. In February 1983, the Xi'an city construction committee was set up, guaranteeing the protection of the city walls thereafter.

"The ancient city walls in Xi'an were badly destroyed in the Cultural Revolution," said Zhang Jinqiu, an academic at the Chinese Academy of Engineering. "At that time, many sections had collapsed, and bricks were removed to build air-raid shelters, causing many large gaps to appear in the walls. The situation was reported to Xi Zhongxun, who gave instructions to the Shaanxi and Xi'an authorities to protect the ancient city walls and carry out repairs of the destroyed sections. The ancient city walls in Xi'an were revitalised in a true sense at that point."[1]

Between the late 1980s and early 1990s, two reports on the conservation of the ancient city walls in Xi'an were given to Xi Zhongxun. He gave enthusiastic encouragement to preserve the walls, saying that China is a country with an ancient civilisation and its properties that have been handed down from previous generations must be well preserved; otherwise, foreigners would not believe in our cultural heritage if there was no material evidence of it. He also hoped the remaining gaps in the wall could be filled in. He stated that, once the connected walls were complete, they would remain historical relics for another two centuries.

Chapter 30

Appreciation of Shaanxi Opera in Beijing

Shaanxi opera is known as the 'living fossil' of Chinese opera. The 10 *Shaanxi Ballads* from *The Book of Songs* (actually a book of ancient Chinese classical poetry) and *Records*: *A Biography of Li Si* include this summary of Shaanxi opera: "Music requiring the listener to strike earthen jars, play a stringed instrument, beat on the thigh and cry is the authentic music of the Shaanxi style." It is characterised by vigour, magnificence and extreme sentimentality. The high-pitched sounds are chanted in a sonorous, unrestrained, loud and strong voice, while the quieter sounds are chanted in a soft, sweet and deeply touching voice.

Xi Zhongxun receives a Shaanxi opera troupe

In early 1942, the Guanzhong party branch supported by Xi Zhongxun set up an army opera troupe to actively create new repertoire, put on shows for the troops and the people, and even perform an excellent repertoire in Yan'an. During his time in Suide, Xi founded the Suide song and dance troupe, approved the purchase of stage property and costumes and gave special instructions to ensure performers were equipped with special shoes and socks. At that time, the song and dance troupe performed at village temple fairs, playing a leading role in cultural life and paying its way in the process. It earned as much as 1,000 silver dollars from its performances in a single season.

After liberation, the northwest military and administrative committee set up an opera improvement committee to promote and develop drama, including Shaanxi opera. In 1951, the Yisu Company, a famous professional Shaanxi opera troupe, took the lead in becoming a publicly operated opera troupe. On 13 July 1951, Xi Zhongxun attended a meeting to celebrate its transformation. "Xi Zhongxun made it clear from the outset that the Yisu Company was set up by progressive figures in the olden days and was a product of the 1911 revolution," recalled the old actor, Lei Zhenzhong. "The dramas put on by the Yisu Company were progressive, and they had an influence on my devotion to revolutionary life."[1] At that time, Xi Zhongxun was aware of the saying 'Take over Yisu Company' but he was quick to correct this view. "The Yisu Company is not a reactionary organisation," he said. "It should not be 'taken over' but 'continue to operate'. It's just that it should be well run, not badly run."[2]

During the late 1950s and early 1960s, Xi Zhongxun and several public Shaanxi figures in Beijing staged an opera gala "to promote the three major Shaanxi opera troupes in Beijing". It was a spectacular event in the history of Shaanxi opera.

In November 1958, the second troupe (youth elite troupe) of the Shaanxi traditional opera institute, the third troupe (Meiwan troupe) and the Yisu Company went to perform in Beijing. Xi Zhongxun handled many of the arrangements, including overseeing the repertoire, selecting the site and inviting distinguished guests. On the night of 9 November 1958, Xi and his compatriots Yang Mingxuan, Wang Feng and Zhang Xiruo held a special banquet in honour of the performers. Since Shaanxi opera is made up of

Xi Zhongxun and Zhang Zhizhong (second from right, front row) join members of a Shaanxi opera troupe performing *Liang Qiuyan* in Beijing, November 1958

diverse schools, there were different views on which school should perform first. Xi listened carefully to everyone's viewpoints before deciding that the first performance should be one that would make leaders in literature and art circles stand up and take notice, and that the first play should be *The Gold Hairpin* of the Wan Wan opera style because it was a daring innovation to showcase an opera style on a grand stage that originated from leather-silhouette shows. Their debut in the auditorium of the China federation of literary and art circles brought the house down.

On 12 November 1958, the drama *Three Drops of Blood* was performed in a small auditorium of the state council. Xi Zhongxun invited and accompanied the leaders of the CPC central committee, including Zhou Enlai, Zhu De and Chen Yi, to watch the performance and meet the performers. Just over a month later, on 20 December, Liu Shaoqi returned from an inspection visit to other parts of China. He had heard good reviews of *Three Drops of Blood* and invited Xi Zhongxun to accompany him to watch it in the auditorium of the ministry of public security.

The three major Shaanxi opera troupes performed in Beijing for one month, and they were a resounding success. Premier Zhou Enlai held a banquet for all the performers. Ouyang Yuqian, Mei Lanfang, Tian Han, Cao Yu and Ma Shaobo wrote articles to extol the virtues of Shaanxi opera.

Shaanxi opera artist Li Ruifang was deeply moved. "Without Xi Zhongxun, the three major Shaanxi opera troupes could not have performed in Beijing," he said. "He invited us to dinner at the Qianmen restaurant and took photographs with us, together with Mei Lanfang."³

In the autumn of 1959, at the instigation of Xi Zhongxun, the Shaanxi opera troupe again performed *Three Drops of Blood* in Beijing as well as an adaptation of *Tour on West Lake* before embarking on a tour to perform in 13 provinces and cities. These 15 performances by the three major Shaanxi opera troupes in a region south of the Yangtze river were a major cultural event.

In 1961, Xi Zhongxun invited the E'gong opera troupe from his hometown to perform in Beijing. E'gong was an ancient, traditional style

Xi Zhongxun receives actors of the E'gong opera style from his hometown, October 1961

Appreciation of Shaanxi Opera in Beijing

Xi Zhongxun and Vice Premier Chen Yi hold a banquet for the actors of the E'gong opera style of Fuping county troupe, Shaanxi province, in Beijing, October 1961

of Chinese opera. But it was very difficult for a county-level troupe to perform in Beijing. They gave more than 10 performances in Beijing, attended by Xi Zhongxun. During this time, Xi invited his townsmen to visit his home and offered them grapes grown in his courtyard. He praised the young actors and advised them to rest well, protect their voices and give good performances. He also urged them to rehearse more operas to perform in Beijing in later years.

Xi paid much attention to the innovation and development of Shaanxi opera. In the early 1980s, he eagerly told senior leaders of the Shaanxi provincial party committee that the Shanxi and Henan operas are both highly regarded, whereas Shaanxi opera deserves greater recognition as the originator of opera. On 23 September 1985, Xi watched a video recording of a large-scale Shaanxi opera called *The Emperor of the Qin Dynasty* in the state guest house. Later that year, on 5 December, this opera was performed in Beijing. On the eve of the performance, Xi made a series

Xi Zhongxun and Deng Liqun (far right) greet the performers of *The Emperor of the Qin Dynasty*

of calls to invite leaders of the CPC central committee, those in charge of the publicity department of the CPC central committee and the ministry of culture, as well as leading figures in the world of literature and the arts. The opening performance of *The Emperor of the Qin Dynasty* in Beijing was a huge success. Xi Zhongxun and the CPC central committee leaders received all the troupe staff. Xi said: "You see how wonderful our Shaanxi opera is!"

Xi Zhongxun cared about innovation in opera. On returning to Shaanxi in December 1986 to take part in events commemorating 'the Xi'an Incident' he stated that Shaanxi opera should undergo innovation without changing its original flavour.

Xi also loved other genres of drama, including Beijing opera. When he served as director of the publicity department of the CPC central committee, he led and formulated the opera reform programmes of the new China and made vital contributions to the sound growth of this art form. When he assumed the post of secretary general of the state council, he often accompanied Premier Zhou Enlai to watch operas from various areas performed in Beijing and established deep friendships with many artists. Whenever artists such as Guo Moruo, Tian Han, Xia Yan, Cao Yu, Wu Zuguang, Ouyang Yuqian, Yang Hansheng and Ma Shaobo created new works, they graciously invited Xi Zhongxun to watch the performances and were receptive to his ideas.

As the opera artist Du Jinfang recalled, in the spring of 1958, the Matsuyama ballet troupe performed a ballet adapted from the Chinese opera *The White-Haired Girl* and made it a hit. Chinese opera artists were inspired and put on their own performance of the Beijing opera. Li Shaochun played Dachun and Du Jinfang played Xi'er.[4] Many difficulties needed to be overcome in rehearsing a modern opera in an art form as ancient as Beijing opera. Xi Zhongxun often accompanied Premier Zhou Enlai to watch their rehearsals and energetically encouraged the Beijing opera artists to adopt daring, innovative practices.

In the turmoil of the Cultural Revolution that lasted a decade, many old

In January 1980, Xi Zhongxun became first political commissar of Guangzhou military region. Here, he receives actors of the troops of Guangzhou military region

artists experienced mental or physical injury. After working in the central government, Xi Zhongxun gave instructions to relevant departments to work out policies offering practical care for old artists and to solve their everyday needs. For example, playwright and screenwriter Xia Yan was unable to move freely and had to get about in a wheelchair in his later years. When Xi Zhongxun paid him a visit, he found that Xia Yan's courtyard was very small and inconvenient for a wheelchair user. He immediately instructed the relevant department to find a bigger courtyard for Xia Yan.

Xi Zhongxun was in charge of the ministry of culture, the China federation of literary and art circles and the Chinese writers' association for a long period in the 1980s. In those years, numerous troupes from all corners of China performed in Beijing. Xi attended many performances and received and greeted performers on behalf of the CPC central committee and the state council. During this period, he personally concerned himself with and directed changes in the terms of office of the China federation of

Xi Zhongxun pictured with Guo Suying (centre), who was Cheng Yanqiu's wife, and Wang Yinqiu (far right), a famous actor, 29 April 1983

literary and art circles, the Chinese writers' association and the Chinese dramatists' association.

Renowned dramatist Ma Shaobo recalled that Xi Zhongxun was an open-minded and modest leader. His care and love for artists warmed the hearts of others. However, he also did not hesitate to criticise what he regarded as unhealthy trends. Although the criticism was sometimes serious, it was never condescending but done in a comradely, friendly way that did not cause offence. "Xi Zhongxun, just like Premier Zhou Enlai, was a leader and bosom friend closest to the literary and art workers."[5]

Chapter 31

The Liu Zhidan Novel Incident

When the central working conference in the seaside resort of Beidaihe was about to end on 24 August 1962, someone rose in revolt against Xi Zhongxun under the pretext of the novel *Liu Zhidan*. This person regarded it as a work that reversed the verdict on Gao Gang and framed Xi Zhongxun as "the first author" of the novel. On 8 September, during the preparatory meeting of the 10th plenary session of the eighth central committee of the CPC, Kang Sheng took advantage of the novel *Liu Zhidan* and stated at the southwestern group meeting that: "The central problem is the reason for publicising Gao Gang at this moment." Xi Zhongxun immediately became a target of the criticism of Peng Dehuai's "tendency to reverse verdicts" and was framed as a "big anti-party plotter and schemer".[1]

Up to that point, Xi Zhongxun had been entrusted by Premier Zhou Enlai to chair a conference in Beijing on the work of 36 cities nationwide. When he attended the preparatory meeting of the 10th plenary session of the eighth CPC central committee, he was completely unaware of what was about to happen. When he was told he would be personally criticised at the session, he could not believe it was true.

"It was a bolt from the blue and baffling." Xi Zhongxun decided to write a letter to the central government to clarify the case.

Li Jiantong, the author of the novel *Liu Zhidan*, was the wife of Liu Jingfan, who was the brother of Liu Zhidan. Around 1956, at the suggestion of the China Workers Publishing House, Li Jiantong decided to write a novel that reflected the history of the revolutionary struggles in northwest China and the revolutionary deeds of Liu Zhidan. When she asked for Xi Zhongxun's opinion before starting the project, Xi strongly advised her against writing a novel based on the serious and complicated revolutionary history of northwest China.

After the third draft of the novel was completed, Xi Zhongxun still gently tried to persuade Li that the many historical problems of the party in northwest China would trigger disputes if they were not handled properly. Many old comrades in the northwest urged him to support the writing of the novel, but Xi was unmoved. "A book on the revolution in northwest China should cover the whole era," he said. "What's the ideology of it? The correct ideology of Chairman Mao leading the revolution should be specifically reflected through Liu Zhidan. The last paragraph is only about the Shaanxi-Gansu soviet zone." He went on: "The last part should focus on Chairman Mao finally coming to lead the revolution. Otherwise, everything could have been over!"

Xi Zhongxun in his office in Zhongnanhai

On 19 September 1956, the preparatory meeting of the 10th plenary session of the eighth CPC central committee publicised a long article framing Peng Dehuai and Xi Zhongxun. As a result, Xi attracted further criticism and he had no alternative but to ask Zhou Enlai for permission to leave the meeting.

On 24 September, the preparatory meeting of the 10th plenary session of the eighth CPC central committee opened. When Mao Zedong gave a speech, Kang Sheng passed a message stating: "It is highly original to launch anti-party activities through novels." Mao read the message and went on: "Now, novels and magazines prevail. It is an invention to stir up anti-party activities through novels."[2] Later, he added: "It was Kang Sheng who discovered the practice of opposing the party through writing novels." At the meeting, Mao Zedong advocated "talking about class struggle year after year, month after month and day after day". The plenary session made a final decision to set up "special investigation committees" on Peng Dehuai and Xi Zhongxun, to be overseen by Kang Sheng. The 'charges' against Xi Zhongxun were that the novel *Liu Zhidan* "falsified party history", described the Shaanxi-Gansu border region as if it were the "centre of orthodoxy of the Chinese revolution" and "attributed Mao Zedong's ideology to Liu Zhidan's ideology"; "Luo Yan and Xu Zhong in the novel represented Gao Gang and Xi Zhongxun, respectively", aiming to "reverse the verdict on Gao Gang" and "lavish praise on Xi Zhongxun".

Xi Zhongxun felt miserable and kept silent all day. Zhou Enlai and Chen Yi talked with him on the recommendation of the CPC central committee and

Xi Zhongxun and his sons Xi Jinping and Xi Yuanping in 1958

The Liu Zhidan Novel Incident

Xi Zhongxun and his family in 1959

Mao Zedong. "The CPC central committee and Chairman Mao still trust you," said Zhou, "and have assigned you to do much work on behalf of the government despite the occurrence of the *Liu Zhidan* incident. You can correct your mistakes! We are still good friends. You really must not let this one mistake get you down!"

Peng Dehuai didn't attend the 10th plenary session of the eighth CPC central committee. He asked his wife, Pu Anxiu: "How come my problem got Xi Zhongxun into trouble?"

Xi Zhongxun kept to himself, pondered his mistakes and submitted himself to investigation. In the autumn of 1963, he began to write 'a self-criticism report'. "Zhongxun attached top priority to the party's interests and assumed responsibility for his actions," recalled Qi Xin. "He wrote down his reminiscences over 36 years in the self-criticism, from 1926 when he participated in the communist youth league to 1962. Although he suffered awful misery from a fabricated accusation, he considered the interests of the party. In those years, the children were still young and could not understand what had happened."[3]

Soon afterwards, Xi Zhongxun moved to live in a courtyard known as 'the Western Guild Hall' not far away from the central committee party school. There, he began life as a 'student' for more than two years. The Western Guild Hall covered more than two-thirds of a hectare and was divided into a front and back yard. There was no house in the front yard overgrown with flowers and grass. He did not attend classes in the party school and was not allowed to step out of the gate. He had to read books in the morning and work in the afternoon.

Xi Zhongxun and Qi Xin with family and friends in Beihai Park, 1960

Xi Zhongxun led his family members in planting a large area of corn, castor-oil plants and vegetables in a clearing in the back yard and handed over most of the produce to the state. Previously, on festivals and holidays, he would take his children to play in Tiananmen Square. When May Day 1964 came, his youngest son Yuanping asked: "Dad, are you going to take us to Tiananmen Square this year?" Xi Zhongxun answered loudly: "Come on, my children! We will celebrate a real Labour Day." He led them in a day of labour, with the children vying with each other to work harder; it was a busy and unforgettable May Day.

One day, Xi Zhongxun's sister Xi Yanying called round and broke out in tears at the sight of him. Xi Zhongxun soothed her. "You are still so weak despite having been educated by the party for so many years," he said. "How can you break down and burst into tears so easily? Whatever may happen, you should follow the party's instructions and do your work well." Xi Yanying recalled: "I had originally planned to console him and raise his spirits. But it was he who gave me a lesson instead. He did not bear any grudge against the party and he told his family members to strengthen their conviction and carry out our duties well."[4]

"I did not hurl myself into revolution in order to become an official," Xi Zhongxun told his wife. "I can still work for revolution by tilling the land." In the summer of 1965, he wrote a letter to the CPC central committee and Mao Zedong. In addition to criticising his 'mistakes', he proposed: "Please allow me to take part in the collective work of a rural production team and rebuild myself as an ordinary labourer as advocated by Mao Zedong thought. I would not be transformed if I was long confined to a house and divorced from reality."

Mao Zedong advised Xi Zhongxun to go and temper himself in a factory and "return two or three years later".[5]

Xi Zhongxun, his wife Qi Xin and his youngest son Xi Yuanping

The central government finally decided to transfer Peng Dehuai to work in the third line of defence in the southwestern region and Xi Zhongxun to work for Luoyang Mining Machinery Factory, given that no long-term conclusion had been reached on their cases. The two comrades-in-arms of the northwestern battlefield left Beijing convicted of similar crimes. From then on, they lived far apart and never saw each other again.

Chapter 32

Being Wronged for 16 Years and Twice Sent Down to Luoyang

On 7 December 1965, Xi Zhongxun was transferred to Luoyang, Henan province for the first time and worked as vice manager of Luoyang Mining Machinery Factory. It was a drastic change from being vice premier of the state council to a factory vice manager. But he showed no trace of frustration or depression.

Xi Zhongxun in Luoyang

Xi Zhongxun worked in an electricity team of the second metal workshop every morning and read books and newspapers in the afternoon. He was able to maintain two of his lifetime habits: taking a bath and walking. He took a bath together with the workers in a big pool and liked to chat with them. After supper, he would walk to a nearby apple orchard and talk with people in the fields.

Unfortunately, this relatively tranquil life lasted only a short time until the start of the Cultural Revolution.

The Cultural Revolution rapidly swept all corners of the country. Xi Zhongxun felt baffled and confused from the very beginning and reacted furiously to the 'vandalism' carried out by the Red Guards. Ding Hongru, who was once Xi's hairdresser, remembered: "Once, when he was having his hair cut, he saw rebels take out and burn the cigarettes and alcohol belonging to some state-owned stores. He was outraged and told secretary Fan to write an account and send it to the premier – how could such behaviour be condoned! I advised him not to get involved because the rebels were all Red Guards, who refused to see reason. He said he was not afraid of them and he had never seen anybody dare to burn state property."[1]

On 1 January 1967, the magazine *Red Flag* published an article entitled *Review on the Two-Faced Counterrevolutionary Zhou Yang* written by Yao Wenyuan. The article criticised Zhou Yang by name and the novel *Liu Zhidan* and once again focused critical pressure on Xi Zhongxun.

One dark night, Xi Zhongxun was forcibly transferred to Xi'an by Red Guards from Shaanxi where he was put into prison, criticised and denounced.

At Northwest University, he and a Red Guard jailor became confidantes. His family members in Beijing received a hardback edition of *Quotations from Chairman Mao Zedong* and a letter mailed from Xi'an. They provided hard-won sustenance during those difficult years.

At a criticism and struggle meeting, Xi Zhongxun met with his 'mentor' and the former governor of Shaanxi province, Zhao Boping. At the northwestern group meeting of the 10th plenary session of the eighth CPC central committee, Zhao Boping insisted that "Zhongxun is a good comrade". He persisted in neither exposing, criticising nor revealing his attitude toward Xi, and was implicated as a consequence. Staring at the 65-year-old Zhao, Xi Zhongxun felt extremely sad. "Alas!" said Zhao with a sigh. "I didn't expect to bring such ruin on myself in my old age!"

Xi Zhongxun wrote to Zhou Enlai to reflect on the criticism and denunciation he had received and his misunderstanding of the Cultural Revolution. Xi's circumstances captured the attention of Zhou Enlai. When receiving representatives of the rebels in Xi'an in mid-February 1967, Zhou was critical of them. "None of us know why you grabbed Xi Zhongxun and brought him to Xi'an", he said, before asking, cryptically: "Did you think that by seizing Xi Zhongxun you would be eligible for some sort of reward? In fact, you've only succeeded in grasping a hedgehog."

On 19 March 1967, the authorities in Shaanxi military region immediately followed Zhou Enlai's instructions by putting Xi Zhongxun under military supervision, transferring him to institutions of the provincial military region and temporarily offering him protection.

On 2 October 1967, the rebels took Xi Zhongxun to the playground of Yishan middle school, Fuping county, to criticise and struggle with him. The secretary of Fuping party committee, Zhou Dun, accompanied him to receive criticism and struggle. When Xi Zhongxun stepped on the makeshift platform, a crowd of thousands of people from nearby villages focused their eyes on him. Every one of them was concerned for their hometown hero. Due to the sultry weather, Xi had to wipe the sweat from his face on a number of occasions. On seeing this, a member of the crowd hurried to find an umbrella and held it for him. The masses reprimanded those who criticised and struggled against him. "What are you shouting for?" they asked. "But for him who asked the people to carry provisions from northern Shaanxi and allocated relief food supplies to the counties in Guanzhong during the famine of spring 1962, countless people would have died."

The criticism and struggle meeting had to be hastily curtailed. "I was criticised and struggled against in Yishan middle school," Xi recalled. "For fear that I would faint in the intense heat, someone held an umbrella for me. After the meeting, I told them 'I'm back' and said jokingly that they should treat me to a meal in my hometown. They cooked me local snacks such as minced green bean paste and red bean noodles."[2]

Xi Zhongxun wrote to Mao Zedong on 31 October 1967 and to Zhou Enlai in early November to report the criticism and struggle situation and the changes in his thinking. On 3 January 1968, the central government dispatched a special plane to take him back to Beijing. From then on, a long period of house arrest began.

During the eight years from early 1968 to May 1975, Xi Zhongxun was kept under house arrest in a small, isolated house of only seven to eight square metres in Beixinqiao communications cadre school. Luckily, he was allowed to read *People's Daily* every day.

Xi Zhongxun disciplined himself to undertake a twice-daily routine of walking round the perimeter of his tiny room, counting from one to 10,000 circuits in one direction and then the other. He strengthened his conviction that he had to move back and forth in this way to maintain his perseverance and physical health so as to be able to serve the party and the people again in future. "I had full confidence in the party. I believed that the CPC central committee would ultimately arrive at a correct conclusion about me."

In the winter of 1972, Zhou Enlai gave Xi permission to see his family. In the seven years since December 1965, when he was transferred to Luoyang, he had been parted from his family and he was unable to distinguish Jinping from Yuanping. On seeing them once again, tears welled in Xi Zhongxun's eyes.

After the Cultural Revolution began, Red Guards took Xi Zhongxun from Luoyang to Xi'an to criticise and struggle against him. One year later, Xi was put under house arrest in Beijing and subjected to investigation by a special group. He was kept separated from his family for seven years. In the winter of 1972, Qi Xin was allowed to take their children to see Xi Zhongxun where he was being detained. To commemorate the event, Qi Xin and the children travelled to Beijing and had their photograph taken in the Wangfujing (China) Photo Studio. At that time, Qi Qiaoqiao was working at the Inner Mongolia Production and Construction Corps, Xi An'an lived and worked in a production team in Linyi, Yuncheng, Shanxi province, Xi Jinping lived and worked in a production team in Liangjiahe village, Yanchuan county, Shaanxi province, Xi Yuanping had just graduated from the '57' middle school of the CPC central committee in rural Huangfan district, Xihua county, Henan province and Qi Xin worked at the same school. Pictured from left to right front row: Xi An'an, Qi Xin and Qi Qiaoqiao. Back row: Xi Yuanping and Xi Jinping

Xi Zhongxun in Luoyang in 1975

On 21 December 1974, Mao Zedong gave instructions regarding the novel *Liu Zhidan*: "The case has been examined for such a long period and there is no need to drag it out any longer. I propose we announce Xi Zhongxun's freedom and exemption from any further investigation." Around the spring festival of 1975, a special group to examine Xi Zhongxun's case declared an end to the supervision over Xi and let him "have a change of scenery for rest and recuperation". Xi chose to return to Luoyang.

On 22 May 1975, in the company of his wife Qi Xin, Xi Zhongxun returned to Luoyang and lived a life of 'neither a party member nor a worker'. They inhabited a small house of merely 24 square metres at the western end of the second floor of a residential building in Luoyang Fire-resistant Materials Factory. Xi Zhongxun received no salary but he had a periodic allowance of Rmb200 from the factory to cover living expenses.

To save money, Xi Zhongxun made a coal machine by hand and learnt to make honeycomb briquettes. One day, a neighbour called Li Jinhai came to help him move coal. They drank some alcohol that day and a minor event left a deep impression on Li. "A peanut fell on the floor," he said. "He quickly picked it up, blew off the dust and ate it."[3]

"When people found out that our children lacked the travelling expenses to see their father, the old workers of the fire-resistant factory silently lent us money from their meagre wages," recalled Comrade Qi Xin. "Song Futang, an old worker at the mining machinery factory, invited me to his home to a delicious meal of pork-and-leek dumplings and big peanuts from their hometown in Shandong. At that time, nothing could warm my heart more."[4]

Xi Zhongxun noticed that it was difficult for the workers to commute. He went to the municipal party committee to reflect the problem but was turned away by the doorkeeper. He told the doorkeeper that he was Xi Zhongxun and that he had come to reflect problems to the leaders of the municipal party committee. After seeing the secretary of the municipal party committee, he explained the situation and finally got the problem tackled.

Xi Zhongxun, his wife Qi Xin and their children photographed at the Luoyang Red Flag Photo Studio in 1975. From left to right back row: his son Xi Jinping, daughter Xi An'an and son-in-law Wu Long

Xi Zhongxun and his youngest son Xi Yuanping in Luoyang in 1975

On the morning of 9 January 1976, Xi Zhongxun heard of the death of Premier Zhou Enlai from the radio and stood transfixed. Oblivious to the obstructions of the departments concerned, he sent a telegram to Deng Xiaoping, director of the funeral committee, who forwarded it to the grieving Deng Yingchao: "Hearing the bad news, I could not be sadder! Unable to attend the funeral in person, I feel eternal regret!" Watching the portrait of Premier Zhou, he burst into tears repeatedly.

1976 was the year of the dragon according to the Chinese lunar calendar. On 6 July, Zhu De, one of the founding fathers of the people's army and commander-in-chief of the Red Army, the Eighth Route Army and the PLA, passed away; on 28 July, the Tangshan earthquake occurred; on 9 September, Mao Zedong, the main founder and leader of the CPC, the PLA and the PRC, passed away. These seismic events made Xi Zhongxun apprehensive about the future of the country.

After Mao died, Xi Zhongxun was in grief. He walked the hills of a suburb alone, picked a flower, wore it on his chest and stood in silent tribute. Two years later, he recalled his feelings with deep emotion in an article entitled *The Red Sun Shone over the Shaanxi-Gansu Plateau*. "I worked in the local area for a long time," he wrote. "Chairman Mao asked me to study in the central committee party school and to work in local areas, the party school, among the troops and for leading authorities. In more than a decade of contact with Chairman Mao, he showed his loving care for me. He sometimes let me attend CPC meetings, talked with me, wrote to me and wrote inscriptions to encourage and educate me."

In October 1976, the 'Gang of Four' who stirred up trouble during the Cultural Revolution, fell from power, which delighted Xi Zhongxun no end. In August 1977, the 11th NPC of the CPC was convened in Beijing, which declared an end to the 10-year-long Cultural Revolution. Xi Zhongxun wrote to the CPC central committee after the fall of the Gang of Four, requiring the committee to redress fabricated cases, rehabilitate him after he was wronged and arrange suitable work for him. Qi Xin and their children also campaigned for the rehabilitation of Xi Zhongxun.

In mid-February 1978, the general office of the central committee made a phone call to instruct Henan provincial party committee to escort Xi Zhongxun to Beijing without delay. On 22 February, Xi arrived in Zhengzhou from Luoyang by train. Wang Hui, secretary of Henan provincial party committee, met Xi Zhongxun on the platform. The moment he got off the train, Xi Zhongxun embraced Wang Hui tightly and said excitedly: "Wang Hui, this is the first time I have hugged someone for 16 years!"

Chapter 33

Sent South at Age 65 to Govern Guangdong

In early 1978, Xi Zhongxun attended the first session of the fifth national committee of the CPPCC as a specially invited member and he was elected as a member of the CPPCC's standing committee. It was the first time in 16 years that he had entered the familiar Great Hall of the People. He met many old friends and comrades-in-arms. They clasped hands for a long time and hugged each other tightly.

Xi Zhongxun in the early stage of reform and opening up

Burhan Shahidi, an Uygur from Xinjiang, held Xi Zhongxun tightly the moment he saw him, shedding tears as he did so. During their talks, Xi did not mention his own experiences but showed deep concern for Burhan. "When he knew that many of my father's problems had not been resolved, he consoled my father, urging him to trust the central government and assuring him that they would arrive at a fair and just conclusion to his case," recalled Burhan's daughter, Erie Suja.[1]

Ye Jianying[2] was left dumbfounded at the sight of Xi Zhongxun. He was surprised to see him in such good health after all the suffering and tribulations he had endured. Soon afterwards, Ye proposed to Hua Guofeng and Hu Yaobang,[3] who had recently been elected as director of the organisation department of the CPC central committee, to let Xi Zhongxun work in Guangdong.

The 65-year-old Xi quickly assumed the historic duty to "safeguard the southern gateway to China". Before doing so, Hua Guofeng, Ye

Well-wishers join Xi Zhongxun before he departs Beijing for Guangdong to take office, 5 April 1978. From first to fifth from left: Xi Jinping, Wu Qingtong, Song Yangchu, Qi Xin and Qu Wu. Qi Qiaoqiao is second from right and Xi Yuanping is third from right

Sent South at Age 65 to Govern Guangdong

Xi Zhongxun welcomes Ye Jianying, who had travelled to Guangdong for an inspection tour

Jianying, Deng Xiaoping and Li Xiannian met Xi Zhongxun, placing high expectations on him, emphasising the great significance of the task in Guangdong and asking him to work audaciously and with a free hand.

"Yaobang praised Zhongxun for his qualifications, experience, competence, calibre and reputation," comrade Qi Xin recalled. "Ye Jianying also firmly supported Zhongxun to work in Guangdong... After the talk with Deng Xiaoping, the CPC central committee decided to send him on the mission to work in Guangdong. As Yaobang said: 'You are being dispatched to safeguard the southern gateway of China'."[4]

Guangdong was severely afflicted by the Cultural Revolution. Its former advantages of "proximity to Hong Kong and Macau and being home to many overseas Chinese" became disadvantages and the overseas relations became 'illegal relations'. It was not only economic development that regressed, but there was an increasing tendency in coastal areas toward illegal emigration to other countries. What awaited Xi Zhongxun was a hefty burden.

On 5 April 1978, Xi arrived at Guangzhou airport. That afternoon, he attended the fourth congress of Guangdong party representatives. On the following morning, Xi delivered a gracious and eloquent speech at the third plenary session of the fourth Guangdong CPC congress of representatives. He solemnly stated that he had grown up and lived in northern China during his early years and that he would spend the rest of his days in Guangdong.

Fang Bao was deputy secretary of Huiyang prefectural party committee and secretary of Bao'an county party committee. "He made an impromptu speech, in stark contrast to all the other leaders after the Cultural Revolution," recalled Fang. "It surprised me because it was his first time to come to Guangdong and talk to all the committee members. His straightforwardness filled me with hope for the province."[5]

Xi Zhongxun in Sanya, Hainan in January 1979

Xi Zhongxun was elected as second secretary of Guangdong provincial party committee at the first session of the fourth provincial party committee on the afternoon of 6 April 1978. Meanwhile, the CPC central committee also appointed him as deputy director of Guangdong provincial revolutionary committee. He was also appointed as first secretary of Guangdong provincial party committee and director of Guangdong provincial revolutionary committee in December 1978. He mainly focused his attention on the work of the Guangdong provincial party committee and

Xi Zhongxun and Xu Shiyou arm-wrestling through a vehicle window flanked by Yang Shangkun on the left, June 1979

Xi Zhongxun, Su Yu and Xu Shiyou in Guangzhou, January 1980

Xi Jinping and Xi Zhongxun in Hainan, 1978

gave a free hand to Liu Tianfu, who was secretary of Guangdong provincial party committee and deputy director of Guangdong provincial revolutionary committee, to handle the affairs of the revolutionary committee.

Just one week after Xi Zhongxun took office, the 81-year-old Ye Jianying went on an inspection visit to Guangdong. After listening to Xi's work report, Ye advised him to "make in-depth investigations, formulate sound plans, report to the CPC central committee without delay, implement the plans step by step and in order of priority, and emphasise confidentiality and security".[6]

Xi Zhongxun summarised the rectification of incorrect styles of work of the Guangdong provincial party committee at an enlarged session of the standing committee of the first session of the fourth provincial party committee on 30 June 1978. He reminded everyone present to "read articles in recently published newspapers, such as *One of the Most Fundamental Principles of Marxism* and *Practice is the Sole Criterion for Testing Truth*; to combine theory with practice, because theory can guide practice, which in turn can enrich theory and that theory on its own, without practice, is not worth a farthing."

On 20 September 1978, *People's Daily* published an article entitled *Seek Truth from Facts, Emancipate the Mind and Accelerate Progress* to report that Xi Zhongxun chaired a conference of the Guangdong provincial party committee to discuss the criterion of truth. The article said that the conference was held for deputy directors of the standing committee of Guangdong provincial party committee and Guangdong provincial revolutionary committee to discuss the issue of linking theory with practice. Xi Zhongxun pointed out that practice was the sole criterion for testing truth and it was absolutely not a theoretical issue but an issue of vital practical significance. At that time, Xi was one of the few principal

Xi Zhongxun with leaders of the 124th division in Luofu mountain, Boluo county, in August 1978. Xi Jinping is second from the left in the front row

provincial leaders nationwide to publicly support discussion on the criterion of truth in a newspaper.

Xi Zhongxun took on the additional position of first political commissar of the Guangzhou military region in January 1980. With his help, the unjust, false and erroneous cases during the Cultural Revolution in the region were quickly redressed.

During his administration in Guangdong, Xi Zhongxun attached high importance to unity between the army and the people and fostering good relations between local government and the army. As primary political commissar of the Guangzhou military region, he earnestly practised what he preached. He was candid and on good terms with Xu Shiyou and Wu Kehua, who were successive commanders of the Guangzhou military region. Xu Shiyou had a colourful personality and he liked to participate in drinking competitions. At their first encounter, Xu Shiyou poured three large glasses of alcohol for both himself and Xi Zhongxun, expecting to unsettle Xi. Unexpectedly, Xi downed the three large glasses with no visible signs of distress, which changed Xu's opinion of him from then on.

Chapter 34

Decisive Action to Redress Miscarriages of Justice

Xi Zhongxun chaired the second plenary session of the standing committee of the fourth provincial party committee to convey the spirit of the third plenary session of the 11th central committee of the CPC between 8 and 25 January 1979. At the session, Xi made a thorough review of the problems left over in Guangdong's history before the Cultural Revolution and highlighted 11 areas related to redressing unjust, false and erroneous cases. When it came to the problem of the struggle against the rightists, he said that Guangdong should rectify all its wrong cases in accordance with the direction of the CPC central committee.

Xi Zhongxun's speech was interrupted by repeated applause. It was later described as a true southern China spring!

Xi acted decisively to redress those unjust, false and erroneous cases, the most important of which included

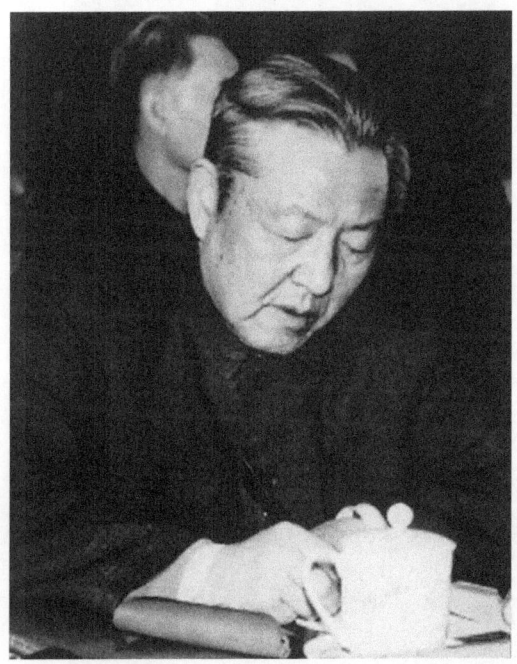

Xi Zhongxun attending the third plenary session of the 11th CPC Central Committee in December 1978, where he was admitted as a central committee member

the 'anti-localism campaign', the 'Li Yizhe case' and the 'anti-Peng Pai martyrs incident'.

A report in the 12 February 1979 edition of *People's Daily* on Guangdong's political rehabilitation of people wronged in unjust, false and erroneous cases

Decisive Action to Redress Miscarriages of Justice

Peng Pai was celebrated as the 'king of the peasant movement'. In the 'four clean-ups' campaign of the 1960s, an upsurge of 'anti-Peng Pai martyrs' sentiment was aroused in Haifeng county, Guangdong province. During the Cultural Revolution, several family members and relatives of Peng Pai, including his son Peng Hong, were killed. Hosts of innocent cadres and ordinary people were implicated, thrown into prison, criticised, denounced and even beaten to death or left disabled. It was an unjust case that became a sensation throughout the country.

On 18 June 1978, more than two months after his arrival in Guangdong, Xi Zhongxun listened to the report on the 'anti-Peng Pai incident' and explicitly instructed that the case be reviewed and redressed. Some rebels stubbornly opposed redressing the incident and threatened to report it to the CPC central committee. Upon hearing this, Xi Zhongxun said angrily: "You're a son of a bitch if you make such a report!"

Wang Ning was then head of the public security department of Guangdong province. "According to the instructions of Secretary Xi," he recalled, "the Guangdong provincial party committee and the Guangdong provincial revolutionary committee, together with the party committee of the Guangzhou military region, dispatched a joint working team to assist the prefectural party committee in a thorough review of the anti-Peng Pai martyrs incident. I headed the investigation team of roughly 30 members, who were cadres of a rank above department level in all units. The whole investigation lasted more than six months."[1]

At the second plenary session of the standing committee of the fourth provincial party committee, Xi Zhongxun stated that the anti-Peng Pai incident was nothing more than a conspiracy by Lin Biao and the 'Gang of Four' to target the old generation of proletarian revolutionaries, including Premier Zhou and Deputy Chairman Ye, to usurp party leadership and seize state power; it was a counter-revolutionary event, pure and simple.

There were two 'anti-localism campaigns': the first one occurred between 1952 and 1953, when the CPC central committee and Mao Zedong rigorously criticised Guangdong for 'losing its direction' in the land reform and held that Fang Fang, head of the CPC central committee in south China, made mistakes of 'localism'. The second happened in late 1957, when Guangdong provincial party committee believed there was a 'Hainan localist anti-party alliance' headed by Feng Baiju, who was secretary of

Hu Yaobang and Xi Zhongxun greet each other at Guangzhou Baiyun international airport, spring 1980

Guangdong provincial party committee, and Gu Dacun, and reported it to the CPC central committee, which gave approval. These two campaigns had disastrous results involving more than 27,000 local cadres.

Xi Zhongxun withstood the pressure and persisted in reviewing 'anti-localism'. "There might be two possible outcomes," he said, frankly. "The first is that I will be exiled from Guangdong and the other is that I can succeed in redressing the unjust, false and erroneous cases involving 'anti-localism'."

In August 1979, Guangdong provincial party committee issued *The Notice to Review the 'Anti-Localism' Incident*. The notice stated: "It was firmly believed that Gu Dacun and Feng Baiju 'united to conduct anti-party activities' and that there was a 'localist anti-party clique in Hainan headed by Gu Dacun and Feng Baiju'; some localist and anti-party cliques were also identified in other places. Reviewing the circumstances again now, these conclusions were incorrect and should be repealed."

After he was transferred to work in the CPC central committee, Xi Zhongxun continued to follow the progress of the case. Under the

Xi Zhongxun reading letters from the public

tutelage of Xi Zhongxun, Chen Yun and Huang Kecheng, the CPC central committee issued *The Notice to Rehabilitate the Reputation of Feng Baiju and Gu Dacun* on 9 February 1983. Afterwards, it repealed Fang Fang's punishment and rehabilitated his reputation. After a period of 30 years, the unjust case of 'anti-localism' in Guangdong was at last completely redressed.

The 'Li Yizhe' case, or so-called 'counter-revolutionary clique incident', was well known across Guangdong during the Cultural Revolution. On 10 November 1974, a big character poster headed *On Democracy and the Legal System Under Socialism — For Chairman Mao and the Fourth National People's Congress* was put up by Li Yizhe in Guangzhou. The poster was intended to publicly disclose the conspiracy of the Lin Biao clique to destroy democracy and the legal system and it criticised the severe

Liu Tianfu, Wu Kehua, Xi Zhongxun, Yang Shangkun and Li Jianzhen attend a military forum in the spring of 1980

crimes of the Gang of Four but not by name, which gave rise to a strong reaction. Soon after Xi Zhongxun came to Guangdong, the imprisoned Li Zhengtian, who was associated with 'Li Yizhe', twice wrote in appeal to Xi Zhongxun. Xi held several meetings to discuss the issue of 'Li Yizhe' and concluded that it was not a counter-revolutionary clique and that the case should be redressed. Li Zhengtian and others were set free on 30 December 1978.

On the afternoon of 24 January 1979, Xi Zhongxun met Li Zhengtian and the others who had been released. "You have a long way to go," Xi told them. "I hope you will take the right path and grow healthily." Xi talked with them on a number of occasions over the following two months and the minutes from these discussions amounted to more than 200,000 words.

What many people didn't realise at the time was that when Xi Zhongxun redressed the unjust, false and erroneous cases in Guangdong, his own unjust cases, namely 'The *Liu Zhidan* novel incident' and the 'Xi Zhongxun anti-party clique' had not been redressed. The CPC central committee endorsed *The Report on the Redressing of 'The Liu Zhidan Novel Incident'* made by the organisation department of the CPC central committee on 4 August 1979 and issued *The Notice to Redress the Unjust Case of the So-called 'Xi Zhongxun Anti-Party Clique'* on 25 February 1980. Wrong cases involving Xi Zhongxun were redressed two years after he began to govern Guangdong.

Xi Zhongxun's journey southwards to govern Guangdong came after 16 years of trials and tribulations. A sense of urgency and mission drove him to immerse himself in work. After a long day's work, he often read books and newspapers to learn about developments at home and abroad. In his own words, he accomplished in one day what should have taken two days to complete. All this could not escape the notice of Qi Xin. "As his wife, I could understand him," she said. "He wanted to recapture the lost 16 years to perform more real deeds for the party and the people."[2]

Chapter 35

Tackling the Root Causes of the 'Illegal Emigration' Frenzy

'Illegal emigration' was a chronic and intractable problem in Guangdong and a major challenge when Xi Zhongxun came to administer the province.

Statistics indicated that more than 150,000 people fled from Guangdong to Hong Kong during the 1960s and 1970s. More than 40,000 people fled from Bao'an alone, a county adjacent to Hong Kong that would later be

Xi Zhongxun visits Huaqiao farm in Guangdong, July 1978

transformed into the thriving industrial zone of Shenzhen. Some places experienced an almost total exodus of working-age men. Shatoujiao commune on the Guangdong/Hong Kong border (known as Sha Tau Kok in Hong Kong) for example, had a population of fewer than 1,200 after more than twice that number fled to Hong Kong; only the old, weak, ill and disabled, and women were left. Many fled again the moment they were repatriated.

One scorching summer day in early July 1978, Xi Zhongxun braved the heat to inspect Bao'an county bordering Hong Kong. No young people could be seen in the border villages. He was informed when he was in Nanling that the village originally had more than 600 inhabitants, but that more than 500 of them had fled to Hong Kong, leaving nothing but empty houses and wilderness. Two men were tied up beside a road near Sha Tau Kok. Xi Zhongxun asked why and was told by Fang Bao, secretary of Bao'an county party committee: "They tried to flee only to be caught by the border guards, who had no time to send the fugitives away under escort because they were busy trying to catch other fugitives there."

Xi Zhongxun persisted in investigating the holding centres. "Dozens of people from Shanwei and Shantou were locked up in the holding centres at the lotus pond," recalled Fang Bao. "Comrade Zhongxun asked why they had fled. The peasants did not know who he was and told him everything. They said they had fled simply because their lives were hard and that the opportunities in Hong Kong were better for them to make money."[1]

His mind was weighed down with all that he had heard and seen.

After Fang Bao accompanied him on a visit to two factories processing semi-finished materials, Xi Zhongxun said with deep feeling: "You should place high priority on the development of Shatoujiao. Two worlds are bisected by a single street: prosperous on their side and desolate on our side. How can this reflect the superiority of socialism? Methods should be worked out to develop Shatoujiao." He added: "It seems to me an issue of policy. As long as we adopt the proper policies, the economy will expand in no time. It is the southern gateway of our country and you should strive for the glory of the country so that foreigners will notice a new image of socialism the moment they set foot in Guangdong."

Xi Zhongxun made it widely known that issues such as fleeing across

Xi Zhongxun visits a cigarette factory in Mei county, July 1978

the border, letting capitalists from Hong Kong import equipment and source gravel for export, absorbing foreign capital to develop industry and resuming small-scale border trade should be "handled immediately, without any delay". He added: "Whatever can develop production should be done. Don't worry about doctrinairism or opposing any other 'isms'. They are capitalists but we can still learn some good methods from them." He further encouraged them by saying: "You can raise and plant whatever is needed in Hong Kong and whatever can earn more foreign exchange."

Act first, get rich first, "lay aside doctrinairism in whatever form"… these words were earth-shattering and shocking to people like Fang Bao. Xi's "effective methods" fundamentally eradicated illegal emigration.

Nonetheless, results could not be achieved overnight. Illegal emigration worsened in the second half of 1978. From 14 to 18 October that year, a Guangdong anti-illegal emigration conference was held in Shantou. It proposed measures to address these problems, stimulate production, develop the economy, improve people's living standards, rigorously reinforce border defence management and intensify interception.

Tackling the Root Causes of the 'Illegal Emigration' Frenzy

At the session of the standing committee of Guangdong provincial party committee, Xi Zhongxun clearly articulated his view: illegal emigration was not class struggle but should be classified as internal contradictions among the people. Hong Kong is also part of China's territory. The actions of people unable to make a living here fleeing to Hong Kong should be called "external flow" rather than "external escape"!

However, a large number of people continued to escape, which put huge pressure on the authorities. Up to 200 people were crowded in a very small house, with no room to sit down. From January to early June 1979, the number of people in holding centres in Shenzhen exceeded 100,000, double the total during the whole of the previous year. "The people in external flow should not be treated as enemies," Xi Zhongxun said. "You should set them free. Instead of taking them into custody, we should adopt measures to make Guangdong a better place so that they will run to reside here."[2]

On 14 June 1979, the State Council and the CMC issued instructions to firmly crack down on illegal emigration from Guangdong. Xi Zhongxun chaired two provincial party committee meetings, on 17 and 18 June, to research and implement the crackdown and set up a 10-member anti-illegal

Xi Zhongxun visits the village of Huiyang in Guangdong, August 1978. Xi Jinping, pictured far left, was then studying at Qinghua University. He accompanied his father to the village and participated in social work in Guangdong during his summer vacation

Xi Zhongxun visits Boluo county in Guangdong, August 1978, with Xi Jinping pictured in the centre

emigration leading group headed by Xi himself. He persisted in not treating the so-called 'fugitives' as 'enemies' and instructed the release of many imprisoned people even at what was a sensitive time during the campaign.

On 20 June 1979, Xi Zhongxun stressed at an anti-fugitive conference of Huiyang prefectural party committee that illegal emigration should be eradicated in an appropriate way; the best way to curb the practice is to lay material, spiritual and organisational foundations and to fortify the position of socialism. As long as production levels were developed and people's incomes improved, the numbers trying to leave would fall drastically.

On 7 July, Xi Zhongxun wrote telegrams to Vice Premiers Li Xiannian and Chen Muhua as well as the central committee to report on the measures taken to curb illegal emigration since the end of the previous year. He also proposed to improve reception work rather than treating those caught as criminals.

Tackling the Root Causes of the 'Illegal Emigration' Frenzy

Xi Zhongxun delivers a speech at a standing committee session of Huiyang prefectural party committee

On 27 August, Guangdong provincial party committee issued instructions for further work to combat illegal emigration, requiring party committees at all levels to tackle the problem as a long-term political task, practically improve the work relating to reception and repatriation, and to help people out of their difficulties under the "guidance of addressing the problems appropriately and fundamentally".

During this time, with the help of Xi Zhongxun and Guangdong provincial party committee, the CPC central committee and the state council issued Document No.50 (on 15 July 1979) and decided to initiate pilot special economic zones (SEZs) in Shenzhen and other coastal locations in the province. China's SEZs had officially been launched, which would ultimately lead to an increase in production and incomes and the eradication of illegal emigration.

Xi Zhongxun investigates the living conditions of farmers in Lingnan village in Shenzhen on 14 February 1987, seven years after he left Guangdong. He was pleased to witness the improvements in rural life following the reform and opening up

Chapter 36

'Lobbying' the Central Government to Let Guangdong 'Take the First Step'

On the afternoon of 8 April 1979, Hua Guofeng, Li Xiannian and Hu Yaobang attended a discussion of the south central China group during a central government work conference (5-28 April 1979). As chair of the discussion, Xi Zhongxun delivered a meticulously crafted speech, solemnly explaining the need for the central government to delegate powers to Guangdong.

After talking about problems such as centralised power in the economic management system, Xi came up with an important recommendation.

Xi Zhongxun looks out over the South China Sea

"Many overseas Chinese live in Guangdong, which is close to Hong Kong and Macau," he said. "This advantage should be fully utilised in order to promote foreign economic and technical exchange. The Guangdong provincial party committee has already discussed this matter. We came here in the hope that the central government can authorise Guangdong to take the first step and give us a free hand."

In making his case, Xi drew a vivid comparison. "'Despite its small size, the sparrow possesses all the internal organs — small but complete'. Guangdong province, like a big sparrow, is the equivalent of one or even several countries in size. But it lacks flexibility. It is still hampered by the restrictions imposed by the state and central departments, which is not good for the growth of the national economy. We hope to be granted flexible local management under the nationally centralised and unified leadership, which will be good for both regional and national development." He boldly went on to hypothesise: "If Guangdong was an 'independent state' (definitely a hypothetical assumption), Guangdong might be able to be developed in only a few years. But under the constraints of the current system, it is not easy to make any progress."[1]

Xi Zhongxun on a visit to Huiyang, 5 August 1978

'Lobbying' the Central Government to Let Guangdong 'Take the First Step'

Xi Zhongxun delivers a speech to the Guangdong provincial party committee work conference in December 1978. Liu Tianfu is seated left

This was Xi Zhongxun's urgent wish on behalf of the 56m people of Guangdong. He proposed that "the central government should delegate some power to Guangdong provincial government to take the first step". When Ye Jianying returned to Guangdong in January 1979, he beseeched the leaders in charge of Guangdong, including Xi Zhongxun, to make the necessary reform. "Guangdong is in such abject poverty," he argued. "You should work out some measures to invigorate its economy."

At a central government work conference in mid-November 1978, Xi Zhongxun explicitly proposed in his speech that the central government should give local authorities more scope to handle their own affairs. Guangdong, he argued, should be allowed to establish an office in Hong Kong, absorb capital from Hong Kong, Macau and overseas Chinese, introduce advanced technology and equipment, and make independent decisions in processing trade and compensation trade. Xi's heartfelt 'request for limited powers' chimed with the views of Deng Xiaoping at that time, who advocated the "delegation of powers from central to local governments" and allowing certain areas to "get rich first".

On 17 April 1979, the political bureau of the CPC central committee held review meetings involving the conveners of all groups along with Hua Guofeng and Deng Xiaoping. Xi Zhongxun reiterated in his report: "Guangdong provincial party committee has already discussed this issue. We have come to the conference hoping that the central government could delegate some power to us so that Guangdong could take the first step and exploit its advantages." He made another bold prediction that: "If Guangdong were an 'independent country', it would surpass Hong Kong." He also proposed that Guangdong should plan to learn from and replicate foreign processing zones, and establish areas in Shenzhen, Zhuhai (close to Hong Kong and Macau, respectively) and Shantou (an important town of overseas Chinese) for inward investment and production according to the demands of the international market. They were initially called 'trade cooperation zones'.

Xi Zhongxun and Ye Jianying in Hainan, 1979

'Lobbying' the Central Government to Let Guangdong 'Take the First Step'

Guangdong provincial party committee held a three-level cadre conference in June 1979 at which Xi Zhongxun conveyed the approval of the central government for Guangdong to become a pioneer in the country's reform and opening up. This photo shows Xi Zhongxun, Ye Jianying, Xu Shiyou and Yang Shangkun walking into the meeting

The 'request for power' 'to take the first step' and establish 'trade cooperation zones' received a positive response and the approval of major leaders in the central government. "The practice of Guangdong and Fujian adopting special policies, making use of capital and technology from overseas Chinese and even setting up plants will not lead to a slide to capitalism because the gains will not belong to either Comrade Hua Guofeng or any one of us," said Deng Xiaoping. "We adhere to the system of ownership by the whole people. So it will do us no harm if the 80m people in Guangdong and Fujian provinces get rich first."[2]

Xi Zhongxun's proposals at the central work conference to 'request authorisation' to 'take the first step' were the catalyst for Guangdong and Fujian adopting 'special policies and flexible measures for foreign economic activities' and establishing the four SEZs in Shenzhen, Zhuhai, Shantou and Xiamen.

Xi felt that anyone who doesn't investigate has no right to speak.

He travelled the length and breadth of Guangdong and was constantly thinking about the crucial issue of how to accelerate construction of the 'four modernisations' (a policy to modernise agriculture, industry, national defence, and science and technology introduced by Deng Xiaoping in 1978) and how to fully leverage the advantages of Guangdong's proximity to Hong Kong and Macau.

When Xi Zhongxun made a visit to Bao'an county, Fang Bao, secretary of Bao'an county party committee, told him that many of those who had been smuggled to Hong Kong could send money home after working there for one or two years so that their family could afford to build new homes.

In Puning county, he was saddened to see three men working in the fields with a single plough. "'Slash-and-burn' agriculture is still practised even today, 29 years after the liberation of China," he said.

Xi Zhongxun also twice raised the issue of the 'decision-making process' regarding 'authorisation' and 'permission' at the central government work

Xi Zhongxun visits farmland and, later, a water conservation construction site, in Zhanjiang, Guangdong province, between late August and early September 1980

'Lobbying' the Central Government to Let Guangdong 'Take the First Step'

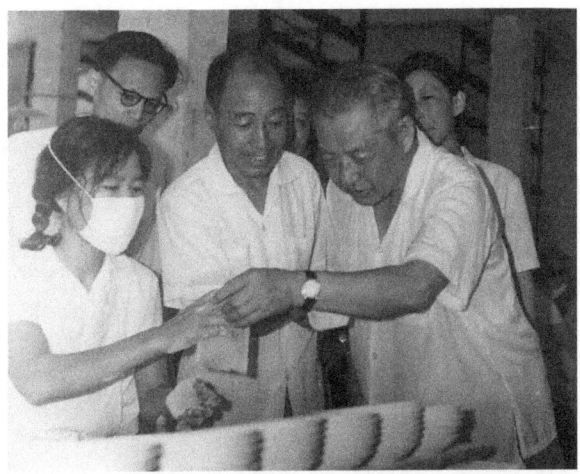

Xi Zhongxun closely analysed state-owned-enterprise (SOE) reform and promoted the 'experience of Qingyuan' to extend decision-making power among enterprises and enhance productivity. Here, Xi visits an enterprise to find out about its production and reform plans

Xi Zhongxun talks with young locals on a visit to Zhanjiang, Guangdong province, between late August and early September 1980

Xi Zhongxun meeting disaster-stricken people in Zhanjiang between late August and early September 1980

conference to deal with numerous problems relating to economic reform. His enthusiasm was apparent to all who attended. The moment the work conference ended, Xi returned to Guangdong and conveyed the essence of the conference and the process of applying to the central government for 'authorisation' to be granted to the standing committee of Guangdong provincial party committee. "The need for Guangdong to take the first step is not just a Guangdong matter," he stressed. "It is a matter of vital significance for the entire country. So this is a matter of widespread significance." He went on to say with conviction: "This Guangdong issue won't go away. If we don't tackle it today, it'll have to be tackled tomorrow and if it's not tackled tomorrow, it'll have to be tackled the next day. The development of Chinese society has been one of constant evolution. If you

'Lobbying' the Central Government to Let Guangdong 'Take the First Step'

Xi Zhongxun headed a Guangdong friendship delegation to Australia from 22 November to 6 December 1979. Here, he visits an iron ore production facility

Xi Zhongxun visits a securities company during his trip to Hong Kong, December 1979

don't tackle the issue, the central government will have to tackle it anyway. We must do everything within our power to make it happen while we have breath in our bodies."

Ye Jianying applauded Xi Zhongxun's application to the central government for 'authorisation' and 'taking the first step'. When he met the secretaries of the prefectural, municipal and county party committee attending the three-level cadre conference in Guangzhou on 1 June 1979, he encouraged the cadres: "If Guangdong succeeds, it can promote the development of the whole country. If it doesn't succeed, it could mess up the entire country. Therefore, it is of great significance. You should work harder to achieve success."[3]

Chapter 37

'Blazing a New Trail' to Advocate the Establishment of SEZs

The formulation and implementation of special economic zones (SEZs) was closely associated with Xi Zhongxun. As spring turned to summer in 1978, an investigation team from the state development planning commission (SDPC) and the ministry of foreign trade travelled to Hong Kong and Macau and subsequently recommended the upgrade of

Xi Zhongxun during his time as governor of Guangdong

Bao'an and Zhuhai counties into provincially administered municipalities in order to develop the building materials and processing sectors. The leaders in charge of Guangdong provincial party committee, including Xi Zhongxun, pledged their support to the plan and energetically began to make preparations.

In October 1978, the Guangdong government submitted to the state council *The Plan to Establish Foreign Trade Business Bases in Bao'an and Zhuhai Counties* and came up with the goal of 'three establishments': to establish Bao'an and Zhuhai as bases for commodity exports of an appropriate technological level, as tourist areas to attract visitors from Hong Kong and Macau, and as prosperous new border cities.

On 6 January 1979, Guangdong provincial government and the ministry of communications jointly submitted to the state council a *Report on the Establishment of the Industrial Park in Bao'an, Guangdong by the Hong Kong Branch of China Merchants Holdings.* Guangdong upgraded

On a visit to Bao'an in July 1978, Xi Zhongxun asked for permission to establish a foreign trade and commodity production base in the county. Xi is pictured standing next to his wife Qi Xin, with the deputy director of Guangdong provincial planning commission, Zhang Xunfu, far left

Xi Zhongxun meets a farmer in Sihui county, Guangdong province, in the spring of 1979

Bao'an county to become Shenzhen city and Zhuhai county to become Zhuhai city on 23 January and made preparations to set up an export base. The state council agreed to upgrade the two counties into provincially administered municipalities on 5 March 1979.

In his discussions with Zhang Xunfu and Wu Jianmin, who would take office in Shenzhen and Zhuhai respectively, Xi Zhongxun encouraged them to initially set about boosting average incomes. As the first secretary of Shenzhen municipal party committee, Zhang Xunfu recalled: "Xi Zhongxun asked us secretaries to come up with suggestions for the work and for the leading group. I was to hold primary responsibility while Fang Bao would be second in command. He asked me to improve people's livelihoods and boost prosperity because only in that way could we solve the problem of illegal emigration. If we simply captured those who fled, they would leave again sooner or later. The people told us that they left because it was much more prosperous [across the border]. For that reason, and with the support of Xi Zhongxun, we developed a 'get rich first zone'."[1] With Xi Zhongxun's support, the pilot 'get rich first zone' was 'the first step' towards the creation of China's SEZs.

The term 'special zone' came into being because of a famous exchange between Xi Zhongxun and Deng Xiaoping.

During a central government work conference held between 5 and 28 April 1979, Xi Zhongxun reported to Hua Guofeng and members of the standing committee of the political bureau of the CPC central committee.

Later, he submitted a special and detailed report to Deng Xiaoping on the plan to establish 'trade cooperation zones' in Shenzhen, Zhuhai and Shantou. Xi started by saying that no decision had been reached on what to call these zones. Everybody reckoned that 'export processing zone' was a Taiwanese term, while 'free trade zone' was thought to be too capitalist. So finally the term 'trade cooperation zone' was settled upon as an intermediate measure. "It is good to call it a 'special zone'," Deng told Xi, "because Shaanxi-Gansu-Ningxia region was called a special zone at the very beginning!"

Deng encouraged Xi Zhongxun to forge ahead with his work. "The central authorities have no money but can offer you policy support," he said. "You need to take the initiative yourselves and blaze a new trail."[2]

During the agrarian revolutionary war, the teenage Xi Zhongxun hurled himself into building the Shaanxi-Gansu border region revolutionary base. In the early stages of the war of resistance against Japan, Xi safeguarded the southern gateway to Shaanxi-Gansu-Ningxia special zone (later called the

Xi Zhongxun visited Zhuhai in June 1979. He is pictured here with Wu Jianmin, secretary of Zhuhai municipal party committee, far left

The oil painting *Xi Zhongxun and Deng Xiaoping in 1979* by Liao Xiaoming

border region). He established contact with Deng Xiaoping when he was secretary of Guanzhong special zone. Therefore, it was quite appropriate that they should once again discuss the creation of a new type of special zone.

'Blazing a new trail' meant the need to deploy a heroic and indomitable spirit and a selfless sense of responsibility in order to achieve ideological breakthrough and system reform. For this reason, Xi Zhongxun responded with determination: "I will risk my old bones to do a good job of this pilot system reform in Guangdong."

In mid-May 1979, Gu Mu, vice premier of the state council, headed a central government work team to Guangzhou. The leaders in charge of Guangdong province, including Xi Zhongxun, exchanged in-depth views with Gu Mu on the contents of a draft report to the central government and the state council. Afterwards, on 6 June, Guangdong provincial party committee submitted its *Report on Optimising Guangdong's Advantages to Expand Foreign Trade and Accelerate Economic Development* to the central government and the state council. Fujian provincial party committee also submitted a similar report three days later. The CPC central committee and the state council promptly endorsed the two reports in the form of the long-awaited Document No. 50 for cadres and the people of Guangdong on 15 July. The document stated: "Special policies and flexible measures should be applied to foreign economic activities in the two provinces and more initiative should be given to the two provincial governments so as to make the most of their advantages, seize the prevailing beneficial international situation and take a first step to invigorate the economy. It is a vital decision for the acceleration of China's four modernisations drive."

Yang Shangkun, Xi Zhongxun, Ye Jianying and Hu Yaobang hold an informal discussion in the spring of 1980

Xi Zhongxun and Gu Mu

Li Hao, deputy secretary-general of the state council, was one of the drafters of Document No. 50. "Comrade Xi Zhongxun came to meet the work team at the railway station," he recalled. "I can still remember it now. You could tell the importance of the team headed by Vice Premier Gu Mu. The formulation of Document No. 50 would not have been successful without Xi Zhongxun's vehement presentation of views at the third plenary session of the 11th CPC central committee, especially at the work conference where he called for Guangdong to be given a free hand to proceed. It played the most important role in taking the first step in the reform and opening up."[3]

Xi Zhongxun gave explicit instructions to implement Document No. 50 at a conference for secretaries of prefectural party committees in Guangdong on 21 September 1979. "Guangdong should proceed from the overall situation of the whole country and do a good job," he said. "Now it is not a question of whether to proceed or not, nor whether to proceed gradually or half-heartedly. We must proceed vigorously and quickly rather than inching forward like women with bound feet." He went on full of confidence: "The situation is pressing, so we should go all out to pioneer new ways of invigorating foreign economic activity and managing the special zones well so that we can be a point of reference for the whole country."

In contemplating how to 'blaze a new trail', Xi said: "We should take the attitude of 'three dos' and 'three don'ts'. Regarding the do's: first, we should be determined and confident without holding back; second, we should bravely take responsibility without fear of making mistakes or taking risks; third, we should uphold the spirit of pragmatism, modesty and prudence. Regarding the don'ts: don't be risk-averse, don't show off and don't be afraid of self-negation. Leaders and cadres at all levels should risk our old bones to succeed in carrying out pilot system reform in Guangdong." He added: "I believe that, as long as we take it seriously and work hard under the leadership of the central government, we will successfully implement Document No. 50. We will blaze a new trail in the experiment of economic and management reform." Meanwhile, he sincerely reminded everyone: "As we move forward, we will encounter many difficulties, a lot of resistance and people may even curse us. We should be prepared for that."

Xi Zhongxun joins voluntary workers in Guangzhou in the spring of 1980

'Blazing a New Trail' to Advocate the Establishment of SEZs

Ye Jianying, Nie Rongzhen and Xi Zhongxun in Guangdong, 1980

Gu Mu held a conference on the issues of Guangdong and Fujian in Beijing's Jingxi Hotel on 17 December 1979. "Comrade Xi Zhongxun once said that Guangdong would see faster growth if it was an 'independent state'," he said. "Now it is basically semi-independent and its further development hinges on you. Some central departments lack sufficient ideological emancipation. We must continue to work on that while you must turn somersaults and jump through hoops."[4]

From 24 to 30 March 1980, Gu Mu held another conference, in Guangzhou, for the leaders in charge of Guangdong and Fujian to review and summarise the situation regarding the implementation of the central government's Document No. 50. *The Guangdong and Fujian Conference Minutes* were developed. The minutes officially referred to 'special export zones' as 'special economic zones'.

"The speeches and advocacy of Comrade Xi Zhongxun at the third plenary session of the 11th CPC central committee, especially at the central government work conference the next year, played a pivotal role," recalled Li Hao. "What was the significance? With China's reform and opening up, the focus of work had changed. The question was whether to unveil the reforms nationwide or whether to let some localities experiment first? It was an issue of vital importance."[5]

Xi Zhongxun, Nuno Viriato Tavares de Melo Egidio (fourth from right, front row), governor of Macau, Liang Weilin (third from right, front row), Huo Yingdong (far left, front row), Ma Wanqi (third from left, front row) and He Xian (fourth from left, front row) on a visit Xi made to Macau from 4 to 7 June 1980

The Guangdong Special Economic Zone Regulations were approved at the 15th session of the fifth standing committee of the NPC on 26 August 1980, by which time Shenzhen SEZ had finished its foundation stone laying ceremony. Establishing the SEZ and 'blazing a new trail' were doubtlessly the most important 'inflection point' in the early stage of reform and opening up. It changed the old system and turned a new page in China's modern history.

To speed up the growth of the new SEZs, Xi Zhongxun decided to "ask the central government for authorisation" once again. From 24 to 25 September 1980, Hu Yaobang chaired a meeting of the central committee secretariat. On the morning of 24 September, Xi Zhongxun, Yang Shangkun and Liu Tianfu reported to this committee the work in Guangdong, especially in Shenzhen and Zhuhai SEZs. They also requested central government approval for more autonomy for Guangdong and for permission for the

'Blazing a New Trail' to Advocate the Establishment of SEZs

Xi Zhongxun and Yang Shangkun (far left), on the eve of their transfer to central government work, travel by bus to the Sun Yat-sen memorial hall together with Ren Zhongyi (far right), autumn 1980

From 20 October to 6 November 1980, Xi Zhongxun headed a delegation of Chinese provincial governors to visit the US. The man sitting next to Xi is Song Ping, deputy head of the delegation

province to learn from the successful experiences of foreign countries and the 'four Asian tigers' to push for the rapid expansion of SEZs.

On 28 September 1980, the central government issued *The Minutes of the Central Committee Secretariat Conference*, which explicitly stated: "The central committee has authorised Guangdong provincial government to flexibly implement the appropriate instructions and requirements of the central departments and ignore the inappropriate ones." This was the 'carte blanche' Xi Zhongxun had always wanted for Guangdong before he was transferred to work in Beijing in November 1980.

Although Xi administered Guangdong for only two years and eight months, he was always concerned about southern China and he frequently asked his old comrades and subordinates to update him on the reform and opening-up process.

In the winter of 1983, Ren Zhongyi left Guangdong to have an operation in Beijing. Xi Zhongxun instructed the hospital to give him the very best treatment. He even waited in the hospital on the day of the operation and

Xi Zhongxun visits Disneyland during the Chinese provincial governors visit to the US, 20 October to 6 November 1980

Xi Zhongxun and other members of the delegation of Chinese provincial governors visit a molybdenum ore enterprise in the US state of Colorado, 20 October to 6 November 1980

Xi Zhongxun and other members of the delegation of Chinese provincial governors visit the North American Aerospace Defense Command, 20 October to 6 November 1980

didn't leave until it had been successfully carried out. In the late 1990s, Xi Zhongxun, by then in his 80s, heard of the hospitalisation of Liu Tianfu, who was formerly governor of Guangdong. He wanted to see Liu in person but a functionary advised him to have someone else see him on his behalf. "He was one of the old guard who contributed to China's reform and opening up," said Xi. "Without their joint efforts, the reform and opening-up process would have been less successful." He would not be swayed from travelling to Guangzhou to see Liu Tianfu in person.

Xi Zhongxun on the recently completed Binhai Avenue in Shenzhen, 2 July 2000

Chapter 38

Return to Zhongnanhai

Xi Zhongxun was elected as vice chairman of the third session of the fifth NPC held from August to September 1980. In November that year, the central government decided to transfer him to Beijing.

Although Xi administered Guangdong for only two years and eight months from April 1978, that period was a turning point in the history of modern China. He strived hard, bravely took responsibility, made efforts to take a first step, advocated the establishment of SEZs and wrote the first chapter of China's reform and opening up with amazing insight and extraordinary courage.

On 28 March 1981, the central government decided to designate Xi Zhongxun to work in the central committee secretariat to assist General Secretary Hu Yaobang in handling the daily affairs of the secretariat. The secretariat, set up during the fifth plenary session of the 11th

Xi Zhongxun at the sixth plenary session of the 11th CPC central committee, June 1981

Members of the central committee secretariat. From left to right: Xi Zhongxun, Fang Yi, Gu Mu, Yang Dezhi, Hu Yaobang, Wan Li, Yao Yilin, Yu Qiuli and Wang Renzhong

CPC central committee, dealt with the committee's routine work. As Hu Qili recalled, to facilitate the leadership, the secretariat set up an interim leading group with Hu Yaobang as group leader and Xi Zhongxun as vice group leader in charge of numerous daily affairs.

In late June, Xi Zhongxun was elected as a member of the central government secretariat at the sixth plenary session of the CPC central committee to take charge of the following central committee organs: the general office, the organisation department, the united front work department and the investigation department. "I was notified in late March 1980 that I had been designated by the central committee to work in the central committee secretariat," Xi said in a speech. "I promised Comrade Yaobang that I would do whatever I could for the party in my remaining years to justify the trust and expectations that the central committee had placed in me. Now I still take this attitude and I'm ready to retire and give room to better and more talented people."[1]

In September 1982, Xi Zhongxun was elected as a member of the standing committee of the political bureau of the CPC central committee and secretary-general of the central committee at the first plenary session of the 12th CPC central committee. Although Xi expressed a desire not to assume a post in the new central committee secretariat and recommended that someone in the prime of life should take on this role, person should take on this role, he was overruled by the central committee because of the value it placed in his integrity and abundant political experience.[2]

Xi Zhongxun and Hu Qili were responsible for the daily affairs of the 12th secretariat of the central committee. As before the 12th NPC, Xi was in charge of the central committee's general office, organisation department and united front work department. He was also responsible for work concerning cadres, human resources, the united front, national religion and workers, youth and women, and for coordination between the NPC, the CPPCC and the CPC central commission for discipline inspection.

It had been six years since Xi Zhongxun and Hu Yaobang started working together, in 1981. "At the beginning of the reform and opening up, Comrade Xiaoping looked far ahead and aimed high as the overall architect of reform and opening up," said Hu Qili. "Comrade Yaobang worked tirelessly in trying to implement the reforms; Comrade Zhongxun was an unwavering advocate and enthusiastic promoter of reform and opening up. Comrade Yaobang had great confidence in Zhongxun and let him deal with numerous important issues."[3]

Xi Zhongxun was an avid reader

Xi Zhongxun working in his office in the Qinzhengdian hall in Zhongnanhai

Among the tasks facing Xi Zhongxun were the need to reform the agencies directly under the CPC central committee, the rejuvenation of provincial leaders and replacing old cadres with younger ones. The 127th session of the central committee secretariat on 15 October 1981 decided that Hu Yaobang and Zhao Ziyang should be in charge of the reform of central government agencies, Xi Zhongxun should head up the reform of agencies directly under the CPC central committee and that Wan Li should head the reform of state council agencies. The same committee made another decision on 28 January 1982: that Xi Zhongxun should be responsible for the reform of agencies directly under the CPC central committee, including: the general office, the investigation department, the laboratory of the secretariat, the party school, the all-China federation of trade unions, the communist youth league, the all-China women's federation and the agencies of the NPC standing committee.

Xi Zhongxun conducted research on each of the units, carefully organised the units, offered them specific guidance and implemented all the reform measures. He often talked with department heads and related cadres and patiently carried out ideological work. He repeatedly stressed adopting interim measures to gradually abolish lifelong tenure of cadres and leaders, and implement institutional reform that would help cultivate and select a large number of outstanding young and middle-aged cadres to take on top jobs so as to ensure continuity and progress for the party and country.

Xi Zhongxun placed special emphasis on establishing a new generation of leaders and encouraging the promotion of young cadres. In a reception of all new leaders of the ministry of state security, he urged them to "take courage and to willingly assume responsibility for whatever might happen".

At the time of the spring festival in 1983, the central committee arranged for Xi Zhongxun to take a holiday in southern China. But instead Xi chose to conduct research in Fujian province. During an informal discussion with cadres in Xiamen on 17 February 1983, Xi said: "The young will never be tempered if they are not allowed to shoulder any responsibility." He proposed requirements as to how to foster young cadres: "From this year on, a group of graduates should be selected in every province, municipality and autonomous region to work in a people's commune, a production

Xi Zhongxun visits a rural area in Yunnan, January 1982

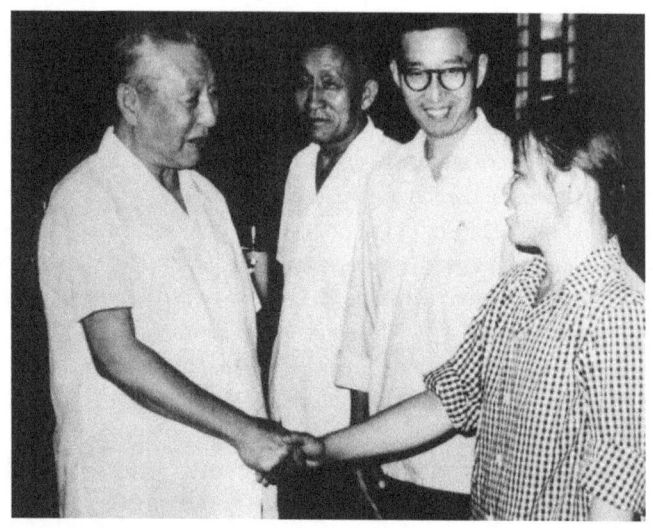

Xi Zhongxun meets pedicure worker Yu Sumei, who was a representative of the 12th NPC, September 1982

Xi Zhongxun visits the port of Xiamen, Fujian province, February 1983

brigade or a factory rather than just letting them be general administrators. After a couple of years' practical work experience, the outstanding ones can be selected to work as leaders at all levels."

From the autumn of 1981 to the spring of 1983, the first round of nationwide system reform was smoothly completed and a normal cadre retirement system was established. Thanks to Xi Zhongxun, the total of bureau-level agencies directly under the CPC central committee declined by 11%, while working staff numbers fell by 17.3% and the number of principals and deputies by 15.7%. Newly selected middle-aged and young cadres in the new leadership accounted for 16% of the total, with the average age falling from 64 to 60.

The central committee fully backed Xi's impartial and upright adherence to the principles in leading the reform of agencies directly under the CPC central committee and the deployment of the provincial leadership. On 14 April 1983, the central committee decided that, in future, reports on the deployment of subsidiaries of the people's congress and the CPPCC in all provinces, municipalities and autonomous regions should no longer be submitted to the secretariat for discussion but reported by the organisation department of the CPC central committee to Xi Zhongxun and Hu Qili for approval. In reporting the deployment of cadres at around this time, the comrades in charge of Shaanxi provincial party committee mentioned a plan to nominate Xi Zhongkai, brother of Xi Zhongxun, as a vice principal. Xi Zhongxun immediately quashed the idea. Xi Zhongkai began his working life before the war of resistance against Japan and had served as a prefectural leader for a long time. It was quite natural for him to be nominated but Xi Zhongxun held that cadres must make an example and he persuaded his brother to give up the chance of promotion to others.

It was also Xi's task to assist Hu Yaobang in taking part in and leading party rectification. The central committee decided to carry out party rectification on a systematic basis over a three-year period from the winter of 1983. The CPC central committee party rectification working committee was set up with Hu Yaobang as chairman, Wan Li, Yu Qiuli, Bo Yibo, Hu Qili and Wang Heshou as vice chairmen, and Wang Zhen, Yang Shangkun, Hu Qiaomu, Xi Zhongxun and Song Renqiong as advisers. Although only an adviser, Xi effectively led party rectification along with Bo Yibo and they worked in a special position in the secretariat.

Xi Zhongxun and his colleagues on an inspection tour of Hunan province in February 1983 pictured in front of the former residence of Mao Zedong in Shaoshan. Fourth from right in the front row is Mao Zhiyong, secretary of Hunan provincial party committee, and third from right is Wang Yuming, chief of the central committee secretariat's research office

From 22 May to 12 June 1984, Xi Zhongxun went to visit Shanghai, Zhejiang, Jiangsu and Shandong. He carefully listened to local reports and held informal discussions with grassroots comrades. While fully and promptly validating good practice, at the same time he helped to clarify a succession of problems that were brought to his attention and talked through with them the main reasons for the problems and possible solutions. Regarding the selection of young cadres, he made it clear during his visit to Shanghai that favouring friends or relatives was absolutely unacceptable and that appointments should be open and above board, based on merit and selected impartially from every corner of the country. As to the objective of party rectification, he pointed out on his trip to Jiangsu that such a measure was essential in order to stimulate the economy, and the reform and opening-up process.

Xi Zhongxun submitted his *Investigation Report on One City and Three Provinces in East China* to the central committee secretariat on 20 June 1984. He believed that initial moves to bring about party rectification would have a significant impact on future work but that undue haste and 'half-cooked rice' (starting a job without finishing it) should be avoided. He also advised extending party rectification to prefecture-level, county and grassroots organisations, and that the new leadership should be replenished and strengthened and the third tier cadre reserve group must be well established. Hu Yaobang gave instructions to forward Xi's report to the governments of all provinces, cities, autonomous regions and party rectification work committees for reference.

The implementation of this policy was the premise and basis for opening up a new situation in unified front work and was also an onerous, substantial, comprehensive and complicated project.

Instigated by Xi Zhongxun, the 15th national united front work conference was held from 21 December 1981 to 6 January 1982. Hu Yaobang stressed that the principal task of the united front was to implement the policy. Xi Zhongxun referred to letters offering different ideas on how to implement the united front policy written by well-known democratic figures Hu

Deng Xiaoping (far left), Deng Yingchao (second from right), and Xi Zhongxun attend a reception banquet on 20 April 1985 in honour of the 70th birthday of Israel Epstein (centre). Epstein had worked in China for 50 years and was a loyal friend of the Chinese people, and a member of the CPPCC standing committee

Xi Zhongxun meets top university graduates, May 1985. Far right is Hu Qiaomu and next to him is Peng Chong

Juewen and Hu Zi'ang to Hu Yaobang during the conference. "The letters were highly relevant to the current united front work," said Xi. "We should learn from their modest work style. We opposed the domineering attitude that held sway over the opinion of other CPC party members in the early 1950s."

On 15 September 1983, Hu Yaobang wrote to Xi Zhongxun on the implementation of united front policy, stating that Xi was needed to implement the policies on behalf of the secretariat and especially the policies for non-CPC friends and returned overseas Chinese. In November, Hu Yaobang proposed to organise a team to conduct inspection tours of the implementation of the policies for non-CPC members over a period of one or two years. As instructed by Hu Yaobang, the central government set up the policy implementation group in early 1984 and Xi Zhongxun was designated as the convener.

On 6 July 1984, Xi Zhongxun held an enlarged meeting of the policy implementation group of the central government. Towards the end of the year, the work of compensating people for confiscated property had almost been completed.

The task of policy implementation lasted several years, touched

Xi Zhongxun visits the poor in rural Jiangxi in November 1985 to hear about their difficulties

every aspect of society and involved tens of millions of households and individuals. Under the leadership of Hu Yaobang and Xi Zhongxun, the task was mostly completed by 1986 and it had a significant impact in righting wrongs and promoting social stability.

"In late November 1980, Zhongxun was transferred to work in Beijing as vice chairman of the fifth NPC, member of the political bureau and secretary of the central committee secretariat," Qi Xin recalled. "During the period when he was assisting Comrade Yaobang, once the working day in Qinzhengdian hall was over, he would often return home and continue to receive comrades from across the country tasked with implementing the policy. In order to abide by his maxim of 'finishing any task that is started on any given day', Zhongxun had to work until midnight."

At the fifth plenary session of the 12th CPC central committee in September 1985, Xi Zhongxun solemnly proposed his resignation as secretary of the central committee secretariat for the second time to make way for a younger, more vigorous person.

At the first session of the seventh NPC in March 1988, Xi was elected for the second time as vice chairman of the standing committee of the NPC

Xi Zhongxun chats with villagers from Danxia, Renhua county, Guangdong province in March 1987

Xi Zhongxun chairs the fifth session of the fifth NPC, 4 December 1982

as well as chairman of the internal affairs and judiciary committee. In these twin roles, Xi made positive contributions to maintaining and perfecting the people's congress system, strengthening the democratic and legal framework and carrying out exchanges and communications between the NPC and foreign parliaments.

Xi Zhongxun attached high importance to construction of the country's legal system. At the fifth session of the fifth NPC on 4 December 1982, Peng Zhen, vice chairman of the standing committee of the NPC, as entrusted by Chairman Ye Jianying, addressed a report on constitutional amendment on behalf of the constitution amendment committee. The session was convened by Xi Zhongxun and voted to approve the amended *Constitution of the PRC*. It was known as the '1982 Constitution' and functioned as the cornerstone for state stability, reform and opening up and the construction of socialism with Chinese characteristics. It turned out to be a good constitution. In 1953, Xi Zhongxun was appointed as a member of the PRC's constitution-drafting committee and participated in the drafting of the first constitution of the new China.

Xi Zhongxun personally participated in and managed the drafting and review of many laws and regulations, such as *Administrative Procedure Law of the PRC, Law of the PRC on the Protection of Rights and Interests of Women, Law of the PRC on the Protection of Minors* and *Law of the PRC on Disabled Persons*.

He also made practical contributions to the sound development of the legal profession in China. In the mid-1980s, three lawyers

Xi Zhongxun accompanies the King of Sweden, Carl Gustaf XVI (centre), on a visit to Xi'an, September 1981

Xi Zhongxun heads a CPC delegation to France, 23 November to 3 December 1983. Third from left is Qiao Shi, deputy head of the delegation

Xi Zhongxun

from Tai'an county, Liaoning province were arrested for their defence of a criminal case. How could the legitimate interests of the lawyers be protected? The problem was finally addressed by the standing committee of the NPC, arousing the close interest of vice chairmen including Xi Zhongxun. In the end, under the supervision and intervention of the standing committee, the three lawyers were acquitted. On 26 March 1988, a commentary entitled *No Infringement of Lawyers' Right to Defence* was published on the front page of *People's Daily*. According to the recollection of Zou Yu, the former minister of justice: "Comrade Zhongxun talked to me and ordered it to be published in a newspaper as soon as possible. At that time, we had drafted the news story but the NPC was not due to be held for another three days. So I called up the chief editor of *People's Daily* that night and said the chairman had instructed this be published, preferably as a front-page headline during the NPC."[4]

Chapter 39

All Rivers Flow to the Sea: Emotional Ties to China

Xi Zhongxun was a model implementer and one of the outstanding leaders of the CPC's united front policy. He once said he devoted 70-80% of his energy to united front work. As far back as the establishment of the Shaanxi-Gansu border region revolutionary base, he helped develop the united front with Liu Zhidan and won over many armed outlaws to the

Xi Zhongxun greets Yang Zhenning (right) and Li Zhengdao (left), winners of the Nobel Prize for physics, at a seminar on the theory of high energy physics in Guangzhou, January 1980

Xi Zhongxun in Zhongnanhai, spring 1981

Red Army. During the war of resistance against Japan, Xi administered Guanzhong and Suide and contributed positively to expanding the united front for resistance against Japan.

Facing the new circumstances of reform and opening up in the early 1980s, Xi Zhongxun made extraordinary contributions to the united front of the CPC in terms of both practice and theory. At the 15th national united front work conference in January 1982, Xi Zhongxun said: "All levels of the united front work departments should be home for non-party figures just like the organisation department is the home of cadres, so that all democratic parties and non-party and non-CPC figures will feel at home there, where they can say whatever they like and raise any question for consultation. We will sincerely help them solve their difficulties."

Under Xi's leadership, the first national united front theory symposium was held in February 1985. He made it clear in his speech that "the united front is a branch of science that includes ethnic nationalities and religion. Its contents are abundant, varied and complicated, but it is a peak of science than can be climbed." He confessed that "the science of the united front

Xi Zhongxun heads an NPC delegation to Scandinavia, May-June 1981

must advance with its practical development rather than keep still or be inflexible; otherwise, it will lose its vigour and vitality."

Xi Zhongxun believed that CPC members in leadership positions should be magnanimous and democratic and make more friends with sincerity. One of Xi's most prominent characteristics was his ability to make friends with those both inside and outside the CPC and from different nationalities and various social sectors, and from across generations. In addition to those already mentioned, Xi made friends with Burhan Shahidi and Seypidin Ezizi from Xinjiang, Yab Gzhis Mgon Po Tshe Brtan from Qinghai, Prince Darijaya of Alashan Banner from Inner Mongolia, Ma Teng'ai from Ningxia, Yang Mingxuan, Ru Yuli and Zhao Shoushan from Shaanxi, and Ma Hongbin and the Living Buddha Kuntangcang from Gansu.

Solving the practical difficulties of others, at any time, was another of Xi Zhongxun's traits. Mnyinuer, former deputy director of Xinjiang Uygur autonomous region people's congress, was the widow of Ehmetjan Qasim, an ethnic minority leader of Xinjiang Uygur nationality. "Xi Zhongxun and Qi Xin were always very kind to me," she recalled. "They greeted me warmly whenever I came to Beijing. Once, I could not find coated printing paper to publish a picture book called *The Sons and Daughters of Xinjiang* during the period of the three years of natural disasters. I told him about it in Beijing. He was then vice premier. To my surprise, he made phone calls on my behalf and solved the problem in person."[1]

When the television play *A Drop in the Ocean* was filmed in the 1980s, the departments concerned were inundated with letters opposing the "pornographic play" because of the "images of the human body" in it. Liu Haisu wrote a letter to Xi Zhongxun and asked for the script to be sent to him. Just three days later, Xi wrote the inscription "A Drop in the Ocean, A Splendid Life". Finally the play could be filmed without interference. As Yan Mingfu remembered, Liu Haisu later proposed to settle in Hong Kong and the arrangements were satisfactorily solved with the personal input of Xi Zhongxun.[2]

Xi Zhongxun was especially concerned about the replacement of old cadres with younger ones and paid attention to cultivating the next

In Fuzhou, Xi Zhongxun receives Taiwanese compatriots settling in Fujian, 11 February 1983. Second from left is Xiang Nan, secretary of Fujian provincial party committee

Xi Zhongxun on the banks of Lake Geneva during a visit to Switzerland, 5 December 1983

Yang Jingren, Seypidin Ezizi, the 10th Panchen Lama Erdeni Choekyi Gyaltsen, Xi Zhongxun, and Ulan-Fu attend the opening ceremony of an ethnic work exhibition following the third plenary session of the 11th CPC central committee in the Beijing Cultural Palace of Nationalities, 28 September 1984

Xi Zhongxun makes a speech at the 40th anniversary of the Jiusan society[3] on behalf of the CPC central committee, 2 September 1985. Front row: Xiao Ke, Xi Zhongxun, Xu Deheng, Qiaoshi and Wang Renzhong

Xi Zhongxun addresses a national united front work conference, 3 December 1986. From left to right: Ngapoi Ngawang Jigme, Xi Zhongxun, Zhu Xuefan, the 10th Panchen Lama Erdeni Choekyi Gyaltsen and Rong Yiren

generation of officials. He talked with comrades in charge of the united front work department about the work assignment of Zhang Yichun, son of Zhang Zhizhong. "Zhang Yichun should be suitably assigned to the revolutionary committee of the Chinese Kuomintang or in Beijing where he can play a greater role," he said.[4] He proposed that Guo Suying, wife of Cheng Yanqiu, and Mei Shaowu, son of Mei Lanfang, should be members of the CPPCC.

Xi also needed to consider and research the question of how to properly handle affairs concerning compatriots in Hong Kong, Macau, Taiwan and overseas, and bring about the reunification of China as early as possible. This was a top priority of the united front-related work.

During Xi Zhongxun's visit to Scandinavia from May to June 1981, Mao Songnian, chairman of the overseas compatriot affairs commission of the 'administration council' of Taiwan, held an 'assembly of overseas Chinese representatives in Europe'. Initially, the diplomatic corps refused

Xi Zhongxun with Chen Jianzhong (far right), former member of the KMT central advisory committee, in Shenzhen in the mid-1990s. Xi's wife Qi Xin is seated while his daughter Qi Qiaoqiao stands

All Rivers Flow to the Sea: Emotional Ties to China

to dispatch delegates to attend the assembly. On hearing this information, Xi Zhongxun said: "More people can be sent to attend it!" He then sent an oral message to Mao Songnian. "This is our internal affair," he said. "You can have a conference and it's no problem if you don't display the 'national emblem of Taiwan' here." He also remarked: "I'd like to talk with Mr Mao Songnian if he wants to."

The work and life of Taiwan compatriots in mainland China had always been on Xi Zhongxun's mind. In April 1982, *Youth Movement Situation* published an article entitled *Sincere Dedication of Taiwan Doctor Zhou Lang to the Service of China Despite the Lack of Trust Due to Him* to reflect the fact that Zhou Lang, a Taiwan expert on blood disease at Hexi district hospital in Tianjin, was not trusted or supported in his work. "How can we implement the goal of uniting with Taiwan without first uniting with our Taiwan compatriots and comrades?" asked Xi after seeing the report. "It is an issue of the guidance and policy relating to the work of Taiwan, which should be treated seriously."

On the afternoon of 27 December 1983, some of the settlers from Taiwan and overseas gathered together to celebrate the new year. In his discussions with Li Dawei, a former major in the KMT and vice president of a PLA aviation academy, Xi Zhongxun said with pleasure: "You work in Shaanxi. I was born in Shaanxi!" Li Dawei retorted: "I learn to do my work while practising and practise while learning. I will manage what I should unceremoniously." Xi Zhongxun was warm in his response: "That's right! Very good!"

Xi Zhongxun proposed that all the departments, not merely the united front work department but also the ministries of foreign trade, commerce, posts and telecommunications, and foreign affairs, should join in the work concerning the united front and Taiwan. The work could not be done satisfactorily without

Xi Zhongxun in recuperation

Jiang Zemin pays a visit to Xi Zhongxun in Shenzhen, 21 February 2000. Far right is Zeng Qinghong, then a candidate member of the political bureau of the CPC central committee

their joint efforts. So the initiatives of all parties should be fully mobilised and given full play.

Xi Zhongxun and Chen Jianzhong, a senior KMT leader, were compatriots and classmates. Chen once worked as vice president of the 'National United Construction Association' in Taiwan and was a member of the KMT central advisory committee. In the early 1980s, he wrote articles advocating an end to cross-Straits hostility. With the approval of the central government, Xi Zhongxun instructed the relevant department to facilitate Chen Jianzhong's visit to mainland China. Accompanied by those in charge of the united front work department, Xi received Chen Jianzhong four times in mid-October 1990 to update him on the situation of reform and development in mainland China and CPC policies relating to Taiwan issues. He also hoped that Chen could contribute more to the course of reunification of China. On the suggestion of Xi Zhongxun, Jiang Zemin, general-secretary of the CPC central committee, also received Chen

Jianzhong. Chen's visit to the mainland was an important contact between the CPC central committee and senior KMT leaders and it therefore had an enormous positive impact on the history of the cross-Straits relationship.

Xi Zhongxun and Hu Jintao, 12 November 1994

Hu Jintao and Xi Zhongxun on national day 1999

In March 1993, Xi Zhongxun stepped down from his post as a national leader but retirement did not stop him from continuing to be concerned about the course of the party and the country.

In the autumn of 1999, the 86-year-old Xi attended celebrations to mark the 50th anniversary of the founding of the PRC in Beijing. He observed the grand military parade and the mass pageants from the Tiananmen gate tower.

Since they were far away in the northwest of the country, neither Xi Zhongxun nor Peng Dehuai was able to attend the founding ceremony of the PRC. Half a century later, among the older generation of proletarian revolutionaries standing on Tiananmen gate tower, Xi was the only founding father to have worked simultaneously as a member of both the CPG commission and the people's revolutionary military commission since the founding of the new China.

Xi Zhongxun attends the 50th anniversary celebrations of the founding of the PRC on 1 October 1999

Jiang Zemin and Xi Zhongxun on Tiananmen gate tower on the evening of 1 October 1999

On the evening of 1 October, Xi Zhongxun walked vigorously to watch the fireworks display from Tiananmen gate tower. Before the party, the central leaders came up one by one to see him, held his hands tightly, chatted with him and asked reporters to take photos. The cheerful scene of the bright, colourful fireworks and the singing and dancing people aroused endless reverie in Xi Zhongxun. "We should always bear in mind that the people are the rivers and mountains (the country), and the rivers and mountains are the people," Xi emotionally told the central leadership comrades that came to greet him.

"The people are the rivers and mountains, and the rivers and mountains are the people" constituted both earnest advice from Xi and the heartfelt wishes of a generation of CPC members.

Xi Zhongxun in his twilight years

All Rivers Flow to the Sea: Emotional Ties to China

Xi Zhongxun and Qi Xin in Shenzhen, October 1999

Xi Zhongxun and his sons Xi Zhengning (left) and Xi Jinping

Xi Zhongxun and his granddaughters

Xi Zhongxun and his family, 15 October 2000

All Rivers Flow to the Sea: Emotional Ties to China

Xi Zhongxun with Xi Jinping and his family, pictured front from left to right: Peng Liyuan, Xi Mingze, Xi Zhongxun and Xi Jinping pushing the wheelchair

Epilogue

Xi Zhongxun died of illness in Beijing at the age of 89 at 5.34am on 24 May 2002.

In *The Life Story of Comrade Xi Zhongxun,* the CPC central committee praised Xi Zhongxun as "an outstanding CPC member, great communist warrior, excellent proletarian revolutionary, remarkable leader of CPC and CMC political work, and one of the main founders and leaders of Shaanxi-Gansu border region revolutionary base", and made the following evaluations:

"During his 76 years of life as a revolutionary, Comrade Xi Zhongxun was firmly faithful to communism and infinitely loyal to the party, the people and the proletarian revolutionary cause. Despite repeated ups and downs as well as adverse circumstances, he was undaunted in his strenuous life. He always kept politically consistent with the third-generation collective leadership of the central committee and unswervingly implemented the basic party line. He tirelessly studied Marxism and was good at keenly discovering and solving problems with a Marxist stance, viewpoints and methods. As to the vital problems relating to the future of the party and the state at the critical moment, he adhered to principle, took a firm and clear-cut stance, placed top priority on the interests of the party and devoted his energy and life to the revolution and construction of China thanks to his strong party spirit."

Xi Zhongxun was not merely one of the main founders and leaders of Shaanxi-Gansu border region revolutionary base but also one of the primary pioneers and advocates of China's reform and opening up. The greatest spirit in all his life was to seek truth from fact.

Epilogue

Qi Xin looks at Xi Zhongxun's portrait in their home in Beijing, May 2005

On the occasion of the third anniversary of Xi Zhongxun's death, his ashes were transferred from Babaoshan Revolutionary Cemetery to his hometown in Fuping county, Shaanxi province on 24 May 2005.

Guanzhong Plain was the starting point of his revolutionary life and also the place his heart yearned for throughout his life. Many villagers in Guanzhong came from all corners and spontaneously stood on both sides of the road to solemnly greet the return of Xi Zhongxun's heroic spirit to his hometown.

Many years later, the people watched the scenes in *Xi Zhongxun*, a docudrama broadcast on CCTV:

When the hearse carrying Xi Zhongxun entered Fuping, Xi Jinping, then secretary of Zhejiang provincial party committee, held the casket containing his ashes covered by a party flag and silently watched the villagers standing on both sides of the road outside the window. Close-up, people could even see the tears welling in the eyes of Xi Jinping and his relatives.

The scene of the return of Xi Zhongxun's ashes was permanently imprinted in the mind of the Chinese people with the popularity of the docudrama.

"Why are my eyes full of tears? Because I love the earth so deeply!" The verses of Ai Qing expressed the love of the Chinese to respect the sages and love the earth underfoot.

In the evergreen cemetery surrounded by bluish-green cypress, a statue of Xi Zhongxun was erected. On the back of the statue is an epitaph engraved by his wife Qi Xin: "Fighting for a lifetime, happy for a lifetime, struggling everyday and happy every day."

It was the motto of Xi Zhongxun and also his valuable spiritual heirloom bequeathed to his descendants.

On 24 May 2005, many villagers in Fuping county, Shaanxi province, spontaneously stood on both sides of the road to solemnly greet the spirit of the returning hometown hero; the banner reads: "In deep mourning for our respected and beloved comrade Xi Zhongxun"

Epilogue

On 24 May 2005, Xi Zhongxun's cremated remains were brought to Fuping county, Shaanxi province

Chronology of Xi Zhongxun's Life

1913

15 October: born to an ordinary peasant family in Dancun village, Fuping county, Shaanxi province

1922-1925

Studied at Ducun primary school

1926

Studied at Licheng higher primary school affiliated to Licheng middle school

May: joined Communist Youth League of China in Licheng middle school

1927

Studied in First Higher primary school, Fuping county

1928

January: studied at Shaanxi Provincial Third Normal University

March: arrested for taking part in student campaigns

April: became a full CPC member in prison

August: freed on bail

1929

Participated in fund-raising and relief campaign in Weibei and secretly recruited party members in his hometown

1930

February: headed west for Changwu to participate in soldier movement

1931

May: garrisoned in Fengxiang and became secretary of CPC battalion party committee

1932

2 April: instigated and led Liangdang mutiny together with Liu Linfu and reorganised troops as the Fifth Shaanxi-Gansu Guerrillas. Worked as secretary of troop party committee

Early September: met with Liu Zhidan and Xie Zichang in Yangliuping, Zhaojin, Yaoxian county, for the first time and stayed in Zhaojin to mobilise the people there

Mid-to-late October: led special agents of Shaanxi-Gansu guerrillas to enter Weibei soviet zone and worked as political commissar of the second guerrilla detachment in Weibei

December: led grain distribution campaign in Dancun, directed and set up CPC Dancun party branch and Dancun guerrilla group

1933

February: worked as secretary of the Communist Youth League in Sanyuan county

March: established Shaanxi-Gansu border region revolutionary base centred in Zhaojin. Worked as member of CPC special party committee and secretary of military committee in Shaanxi-Gansu border region of the CPC

5 April: elected vice chairman of Shaanxi-Gansu border region revolutionary committee and secretary of the parties and other organisations. Later in April, became political commissar of Shaanxi-Gansu border region guerrilla headquarters

14 August: together with Qin Wushan and others, chaired joint conference of Shaanxi-Gansu border region party, administrative and military leadership in Chenjiapo and made correct decision to establish interim Shaanxi-Gansu border region headquarters of the Red Army

16 October: continued to lead struggles in Zhaojin after loss of Xuejia stockade village

1934

January: worked as secretary of the CPC party committee of second guerrilla headquarters and began to set up Shaanxi-Gansu border region revolutionary base with Nanliang as the centre

25 February: elected chairman of reformed Shaanxi-Gansu border region revolutionary committee

October: became political commissar of Shaanxi-Gansu border region military and administrative cadre school

7 November: elected chairman of newly formed Shaanxi-Gansu border region soviet government

1935

5 February: became member of CPC northwest working committee

April: headed more than 100 rear-area workers, guards and guerrillas to move to Luohe valley in Ganquan county

Mid-September: went to Yongning mountain in Bao'an with Liu Jingfan to meet 25th Red Army arriving in northern Shaanxi

October: wrongfully purged, arrested and imprisoned. At the same time, the central Red Army arrived in northern Shaanxi after the Long March and rectified cases of people who were wrongfully purged

December: studied at CPC central committee party school in Wayao village, became head teacher of third class

1936

January: appointed vice chairman and secretary of the political parties and other organisations of the soviet government of Guanzhong special zone

April: worked as secretary of CPC Guanzhong working committee and continued to lead struggles

May: marched with west field army of the Red Army. Set up Quxian-Huanxian county working committee and Huanxian CPC party committee and acted as secretary

September: attended plenary session of central committee political bureau. Went south to Guanzhong for second time and worked as secretary of Guanzhong CPC special committee and as political commissar of the Guanzhong guerrillas

October: worked as political commissar of Guanzhong special zone headquarters

1937

May: attended first people's congress of Shaanxi-Gansu-Ningxia special zone of the central committee and elected as executive committee member

October: Guanzhong special zone renamed as CPC Guanzhong branch. Chaired first congress of party representatives in the branch. Also elected secretary of Guanzhong branch party committee and political commissar of the branch's security headquarters

1939

May: appointed commissioner of Guanzhong's division of administration and supervision

September: elected secretary at second congress of party representatives in Guanzhong

November-December: attended second CPC congress in Shaanxi-Gansu-Ningxia border region

1940

15 March: Second Normal University in Shaanxi-Gansu-Ningxia border region founded in Majia village in Guanzhong branch. Assumed post as president

July: chaired plenary session of Guanzhong branch standing committee in Yangpotou to summarise the experiences in struggle of attrition for more than one year and to research and deploy new tasks for struggle

September: began to serve as member of the central committee's central office in Shaanxi-Gansu-Ningxia border region

1941

April: appointed as member of Shaanxi CPC provincial party committee

August: worked as political commissar of First Police Brigade and Guanzhong garrison headquarters

1942

August: elected president of northwest party school

19 October-14 January 1943: attended Shaanxi-Gansu-Ningxia senior cadre conference held by CPC northwest central office

1943

14 January: at closing ceremony of Shaanxi-Gansu-Ningxia senior cadre conference, recognised for his remarkable achievements in leading

economic construction. Mao Zedong wrote inscription for him: "Putting the party's interests first"

February: acted as secretary of Suide prefectural party committee and political commissar of Suide garrison headquarters

Mid-April: headed team to supervise one-month investigation in Haojiaqiao village, discovered and established labour hero Liu Yuhou as an example and promoted big production campaign in the whole region

Summer: proposed that cultural and educational undertakings should serve the 520,000 people in the entire region and educational reform should be integrated with labour, society, government and family, winning the support of Mao Zedong

1944

28 April: married revolutionary companion Qi Xin in Jiuzhen temple where Suide prefectural party committee was stationed

In examining cadres' personal histories, rectified 'leftist' deviation, which protected cadres and the people

1945

23 April-11 June: attended seventh NPC of the central committee and elected as a candidate member of the central committee

June: attended seminar on history of the party in the northwest

July-August: acted as political commissar of interim headquarters of Yetai mountain counterattack, successfully cooperated with Commander Zhang Zongxun to lead troops

August: appointed deputy director of CPC central committee organisation department

September: became deputy political commissar of Shaanxi-Gansu-Shanxi-Suide joint defence troops

October: took charge of the work of CPC northwest central office

1946

April: elected as permanent member of first session of the third provincial assembly in Shaanxi-Gansu-Ningxia border region

June: began work as secretary of CPC northwest central office

July-September: organised attacks in south to coordinate with the 359th

Brigade breaking out of encirclement in central plains to return to the border region

October: persuaded Hu Jingduo to lead KMT northern Shaanxi security team uprising

13 November: delivered report on mobilisation to safeguard border region and Yan'an at Shaanxi-Gansu-Ningxia border region government cadre mobilisation conference

16 December: with Peng Dehuai entrusted by CPC central committee to chair conference for senior cadres in Shaanxi-Gansu-Ningxia border region, Shaanxi-Suide military region and Taiyue area together with He Long in Gaojiagou, Lishi county, Shanxi province

1947

10 February: political commissar of Shaanxi-Gansu-Ningxia Field Army and headed troops to launch attack in Longdong together with Commander Zhang Zongxun

16 March: Mao Zedong issued CMC presidential order that all border region troops should follow the command of Peng Dehuai and Xi Zhongxun with effect from 17 March

25 March-4 May: Xi and Peng Dehuai led troops to victory in Qinghuabian, Yangmahe and Panlong and killed more than 14,000 enemy troops

21 May-7 July: with Peng Dehuai, directed troops to launch attacks in Longdong, marched to Dingbian, Chichuan and Jingbian where they killed more than 6,200 enemy soldiers and retook Huanxian, Dingbian, Anbian and Jingbian

21-23 July: attended CPC central committee plenary session in Xiaohe, Jingbian county, and elected as political commissar of Shaanxi-Gansu-Ningxia-Shanxi-Suide joint defence force, deputy political commissar of Northwest PLA Field Army and member of Northwest Field Army army front committee

1-25 November: with He Long and Lin Boqu held Shaanxi-Gansu-Ningxia border region cadre conference in Yihe village, Suide to implement spirit of national land conference and deploy land reform and party rectification in border region

25-28 December: attended CPC central committee plenary session in

Yangjiagou, Mizhi county and reported to Mao Zedong the problems in land reform during the meeting

1948

4 January: wrote letter to northwest central office and CPC central committee about land reform. 9 January: Mao Zedong wrote letter of support

19 January: cabled Mao stressing need to overcome 'leftist' sentiments in land reform. 20 January: Mao gave instructions in agreement

6 February: Mao Zedong cabled Xi asking for his ideas about land reform in different areas

8 February: replied to Mao with concept of different land reform measures in three kinds of areas

26 March: with He Long and Lin Boqu jointly issued *The Notice to Protect Cultural Relics and Historic Sites*

26 May-1 June: made speech at second plenary session of Northwest Field Army front committee in Tuji, Luochuan county

14 July: reported to Mao Zedong problems in the newly liberated area. 24 July: central government replied approving all guidance in the report and forwarded it to all central and branch offices

July-August: made themed reports on land reform and party rectification in 1948 at start and end of CPC northwest central office cadre conference

14 November: CPC central committee forwarded report to all central and branch offices

November: worked as political commissar of northwest military region, formerly Shaanxi-Gansu-Ningxia-Shanxi-Suide joint defence military region

1949

17 January: made report *On the Question of Taking Over Cities* at first congress of CPC Northwest Field Army

1 February: elected deputy political commissar of PLA's First Field Army

8 February: recommended as acting speaker of joint conference of permanent representatives in Shaanxi-Gansu-Ningxia border region provincial assembly and government members

5-13 March: attended second plenary session of seventh CPC central committee

8 June: elected as third party secretary of CPC northwest central office with Peng Dehuai and He Long as first and second secretaries, respectively

27 July-4 August: chaired conference of Guanzhong new zone prefectural party committee and made a report *Self-criticism and Current Task of Work in Guanzhong New Zone*

30 September: elected member of CPG commission at CPPCC first plenary session

19 October: appointed as CPG people's revolutionary and military committee member

17-22 November: with Peng Dehuai, chaired plenary session of CPC northwest central office in Lanzhou

30 November: elected political commissar of First Field Army

2 December: with Zhang Zhizhong, appointed as vice-chairmen of northwest military and administrative committee by CPG. Peng Dehuai appointed chairman

1950

19 January: delivered inauguration speech showing devotion to "becoming a loyal servant of the people in northwest China" at founding conference of northwest military and administrative committee

February: worked as second secretary of CPC northwest central office with Peng Dehuai as first secretary

4 March: became political commissar of northwest military region

18 March: made speech *To Fight for the Unification of National Finance* at conference of directors of finance and economics in northwest China

June: attended third plenary session of seventh CPC central committee

10-17 July: reported on land reform at second session of northwest military and administrative committee and recommended as director of northwest land reform committee

October: in charge of party, political and military affairs in northwest China after Peng Dehuai went to direct fighting in North Korea

1951

April: welcomed and sent 10th Panchen Lama Erdeni Choekyi Gyaltsen to Beijing via Xi'an

1 July: delivered a speech *To Win Success under the Leadership of Mao Zedong* at 30th anniversary of the CPC held in CPC northwest central office

22 September: made a speech entitled *Cultural Work Should Serve Economic Construction* at first cultural work conference in northwest China

14 December: went to Xining to see off 10th Panchen Lama who was departing for Tibet on behalf of the CPG and Chairman Mao

22 December: elected as chairman of China-Soviet friendship association northwestern headquarters

1952

6 January: made mobilisation report on fighting corruption, waste and bureaucratism at conference in CPC northwest central office, Shaanxi province and Xi'an

July-August: delivered important instructions of central government and Mao Zedong on work in Xinjiang at second representative assembly of the CPC Xinjiang party committee and tackled problems in the region

7 August: appointed vice chairman of government administration council's culture and education committee

11 August: held reception in honour of Xiang Qian in Lanzhou

3 September: made speech at first forestry working conference in northwest China calling for all soldiers and citizens to make efforts for landscaping

22 September: appointed director of publicity department of CPC central committee

16 November: became SPC member

7-8 December: chaired sixth northwest military and administrative conference and reported on its transformation and task of people's government (military and administrative committee) in greater administrative region

1953

January: became member of PRC constitution drafting committee

13-21 January: chaired national cultural education committee conference and put forward working guidance for cultural education that year

14 January: vice-chairman of northwest administrative commission, formerly northwest military and administrative commission

18 September: became secretary-general of government administration council

1954

12-23 March: chaired national cultural education committee conference

May: made summary report at second national publicity working conference

September: attended second session of first NPC and appointed secretary-general of the state council

1955

January: became secretary of state council party group

27 September: attended PLA military title-conferring ceremony and announced the command for conferring military titles

1956

September: attended eighth NPC of CPC central committee and elected as a central committee member

1957

31 May: made speech at national conference on handling letters of complaint and requests

26 November: discussed with Zhou Enlai about transferring cadres to work at grassroots level

1958

April: accompanied Zhou Enlai on aerial investigation of Three Gorges dam reservoir project and investigated agricultural production in suburbs of Zhengzhou, Henan province together with Zhou Enlai and Peng Dehuai

June: participated in voluntary labour at Ming Tombs reservoir in Beijing

September-October: inspection visit to Shaanxi, Gansu, Ningxia, Qinghai and Inner Mongolia. 6-7 September: inspection visit to Fuping

December: reported to Zhou Enlai issues relating to organisation of the state council

1959

19-25 March: visited Hungary as member of a Chinese party and government delegation headed by Zhu De

April: appointed vice premier and secretary-general of the state council at first session of the second NPC

May-June: headed working team to investigate iron and steel making and state of people's communes

2 July-16 August: attended plenary session of CPC central committee political bureau and eighth plenary session of the eighth CPC central committee held in Lushan, Jiangxi province

Late August-early September: headed Chinese government delegation to the Soviet Union and Czechoslovakia

1960

September: delivered a report on *Streamlining Organisation of All Central Departments* to the CPC central committee

1961

February: inspection trip to Inner Mongolia and celebrated spring festival with Ulan-Fu

April-May: headed central government inspection team in Changge county, Henan province and made two written reports on the problems of people's communes and rural canteens to the central committee

October: accompanied Nepalese King Mahendra on visit to Hangzhou

1962

30 July-24 August: chaired national middle-tier industrial city symposium

September: framed by Kang Sheng at 10th plenary session of the eighth central committee of the CPC and investigated for events arising from the novel *Liu Zhidan*

1963-1964

'Studied' and was investigated in senior party school directly under the central committee

1965

December: transferred to work as vice manager of Luoyang Mining Machinery Factory

1968

3 January: taken back to Beijing by central committee general office as arranged by Zhou Enlai and confined under the military protection of the Beijing garrison

1972

Winter: met family for the first time in seven years as arranged by Zhou Enlai

1975

May: relieved from confinement and took 'sick leave' from Luoyang Fire-resistant Materials Factory

1978

24 February-8 March: attended first session of fifth CPPCC as special committee member and elected as standing committee member of CPPCC

April: appointed second secretary of CPC Guangdong provincial party committee and deputy director of Guangdong provincial revolutionary committee

10 November-15 December: participated in CPC working conference and delivered speech on how to accelerate developments in Guangdong

11 December: worked as first secretary of CPC Guangdong provincial party committee and director of Guangdong provincial revolutionary committee

18-22 December: attended third plenary session of 11th CPC central committee and elected as central committee member

26 December: published an article *The Red Sun Shone over the Shaanxi-Gansu Plateau* in *People's Daily* to mark 85th anniversary of Mao Zedong's birth

1979

15 March: became president of Guangdong provincial party school

5-28 April: attended working conference of central committee and asked central government to authorise Guangdong's accelerated reform and opening up

15 July: CPC central committee and state council officially approved Guangdong's adoption of special policies and flexible measures in foreign economic activities and decided to pilot special export zones in Shenzhen and Zhuhai

4 August: CPC central committee endorsed central organisation department's report on *Redressing the Unjust Case of the Novel 'Liu Zhidan'*

22 November-6 December: headed Guangdong friendship delegation to visit New South Wales, Australia

6-12 December: visited Hong Kong on return trip from Australia

December: appointed governor of Guangdong province

1980

January: became first political commissar of Guangzhou military region

25 February: CPC central committee issued *The Notice to Redress the Unjust Case of the 'Xi Zhongxun Anti-Party Bloc'*

27 April-17 May: accompanied Ye Jianying on inspection tour of Shenzhen, Zhuhai, Hainan and Mei county

4-7 June: visited Macau

September: elected standing committee vice chairman of third session of fifth NPC

20 October-6 November: headed delegation of Chinese provincial governors to the US

9 November: transferred to work in the central committee

1981

March: worked in secretariat of CPC central committee

May-early June: headed NPC delegation visit to Scandinavia

27-29 June: attended sixth plenary session of the 11th CPC central committee and elected secretary of the central committee secretariat

September: accompanied King of Sweden Carl Gustaf XVI on visit to Xi'an, Chengdu and Shanghai

15-25 November: inspection tour of Jiangxi

30 November-13 December: attended fourth session of fifth NPC and later acted as chairman of legislative affairs commission

1982

14-23 January: went to Yunnan to deliver urgent central government message to crack down on economic crimes and conducted inspection tour of seven counties (municipalities) in three districts (provinces) of Yongxi, Honghe and Qujing

26 May: met 10th Panchen Lama en route to Tibet

1-11 September: attended 12th NPC and elected as member of central committee

12-13 September: attended first plenary session of 12th CPC central committee and elected as member of CPC central committee political bureau and secretary of its secretariat in charge of routine work

8-16 October: headed NPC delegation to North Korea

1983

February: inspection tour of Fujian

8 March: addressed symposium of chairmen of NPC standing committees of all provinces, autonomous regions and municipalities

23 November-3 December: headed CPC delegation to France

1984

30 March-6 April: attended funeral of President Sekou Toure of Guinea. On way home, made four-day inspection tour of Xinjiang

20 May-12 June: accompanied delegation of Yugoslavia Communist League to visit Shanghai and went to inspect party rectification work in Hangzhou, Zhejiang province, Suzhou, Wuxi and Nanjing in Jiangsu province and Jinan, Shandong province

30 October-8 November: headed Chinese party and government delegation to celebrate 30th anniversary of Algeria's armed revolution

1985

6 February: made speech at national united front theory symposium and stressed that "the party's united front policy is still a hugely effective weapon"

24 September: resigned as secretary of central committee secretariat at fifth plenary session of 12th CPC central committee

October-December: inspection tour of Jiangsu, Shanghai, Jiangxi and Hubei

1986

January: delivered speech to national conference of religion directors

April: wrote an article *One Year of My Life in Luoyang Mining Machinery Factory*

June: headed CPC delegation to participate in 13th NPC of Yugoslavia Communist League

November: delivered speech to national conference of ethnic affairs directors

1987

11 February-16 March: inspection tour of Guangdong and Hunan

25 October-1 November: attended CPC's 13th NPC

4 December-6 January 1988: inspection tour of Hunan, Guangdong and Hainan

1988

25 March-13 April: attended first session of seventh NPC and elected vice chairman of NPC standing committee and chairman of internal affairs and judiciary committee

20 April: published an article *Wise Decision and Great Success* to mark 40th anniversary of the victorious battle in northern Shaanxi

12-20 June: attended ceremony to open up Waihai Bridge to vehicles in Jiangmen, Guangdong province and conducted inspection tour of Guangzhou and Shenzhen

8-15 July: headed NPC delegation to visit North Korea

December: inspection tour of Guangdong

1989

January: chaired symposium on internal affairs and judiciary

February: inspection tour of Shaanxi

March: with Wang Hanbin, researched issues on modification of draft administrative procedure law

December: inspection tour of Shenzhen

1990

July: chaired founding conference of First Field Army history editorial review board

1995

December: *The Collected Works of Xi Zhongxun* published

1999

30 September: attended state council reception to commemorate 50th anniversary of founding of the PRC

1 October: attended ceremony in Beijing to celebrate the 50th anniversary of the founding of the PRC and national day party that night

2000

May: attended ceremony to commend national care for next generation

November: attended ceremony to celebrate 20th anniversary of establishment of Shenzhen SEZ

2002

24 May, 5.34am: passed away due to illness in Beijing, aged 89

(We would like to sincerely thank Xinhua News Agency, Central Newsreel and Documentary Film Studio, relatives of Xi Zhongxun and comrades who worked alongside him for the images that they supplied for this book.)

Notes

Chapter 1

1. Yang Jue, Wang Jian, Zhang Dan, Sun Piyang, Zhang Qingyun, Jiao Zijing, Zhang Yi'an and Hu Jingyi were all historic figures born in Fuping. They made outstanding contributions in China, starting from the Qin dynasty (221-206BC) to the Republic of China (1912-1949). Liang Yue was an eminent filial son born in Fuping during the Tang dynasty (618-906). Wei Zheng, a minister celebrated for the frank advice he gave to the emperor, stayed in Fuping for a number of years
2. Troops sent by the US, Britain, Germany, France, Russia, Japan, Italy and Austria that forced the Chinese Qing government to sign the *Protocol of 1901*
3. Minutes of an interview with Xi Jinping, 24 December 1996
4. Minutes of talks with Xi Zhongxun, 14 August 1984
5. Born in 1866 in south China's Guangdong province, Dr Sun was a renowned statesman known for his leading role in the 1911 revolution, which overthrew the imperial Qing dynasty (1644-1911) and put an end to more than 2,000 years of feudal rule in China. He died in Beijing on 12 March 1925
6. Hu Jingyi, a famous patriotic general
7. Song Wenmei (1906-1951) was born in Fuping, Shaanxi province. He was enrolled as a student at Huangpu military academy in 1930 and was admitted to the Communist Party of China (CPC) in 1927. He once acted as special task battalion commander of Xi'an pacification headquarters, tasked with detaining Chiang Kai-shek during the Xi'an Incident. In 1946, he was arrested by the Kuomintang (KMT) authorities, charged with 'hijacking the marshal' and was rescued by the CPC. After the foundation of the new China, he served as deputy director general of the government offices administration of the state council
8. Cheng Jianwen (1911-2008), later known as Chen Jianzhong, was born in Fuping, Shaanxi province. He became a CPC member in 1929 and served in Weibei special party committee and Shaanxi provincial party committee in charge of organising the work of the troops. Later, he was arrested, but he managed to emigrate to Taiwan in 1949. He once worked as the 12th KMT central reviewer and secretary-general of the national assembly. In his later years, he paid a visit to mainland China
9. To commemorate 9 May 1915 when the Chinese government caved in to Japan's 21 demands, thereby seriously undermining China's national sovereignty

Notes

Chapter 2

1. Weibei (渭北) refers to the area north of the Wei river (a tributary of the Yellow river) basin encompassing the provinces of Gansu, Ningxia and Shaanxi
2. Chinese coins traditionally had a round or square hole in the middle so they could be strung together in strings of cash to make up larger denominations
3. Ma Hongbin (1884-1960) was an ethnic Hui, born in Linxia, Gansu province. He was once the commander of the 81st national revolutionary army and held the rank of lieutenant general. On 19 September 1949, he took part in a revolt in Tongdian, Zhongning county, Gansu province. After the new China was founded, he served as commander of Ningxia provincial military command and vice-chairman of the first and second Chinese people's political consultative conferences (CPPCC) of Gansu province
4. Huang Ziwen (1909-1947) was born in Sanyuan, Shaanxi province. He became a CPC member in 1926. He once served as chairman of the Weibei revolutionary committee and commander-in-chief of the Shaanxi-Gansu border region guerrilla force. In the spring of 1947, he led the Lingqian town uprising in Sanyuan. In June 1947, he died fighting the KMT army. He was one of the founders and leaders of the Weibei revolutionary base
5. Zhou Dongzhi (1912-1934) was born in Fuping, Shaanxi province. He was admitted to the Communist Party in 1929. He once served as chairman of the Shaanxi-Gansu border region revolutionary committee. He died fighting the KMT army in the autumn of 1934

Chapter 3

1. Yang Hucheng (1893-1949) was born in Pucheng, Shaanxi province. He was a patriotic, high-ranking military officer of the northwest army. He was once the commander-in-chief of the 17th KMT army and director of the Xi'an pacification headquarters. On 12 December 1936 he initiated the Xi'an incident with Zhang Xueliang and was imprisoned by Chiang Kai-shek for a long time. He was killed in September 1949
2. Liu Zhidan (1903-1936) was born in Bao'an county (now Zhidan county) in Shaanxi province. He was recruited by the Chinese socialist youth league in 1924 and became a CPC member in 1925. He went on to serve as secretary of Shaanxi special military committee, commander-in-chief of the Shaanxi-Gansu guerrillas of the Red Army, chairman of the CPC Shaanxi-Gansu border region military committee, commander of the 42nd division of the 26th Red Army, chairman of the CPC northwest military Committee, vice chief and chief of staff of the 15th Army Corps of the Red Army, deputy director of the CPC revolutionary military committee northwest office and commander of the 28th Red Army. He died in the Eastern Expedition in April 1936. As a founder and leader of the northwest revolutionary base and the northwest Red Army, he was regarded as a Robin Hood-like figure by Helen Foster Snow in *Outstanding Figures in Contemporary Chinese History — Liu Zhidan*
3. Wang Shitai (1910-2008) was born in Luochuan, Shaanxi province. He became a CPC member in 1929 and served as commander of the second regiment of the 26th Red Army, the third regiment of the 26th Red Army, secretary of the CPC Jingbian, Dingbian and Anbian prefectural committees, deputy commander of the Shaanxi-Gansu-Ningxia-Shanxi-Suide joint defence army and political commissar of the second corps of the First Field Army. After the new China was founded, he worked as vice-chairman of the Gansu provincial people's government, vice minister of railways, deputy director of the state

development planning commission and director of the standing committee of the Gansu people's congress. He was one of the founders and leaders of the Shaanxi-Gansu border region revolutionary base

4. Liu Linpu (1909-1932) was born in Yaoxian county, Shaanxi province. He became a CPC member in 1929. He learnt military affairs in Huangpu military academy Changsha campus and once assumed the post of secretary general of the CPC Shaanxi provincial military committee. He was killed by the KMT authorities in September 1932

Chapter 4

1. Xie Zichang (1897-1935) was born in Anding (now Zichang), Shaanxi province. He was recruited as a CPC member in 1925. He once served as a member of the CPC Shaanxi special military committee, commander-in-chief of the northwest anti-imperial allies, commander-in-chief of the Red Army's Shaanxi-Gansu guerrillas, political commissar of the 42nd division of the 26th Red Army and chairman of the CPC northwest military committee (Liu Zhidan, according to other sources). He was a founder and leader of the northwest revolutionary base and of the Red Army in northwest China
2. Minutes of talks with Xi Zhongxun, 28 April 1983
3. Jia Tuofu (1912-1967) was born in Shenmu, Shaanxi province. He became a member of the Chinese socialist youth league in 1926 and joined the CPC in 1928. He was once a member of the standing committee of CPC Shaanxi provincial committee, candidate executive member of the temporary central government of the Chinese soviet republic, secretary of CPC Jingbian, Dingbian and Anbian special committee, secretary of CPC Shaanxi provincial committee and mayor of Xi'an. After the new China was founded, he served as deputy director of the financial and economic committee of the state council and deputy director of the state development planning commission
4. Zhao Boping (1902-1993) was born in Lantian, Shaanxi province. He was admitted to the CPC in 1927. He once worked as secretary of the CPC Lantian county committee, secretary of the CPC northern Shaanxi special committee, secretary of the CPC Sanyuan central county committee and a member of the CPC Shaanxi provincial committee. After the new China was founded, he assumed the posts of governor of Shaanxi province, deputy secretary general of the standing committee of the NPC and candidate member of the central committee of the eighth NPC. He was also one of the founders of the northern Shaanxi revolutionary base

Chapter 5

1. Xi Zhongxun. *A Leader of the Masses and a National Hero, The Collected Works of Xi Zhongxun, Volume I*. The Communist Party of China's History Publishing House. October 2013, page 562
2. Minutes of talks with Xi Zhongxun, 28 April 1983
3. Document written by Wang Shitai, April 1994

Chapter 6

1. Zhang Xiushan (1911-1996) was born in Shenmi, Shaanxi province. He joined the Communist Party in 1929. He was secretary of the CPC Shaanxi-Gansu Border Region Special Committee, political commissar of the 42nd Division of the 26th Red Army and secretary of the CPC Liaoning Provincial Committee. After the new China was founded,

Notes

he worked as a member of the standing committee of the CPC northeast central office, the organisation department of the CPC northeast central office and deputy director of the ministry of agriculture

2. Xi Zhongxun. *In Deep Memory of Comrade Wang Taiji, the Collected Works of Xi Zhongxun, Volume II*. The Communist Party of China's History Publishing House. October 2013, page 833

3. Qin Wushan (1914-1971) was born in Heyang, Shaanxi province. He was admitted to the Communist Party in 1932 and worked as secretary of the CPC Shaanxi-Gansu border region special committee. After the new China was founded, he acted as director of the political department of Ningxia provincial military region

4. Gao Gang (1905-1954) was born in Huaiyuan (now Hengshan), Shaanxi province. He became a member of the Communist Party in 1926. He was political commissar of the makeshift headquarters of the Shaanxi-Gansu border region Red Army, political commissar of the 42nd division of the 26th Red Army, secretary of the CPC northeast central office, chairman of the northeast people's government and commander and political commissar of the northeast military region. After the new China was founded, he acted as vice chairman of the central people's government and chairman of the state planning commission. He committed suicide in August 1954 and was posthumously expelled from the party in May 1955

5. Minutes of talks with Xi Zhongxun, 28 April 1983

Chapter 7

1. Zhang Xiushan. *Account of Shaanxi-Gansu Border Region Revolutionary Base, Shaanxi-Gansu Border Region Revolutionary Base*. The Communist Party of China's History Publishing House, November 1997, page 396

2. Minutes of an interview with Jiang Chengying, September 2002

3. Xi Zhongxun. *Unforgettable Teachings — The 90th Anniversary of Comrade Liu Zhidan's Birthday. People's Daily*, 24 October 1993

4. The phrases excerpted here from the Lenin primary school textbook are crafted as rhyming couplets to appeal to young children as they recite the sounds in Chinese-like nursery rhymes:

mǎ kè sī, ēn gé sī,

shì jiè gé mìng liǎng dào shī',

ná dāo shā háo shēn,

ná qiāng dǎ bái jūn.

Chapter 8

1. Minutes of Xi Zhongxun's speech at the CPC northwest central office senior cadre conference, 11 November 1942

2. *The Red Sun Shone over the Shaanxi-Gansu Plateau, The Collected Works of Xi Zhongxun, Volume I*, The Communist Party of China's History Publishing House, October 2013, page 427

3. Minutes of talks with Xi Zhongxun, 7 April 1986

4. Minutes of an interview with Liu Lizhen, March 2003

Chapter 9

1. *A Chronicle of Mao Zedong's Life 1893-1949*, Volume I, People's Publishing House and Central Party Literature Press, December 1993, page 476
2. Zhang Wentian (1900-1976) was born in Nanhui, Jiangsu province (now the Pudong district of Shanghai). He was admitted to the CPC in 1925. He was publicity department director of the CPC central committee and a member of the standing committee of the interim political bureau of the CPC central committee. At the Zunyi conference, he took charge of the general affairs of the central government. After the new China was founded, he became China's ambassador to the Soviet Union and the PRC's first minister of foreign affairs
3. *The Red Sun Shone over the Shaanxi-Gansu Plateau: The Collected Works of Xi Zhongxun*, Volume I, The Communist Party of China's History Publishing House, October 2013, page 428
4. *The Unforgettable Memory: The Collected Works of Xi Zhongxun*, Volume II. The Communist Party of China's History Publishing House. October 2013, page 481
5. Minutes of an interview with Wang Shitai, March 2003

Chapter 10

1. Li Weihan (1896-1984) was born in Changsha, Hunan province. He became a party member in 1922. He once served as a member of the standing committee of the interim political bureau of the CPC central committee, director of the organisation department of the CPC central committee and secretary general of the Shaanxi-Gansu-Ningxia border region government. After the new China was founded, he worked at the united front work department of the CPC central committee, and as vice chairman of the standing committee of the NPC, vice chairman of the CPPCC and deputy director of the CPC central advisory committee
2. Li Weihan, *Reminiscence and Research*, Volume I, The Communist Party of China Historical Data Press, April 1986, page 373
3. Interview with Zhang Guide, May 2004
4. Peng Dehuai (1898-1974) was born in Xiangtan, Hunan province. As a member of the CPC, he led the Jiangping uprising in 1928. He served as vice chairman of the central revolutionary military committee, deputy commander-in-chief of the Eighth Route Army, deputy commander-in-chief of the Chinese PLA, commander and political commissar of the First Field Army and chief secretary of the CPC northwest central office. After the new China was founded, he served as chairman of the northwest military and administrative committee, commander and political commissar of the Chinese people's volunteers, vice premier of the state council, defence minister and vice chairman of the national defence commission

Chapter 11

1. Minutes of an interview with He Zai, March 2003
2. *Brief Introduction to the History of the Communist Party of China in Guanzhong Plain*, The Collected Works of Xi Zhongxun, Volume I, The Communist Party of China's History Publishing House, October 2013, page 20

3. Mao Zedong's speech at the opening ceremony of the CPC northwest central office senior cadre conference, *A Chronicle of Mao Zedong's Life 1893-1949, Volume II* (Revised edition), Central Party Literature Press, December 2013, page 407
4. Xi Zhongxun. *The Red Sun Shone over the Shaanxi-Gansu Plateau, The Collected Works of Xi Zhongxun, Volume I*, The Communist Party of China's History Publishing House, October 2013, page 433

Chapter 12

1. Kang Sheng (1898-1975) was born in Jiaonan, Shandong province. He became a CPC member in 1925 and served as secretary of the secretariat of the CPC central committee, president of the CPC party school and director of the CPC social development department. After the founding of the PRC, he worked as secretary of the secretariat of the CPC central committee and vice chairman of the CPC central committee. During the Cultural Revolution, he participated in the counter-revolutionary conspiracy of Lin Biao and Jiang Qing to usurp party and state power. In October 1980, the CPC central committee decided to expel him from the party
2. Qi Xin. *55 Years of Trials and Tribulations Shared by Zhongxun and I, The Revolutionary Life of Xi Zhongxun*. The Communist Party of China's History Publishing House, April 2002, page 651
3. Minutes of an interview with Yang Heting, June 2002
4. Minutes of a conversation with Bai Zhimin, 13 May 1996

Chapter 13

1. The Lugouqiao (Marco Polo Bridge) incident occurred when invading Japanese troops attacked Chinese forces in the fortress town of Wanping. It marked the beginning of the eight-year anti-Japanese war
2. Minutes of interview with Qi Xin, September 2013

Chapter 14

1. *The Two Fates of China, The Collected Works of Mao Zedong, Volume III*, The People's Publishing House, June 1991, page 1026
2. Zhang Zongxun (1908-1998) was born in Weinan, Shaanxi province. He was recruited as a member of the CPC in 1926. He was commander of the 12th Red Army of the first front army, commander of the 358th brigade of the 120th division of the Eighth Route Army, commander of the Shaanxi-Gansu-Ningxia Field Army and first deputy commander of the Northwest Field Army. After new China was founded, he became deputy general chief-of-staff of the PLA and the general head of logistics

Chapter 15

1. Minutes of an interview with Sidney Rittenberg, September 2012
2. Wang Zhen (1908-1993) was born in Liuyang, Hunan province. He became a member of the CPC in 1927. He served as deputy commander of the Eighth Red Army, commander and political commissar of the 359th brigade of the 120th division of the eighth route army, and commander and political commissar of the first corps of the Northwest Field Army. After the new China was founded, he became first secretary of the CPC central

committee Xinjiang office, deputy general chief-of-staff of the PLA, vice premier of the state council, a member of the political bureau of the CPC central committee, vice chairman of the PRC and deputy director of the CPC advisory committee

3. Xi Zhongxun. *The Red Sun Shone over the Shaanxi-Gansu Plateau, The Collected Works of Xi Zhongxun, Volume I*, The Communist Party of China's History Publishing House, October 2013, page 43

Chapter 16

1. Hu Jingduo (1914-1977) was born in Fuping, Shaanxi province. He was admitted to the CPC in 1946, and later that year he became deputy director of the northern Shaanxi security headquarters. He served as commander of the third battalion of the 500th regiment of the 84th army of the KMT, leading his troops in resisting the Japanese at Zhongtiao mountain for four years. After the foundation of the new China, he became deputy commander of the fourth army of the First Field Army, deputy director of the training department of the PLA first infantry school and deputy director general of the Shaanxi provincial transport department
2. Minutes of an interview with Fan Ming, June 2002

Chapter 17

1. Xi Zhongxun. *Peng Dehuai in the Northwestern Battlefield, The Collected Works of Xi Zhongxun, Volume I*. The Communist Party of China's History Publishing House. October 2013, page 592
2. *The Collected Military Works of Mao Zedong, Volume IV*. The Central Party Literature Press and Military Science Publishing House, December 1993, page 10
3. *A Chronicle of Mao Zedong's Life 1893-1949, Volume III*, The People's Publishing House and The Central Party Literature Press, December 1993, page 192

Chapter 18

1. He Long (1896-1969) was born in Sangzhi, Hunan province. He took part in the Nanchang uprising as commander-in-chief and joined the CPC in 1927. He once served as commander-in-chief of the second army group of the Red Army, commander of the 120th division of the Eighth Route Army and second secretary of the CPC northwest central office. After the foundation of the new China, he worked as third secretary of the CPC southwest central office, commander of the southwest military region, vice chairman of the people's revolutionary military committee, chairman of the northwest military and administrative committee, vice chairman of the national defence commission, vice premier of the state council, director of the state physical culture and sports commission and vice chairman of the central military commission
2. Xi Zhongxun. *Peng Dehuai in the Northwestern Battlefield, the Collected Works of Xi Zhongxun, Volume I*. The Communist Party of China's History Publishing House. October 2013, page 592
3. Minutes of an interview with Zhang Guang, March 2003

Chapter 19

1. *Wise Decisions and Great Victories, The Collected Works of Xi Zhongxun, Volume II*. The Communist Party of China's History Publishing House. October 2013, page 1209

Notes

Chapter 20

1. *A Chronicle of Peng Dehuai's Life*. People's Publishing House, March 1998, page 430
2. Minutes of an interview with Jiang Ping, July 2006
3. *A Cable Concerning the Issue of Democratic Figures Investigating Land Reform, Mao Zedong's Manuscripts Since the Founding of New China, Volume II*. Central Party Literature Press, November 1988, page 173
4. *Work Hard to Green the Northwest, The Collected Works of Xi Zhongxun, Volume I*, The Communist Party of China's History Publishing House, October 2013, page 294
5. Ibid

Chapter 21

1. The 10th Panchen Lama Erdeni Choekyi Gyaltsen (1938-1989) was a Tibetan national, born in Xunhua. He served as the first vice chairman and deputy chairman of the Tibetan autonomous region preparatory committee, vice chairman of the second and the fifth CPPCC and vice chairman of the second, fifth, sixth and seventh NPC standing committees
2. Khenpo in Tibetan refers to a senior monk and spiritual leader of a monastery. The Khenpo chamber, which consists of a group of khenpos, is an organisation designated to manage political and religious affairs in the Tibetan panchen lama system. Approved by the government administration council of the CPG, the committee of the Khenpo chamber was founded in 1953. Later, in July 1961, the state council authorised the committee's application to dissolve the chamber
3. *Several Opinions on the Work in Tibet, The Collected Works of Xi Zhongxun, Volume I*. The Communist Party of China's History Publishing House, October 2013, page 265
4. The '70,000-Word Report' refers to a 70,000-character-long petition written by the 10th Panchen Lama in May 1962. It is a report to the CPC central committee and the state council, pointing out the existing problems in Tibet and other Tibetan-inhabited areas, and giving suggestions on the work in these areas. The main points covered problems with communes and policy implemented on ethnic, religious and united-front affairs
5. *Cherishing the Memory of the Panchen Lama, a Loyal Friend of the CPC, The Collected Works of Xi Zhongxun, Volume II*. The Communist Party of China's History Publishing House, October 2013, page 1230

Chapter 22

1. Xiang Qian (1906-1958), of Tibetan nationality, was born in Jianzha, Qinghai province. He launched armed rebellions between 1950 and the spring of 1952 and surrendered to the people's government in July 1952. Later, he served as a magistrate of Jianzha county people's government and deputy governor of Huangnan Tibetan autonomous prefecture
2. Sherab Gyatso (1883-1968), of Tibetan nationality, was born in Xunhua, Qinghai province. After the new China was founded, he held the posts of vice chairman of Qinghai provincial people's government, a member of the northwest military and administrative committee, deputy director of the nationalities affairs committee and chairman of the Buddhist Association of China

Chapter 23

1. *Central Authority Remarks on Xi Zhongxun's Party Cultural Committee Report on the Struggle Against Bureaucratism, Mao Zedong's Manuscripts Since the Founding of New China, Volume II.* Central Party Literature Press, September 1990, page 74

Chapter 24

1. *A Chronicle of Zhou Enlai's Life, Volume I*, Central Party Literature Press, May 1997, page 424
2. Yuan Shih-kai (1859-1916), born in Xiangcheng County, Henan province. Yuan acquired the position of Provisional President of the Republic of China through a combination of force and political intrigue. The Beiyang Warlord Government under him represented the interests of the landlords and feudalist exploitation class. In 1915, in order to gain Japanese support, Yuan recognized the "21 Demands" which aimed to put China under Japanese suzerainty. He named himself Emperor in December of the same year. He was forced to abdicate in March 1916 after rebellions across the nation led by Yunnan province.

    Tuan Chi-jui (1865-1936), born in Hefei, Anhui, was the head of the Anhui Clique of the Beiyang Warlords. Tuan was named the Minister of War by Yuan Shih-kai in 1912, and from Yuan's death in 1916 through to 1926, he held multiple positions including Premier and Chief Executive (acting president) of the Republic of China, gaining possession of the recognized government in Beijing several times. He was known for his brutal internal repression while maintaining a traitorous and appeasing stance towards foreign powers.
3. *Unforgettable Memories, The Collected Works of Xi Zhongxun, Volume I.* The Communist Party of China's History Publishing House. October 2013, page 490

Chapter 25

1. *The Intimate Contact Between Xi Zhongxun and My Father Deng Baoshan, Collected Essays in Honour of Xi Zhongxun.* The Communist Party of China's History Publishing House, October 2013, page 329
2. *Speech at the 15th Supreme State Conference, Mao Zedong's Manuscripts Since the Founding of New China, Volume VII.* Central Party Literature Press, August 1992, page 378
3. Huang Zhengqing. *A Family Member of the Tibetans, The Revolutionary Life of Xi Zhongxun.* The Communist Party of China's History Publishing House and Chinese Literature Press, April 2002, page 298
4. Minutes of an interview with Jiang Ping, August 2005
5. Minutes of an interview with Tu Zhen, May 2006
6. Minutes of an interview with Shang Changrong, May 2006
7. Qi Qiaoqiao. *My Father Lives Forever in My Heart, Collected Essays in Honour of Xi Zhongxun.* The Communist Party of China's History Publishing House, October 2013, page 778

Chapter 27

1. Ma Yongshun. *Always Care about the People's Hardships, Collected Essays in Honour of Xi Zhongxun.* The Communist Party of China's History Publishing House, October 2013, page 485
2. Minutes of a discussion with Xi Zhongxun, May 1981

Notes

Chapter 28
1. Tian Fang. *A Faithful Servant of the People, Collected Essays in Honour of Xi Zhongxun*. The Communist Party of China's History Publishing House, October 2013, page 585
2. Minutes of a conversation between Xi Zhongxun and Zhou Erfu, May 1981
3. Minutes of an interview with Ma Yongshun, August 2002

Chapter 29
1. Minutes of an interview with Zhang Jinqiu, May 2012

Chapter 30
1. Minutes of an interview with Lei Zhenzhong, March 2003
2. Minutes of an interview with Hu Xinzhong, March 2003
3. Minutes of an interview with Li Ruifang, March 2003
4. Minutes of an interview with Du Jinfang, May 2004
5. Minutes of an interview with Ma Shaobo, June 2005

Chapter 31
1. Minutes of speeches at the 10th plenary session of the eighth CPC central committee, *The No. 72 General Brief Report*
2. *A Chronicle of Mao Zedong's Life 1949-1976, Volume V*, Central Party Literature Press, December 2013, page 153
3. Minutes of an interview with Qi Xin, March 2003
4. Minutes of an interview with Xi Yanying, 2 July 1996
5. Minutes of a discussion between Xi Zhongxun and Kim Il-sung, October 14, 1982

Chapter 32
1. Minutes of an interview with Ding Hongru, June 2012
2. Minutes of a discussion with Xi Zhongxun, 18 April 1984
3. Minutes of an interview with Li Jinhai, June 2004.
4. Wang Hui. *Memoir of a Happy Reunion with Xi Zhongxun. Collected Essays in Honour of Xi Zhongxun*. The Communist Party of China's History Publishing House, October 2013, page 242

Chapter 33
1. Minutes of an interview with Erie Suja, April 2004
2. Ye Jianying (1897-1989) was born in Mei county, Guangdong province. He joined the CPC in 1927. He served as chief of staff of the Eighth Route Army and the CMC, director of Beijing military control commission, mayor of Beijing and first secretary of the CPC central committee in southern China. After the founding of the new China, he took on the posts of chairman of the Guangdong people's government, commander of the south China military region, deputy chairman of the people's revolutionary and military commission, the CPPCC, the CPC central committee and the CMC, and NPC chairman
3. Hu Yaobang (1915-1989) was born in Liuyang, Hunan province. He was recruited

as a communist youth league member in 1930 and a CPC member in 1933. He was once director of the publicity and organisation departments of the youth league of the CPC central committee, director of the organisation department of the general political department of the CMC and director of the political department of the 18th corps. After the founding of the new China, he served as first secretary of the CPC central committee youth league, second secretary of the CPC northwest central office, a member of the political bureau of the CPC central committee, a member of the standing committee of the political bureau of the CPC central committee, and chairman and general secretary of the CPC central committee

4. Minutes of an interview with Qi Xin, March 2003
5. Minutes of an interview with Fang Bao, June 2004
6. *Deep Mourning for Respected General Ye Jianying, The Collected Works of Xi Zhongxun, Volume I*, The Communist Party of China's History Publishing House, October 2013, page 1114

Chapter 34

1. Minutes of an interview with Wang Ning, March 2003
2. Qi Xin. *In Memory of Xi Zhongxun, Collected Essays in Honour of Xi Zhongxun*. The Communist Party of China's History Publishing House, October 2013, page 757

Chapter 35

1. Minutes of an interview with Fang Bao, June 2004
2. Minutes of an interview with Guo Rongchang, 27 December 2004

Chapter 36

1. *Speech to the South Central Group at the Central Government Work Conference, The Collected Works of Xi Zhongxun, Volume I*. The Communist Party of China's History Publishing House. October 2013, page 509
2. *A Chronicle of Deng Xiaoping's Life 1975-1997, Volume I*. Central Party Literature Press, July 2004, page 506
3. *Deep Mourning for Respected General Ye Jianying, The Collected Works of Xi Zhongxun, Volume I*, The Communist Party of China's History Publishing House, October 2013, page 1115

Chapter 37

1. Minutes of an interview with Zhang Xunfu, September 2002
2. *A Chronicle of Deng Xiaoping's Life 1975-1997, Volume I*. Central Party Literature Press, July 2004, page 510
3. Minutes of an interview with Li Hao, September 2004
4. Gu Mu. *Speech After Hearing the Guangdong and Fujian Province Work Reports. The Collection of Central Committee Directives for the Work in Guangdong* (1979-1982) from the General Office of Guangdong Provincial Party Committee, page 53
5. Ibid 3

Notes

Chapter 38

1. Minutes of a speech by Xi Zhongxun at the preparatory meeting of the sixth plenary session of the 11th central committee of the CPC, 24 June 1981
2. *A Chronicle of Deng Xiaoping's Life 1975-1997, Volume II.* Central Party Literature Press, July 2004, page 845
3. Hu Qili. *Comrade Zhongxun as I Knew Him*, 5 August 2009
4. Minutes of an interview with Zou Yu, March 2005

Chapter 39

1. Minutes of an interview with Mnyinuer, March 2011
2. Yan Mingfu. *In Memory of Xi Zhongxun. Collected Essays in Honour of Xi Zhongxun.* The Communist Party of China's History Publishing House, October 2013, page 84
3. The Jiu San Society, formally founded in Chongqing on 4 May 1946, is one of China's eight non-communist political parties whose members are mostly senior and leading intellectuals in the fields of science and technology. The society derives its name from the Chinese characters jiusan (九三) which literally mean '9,3' (in this case, the third day of the ninth month or 3 September) in commemoration of victory in the war of resistance against Japanese aggression and in the world anti-fascist war (World War 2) on 3 September 1945. As of mid-2012, the society had set up more than 5,200 grassroots organisations with more than 132,000 members
4. Yan Mingfu. *In Memory of Xi Zhongxun. Collected Essays in Honour of Xi Zhongxun.* The Communist Party of China's History Publishing House, October 2013, page 83
5. Minutes of an interview with Liu Xiaoping, June 2006